SACRAMENTO PUBLIC LIBRARY

3 3029 03530 9467

CENTRAL LIBRARY
828 "I" STREET
SACRAMENTO, CA 95814

JAN 3 0 1998

D0046518

SIMON AND SCHUSTER

NEW YORK

A STEP-BY-STEP PLAN
FOR REACHING
YOUR FULL POTENTIAL

FINDING

THE

CHAMPION

WITHIN

Bruce Jenner

WITH **Mark Seal**

SIMON & SCHUSTER
Rockefeller Center
1230 Avenue of the Americas
New York, NY 10020

Copyright © 1996 by Bruce Jenner
All rights reserved,
including the right of reproduction
in whole or in part in any form.

SIMON & SCHUSTER and colophon are
registered trademarks of Simon & Schuster Inc.

Designed by Jennifer Ann Daddio

Manufactured in the United States of America

1   3   5   7   9   10   8   6   4   2

Library of Congress Cataloging-in-Publication Data

Jenner, Bruce, 1949–
Finding the champion within : a step-by-step plan
for reaching your full potential /
Bruce Jenner with Mark Seal.
p.   cm.
1. Jenner, Bruce, 1949–   .   2. Self-actualization
(Psychology)—Handbooks, manuals, etc.
3. Athletes—United States—Biography.
I. Seal, Mark.   II. Title.
GV697.J38A3   1996
158.1—dc21   96–39182
CIP

ISBN 0-684-81852-3

To Kris and Kendall, with all my heart

ACKNOWLEDGMENTS

This book would never have been possible if it weren't for one person: my love, my inspiration, the mother of my children and, of course, my best friend—

My lovely wife, Kris.

When we met on September 10, 1990, my life had lost direction. I had given up hope for the future and had forgotten the lessons of the past. But it's amazing what one person can awaken in another. Kris came into my life and brought love, family and a renewed belief in myself and my tomorrow. She is the most loving, kind and giving person I have ever met. With Kris, for the first time in my life, I realized the meaning of love and passion. I love you with all my heart, honey, for all that you have done to make my life an incredible journey.

When our daughter, Kendall, came into our lives on November 3, 1995, she became a living, laughing testament to our love and our deep commitment to our family and our future together. Life is full of many challenges, Kendall, and as your parents we will always love you and be there for you.

I want to thank my cowriter, Mark Seal, who helped me find my voice. This was a very personal and, at times, a very painful book to write. Mark's ability to organize my thoughts with insightful eloquence and style is tremendously appreciated.

To Jan Miller, my literary agent, I give my thanks. Over the last couple of years she has shown incredible persistence in the long and frequently arduous publishing process. Jan was the first person to recognize my potential to write a book that could make a real difference in people's lives, and I feel we have accomplished that mission.

For her invaluable research assistance, I would like to thank Sheri Thompson.

Finally, I would like to pay homage to the Champion Within that is part of us all. It is a tremendous power that can turn an ordinary existence into the stuff of which dreams are truly made. Find it, use it and let the power set you free!

CONTENTS

"Champions aren't made in gyms.
Champions are made from something
they have deep inside them—a desire, a dream, a vision."
—MUHAMMAD ALI

Introduction:
The Decathlon of Life

He stood atop the platform like the personification of victory, one man being crowned the World's Greatest Athlete to the music of anthems and thunder of applause. His name was Nikolay Avilov, of the USSR, and he had just set a new world record, 8,454 points, for the decathlon. Head erect, shoulders back, he stood as triumphant as a heroic statue as the officials hung the gold medal around his neck and the world applauded him to the strains of the Soviet National Anthem.

It was the 1972 Olympics in Munich, Germany, and I was lucky to have even made the team. I was the eternal underdog, the thin-legged, ordinary kid whose youth was spent battling low self-esteem and a reading problem called dyslexia. The just-above-average athlete whose victories were due more to sheer determination than natural ability. I stood off on the side of the stadium, where, during the opening ceremonies one week earlier, thousands of white doves had been released, symbolizing peace to the audience in the stands and raining bird droppings on the athletes in their soon-to-be-stained white uniforms below.

But as I watched the godlike Russian being crowned, I had what you might call a life-altering experience. I saw myself standing on that victory platform at the next Olympic Games four years away. Suddenly, I knew: if I could do the work, I could win the Gold. Victory felt so close it seemed as if I could reach out and grab it.

"What elevates the winners in life," I asked myself as I watched the ceremony, "and what exiles the losers? Why did one man stand on the victory platform while the others stood on the pigeon-stained ground? What made one man a champion and another a perennial contender?" The difference, I decided, was total, undiluted focus on a singular goal. As soon as I realized this, I went from being a "dreamer" to a man obsessed with "doing." I went from being just a member of the multitudes who are content with the self-defeating standard, "It's nice just to be here," to someone who would only be satisfied with victory. On that day in 1972, I made a decision to see what I was made of, to awaken in my twenty-two-year-old body the champion who lives deep down within us all, a champion ready to go from tenth to first place.

"What if I take every second of every day for the next four years to do whatever I have to do to prepare myself to stand on top of that platform?" I asked myself.

The minute I said those words and made the commitment to do the work necessary to get there, I was a different human being. I knew at that instant *exactly* what I wanted and what I would sacrifice to achieve it. I had four years of my life to give, and, as I stood in the shadows, I made myself a promise, a vow, that sunk into every inch of my being: I was going to dedicate the next four years to the goal of standing atop that victory platform, draped in gold. Every decision I would make from that moment forward would be weighed against a singular question: *Will it increase my chances for winning the gold medal for the decathlon at the 1976 Olympic Games?*

I returned to my room in the Olympic Village. It was eleven P.M. I had just spent two days running the decathlon, one of the toughest endurance tests in sport, and I should have been exhausted. Instead, I was exhilarated! My heart pounded, adrenaline flowed and my mind raced with the vision of Avilov atop the platform.

I stared at the clock and listened to its incessant ticking, which seemed to grow louder and louder with every passing second. All of a sudden, the sound of this clock was exploding in my brain. Every time it ticked, I decided, a second had died. Time, I realized, was now my enemy! Each passing second represented an opportunity missed. It was four years until the Games—and the clock was screaming at me: *If you're going to dedicate every second to winning the decathlon, what are you doing wasting your time in bed?*

Possessed, I bolted up and, with my heart pounding in my chest and the clock ticking in my brain, threw on my running gear and began jogging down the streets of Munich. As the rest of the Olympians celebrated their victory or dealt with their defeat, I was preparing for '76 with a full-bore, long-distance run, a run that, for the next four years, would literally never stop.

Looking back, I'm amazed at my single-minded pursuit of my goal. I devoted every hour of every day, 365 days a year, to training for the games, excluding everything else, until I had won each event a thousand times in my mind. This wasn't a business for me. In those days, no athletic company would pay your way, and I never looked at the Games as a career move. I was strictly an amateur: one man against history in a contest that, since Jim Thorpe received the first gold medal for the decathlon in 1912, had determined which individual would be proclaimed the World's Greatest Athlete.

I didn't stop running until the evening of July 30, 1976, when, as Avilov was relegated to third place, I stood atop the winner's platform, receiving the gold medal for the decathlon. It was America's Bicentennial year and, as the country dressed itself in red, white and blue, I brought home not only the gold medal, but a new record—8,634 points—for the decathlon. I was crowned the World's Greatest Athlete, and my life became a flurry of ticker tape and celebration.

It would be nice to say that I stepped off that victory platform and ran through life with equal velocity, a winner forever draped in garlands, a champion of television, film, politics and philanthropy. I could then regale you with tales of gold, of Olympian ideals and the boundless capacities of the human spirit, living proof that man really does have the ability to fly.

It would be a pretty picture. But it would be a lie.

The truth is this: for a long time after I won the Gold, I felt like a failure in real life. After the Olympics—the one arena where I felt comfortable and was the best in the world—I was thrust into a world where I was a rank amateur: the world of lights and cameras, action and celebrity. Literally overnight, I went from feeling like a champion back to being that same dyslexic kid who now had to go out and do uncomfortable things . . . like reading a TV TelePrompTer before a national audience.

Then, as fast as it takes to say "Whatever happened to Bruce Jenner?" I found myself alone and lonely. For twelve years, all I had to do in life was score points. Now I had to deal with people, both personally and professionally, and the results weren't great. Seemingly overnight, I was no longer a winner. I had not only forgotten the secrets that empowered me to win the gold medal; I didn't even remember why I wanted to win in the first place.

Today I proudly stand as a testament to a greater victory than I could ever have achieved in an Olympic stadium, the victory of one man who gained control of his destiny.

But this book is not about me.

It's about you.

It's about a power that lies deep down within us all, a power that most of us don't even know we have. It's about the power that transformed Bruce Jenner, absolutely average American, into Bruce Jenner, gold-medalist, and it's a power that can transform every area of your existence. My victory had nothing to do with bone or muscle mass. My secret was the capacity of my mind, my ability to single-mindedly focus upon a goal and make it a reality. But while it took me four years to win the Olympic gold medal in the decathlon, it would take me twenty years to become a winner in life, twenty years of stumbling in every aspect of my existence.

I am going to show you how to access this power in the Olympics of your own life. Because deep inside each of us lies a champion, a champion who has the ability to race against the clock of life—and win.

> *"I had forgotten that every little action of the common day*
> *makes or unmakes character, and that therefore what one*
> *has done in the secret chamber one has someday to cry*
> *aloud on the house tops. I ceased to be lord over myself."*
> —OSCAR WILDE, THE PICTURE OF DORIAN GRAY

For fifteen years, the gold medal sat in my sock drawer.

The gold medal for the 1976 Olympics, the medal that I had sworn never to do anything to tarnish, the medal that had taken me from the victory platform to hosting jobs on ABC and NBC sports and "Good Morning America," starring roles in numerous feature films, TV shows, and commercials, and hundreds of personal appearances, the medal that signified all that I had accomplished as a human being, did not hang in a hall of honor.

The one thing that I had poured every ounce of my being into achieving was hidden away in a sock drawer.

The annals of glory are filled with tales of bottle rockets, men and women who fire fast and soar high, then come crashing to the ground in an even more startling explosion of fire and noise and light. I never thought that could happen to me.

But it did.

Most people remember me as the Bicentennial-issue Olympic champion who seemed too All-American to be true, the Bruce Jenner of the Wheaties box and the *Sports Illustrated* magazine cover. Well, you wouldn't have recognized me in 1990.

I was living in the hills outside of Los Angeles, in a one-bedroom bungalow where the dirty dishes filled the kitchen sink and a dried-out Christmas tree from the holidays four months ago sat in a clump beside the door, serving as the only attempt at interior decoration. When I ventured out, I drove a 1976 Ford van that hadn't seen a vacuum cleaner since it left the factory, and I dressed in a wardrobe that consisted of ragged athletic gear and one tired old suit. I hadn't worked out with weights since the Olympic Games in 1976, and my diet consisted of my own home cooking—and that's scary. I'd lost between fifteen and twenty pounds, and years of physical inactivity had left me looking a little thin. I probably needed a haircut but, living alone with nobody to talk to, I would have been the last to know.

I was a relic from the era of Farrah and Flip, Howard Cosell and Joe Namath, lost in the world of Tom Cruise and Bob Costas. I had just celebrated my fortieth birthday and I desperately needed help. I'd lost all direction in life. I'd lost interest in business. And after two bad marriages, I didn't even want to think about dating. My self-esteem wasn't exactly soaring. As a matter of fact, I thought I was really unattractive—so unattractive that I spent thousands of dollars that I didn't have on a nose job, only to have the surgeon botch it so badly he had to do it all over again.

So much for self-improvement.

Between personal appearances, my life consisted mostly of golf and learning to play a rented piano, leaving me lots of idle time. I had 200 dollars in the bank and debts of about half a million. My main source of income was talking about the Games, about how I once was a winner, the man proclaimed the World's Greatest Athlete, while valiantly not letting on how much and how long I'd been losing. For somebody who'd won so much professionally, it was amazing how much I was suffering personally. I hoped that nobody could see the defeat and loneliness. But at times, when I stepped up to podiums across America to give my presentation, wearing a circa '76 tuxedo with a big butterfly tie and a Vegas-style ruffled shirt, I felt sure that the defeat and the despair were written all over my face.

I was Mr. Nice Guy.

"Bruce Jenner—what a great guy," everyone would say.

"Bruce'll baby-sit your kids."

"Bruce'll give you his last dollar and not even ask for it back."

Look up "sucker" in the dictionary, and there I am. Do you get the picture? I believed *everybody*. And everybody eventually had taken their pieces of Good Old Bruce. Now Bruce had bottomed out, and they still wanted more.

In so many ways, I was still the dyslexic kid who lived in fear of being called upon to get up in front of the class and read. Perceptually, picking the words off the paper was like reading a billboard while on a roller coaster, and being called upon to read to the class, which would trigger sweaty palms, pounding heartbeat and the assurance that I looked like an absolute idiot, was a fate worse than death. Now, thirty-five years later, I was right back where I started: stripped of self-esteem, doubting my abilities to make intelligent decisions and failing in every area of my life.

I had grown accustomed to a life without: without intimacy, without excitement, without adventure, without growth. I was broken as a

man. And my medal, the golden symbol of all that I'd won, sat in a drawer, now the symbol of how much I'd lost. So wherever you are in your own life, no matter how low you've sunk, I can empathize. *I've been there.* I had given up. I had lost my will.

But once I'd hit bottom, I remembered something from my past: there's no place for losers in sport.

So what was I doing losing in life? That champion who lives down inside each of us, the champion who had the capacity to stand before the world in victory, would no longer allow me to live this lifestyle. *I had to get out!* And once I did, once I made a conscious decision to play the game of life, something extraordinary happened.

I saw light at the end of the tunnel. It arrived in the form of the love of my life and soul mate, my wife, Kris. Suddenly, I realized that I could turn my life around and start anew with a clean slate. Kris reintroduced me to the power that I had experienced, but never understood, so many years before at the Olympic Games. It was a power that I could fully comprehend only after I had sunk into the pit of misery. It was a power that would drive me back to the top with a velocity and speed that exceeded anything I'd experienced before.

It was the power of the Champion Within.

Once again, I could see my goal in front of me, close enough to reach out and grab. Once again, the clock in my head ticked incessantly. This time, the goal had rewards unconnected with sport; this time the goal was *personal.* Absolute personal glory, the gold medal in human development, to become the best person—husband, father, businessman, contributor—I could possibly become. Once again, when I could see my goal I could focus *exclusively* on it until the prize was mine.

Now, six years after leaving my solitary existence, my life has blossomed with an amazing ferocity; it was like the angels arrived, the skies parted and the seas split, allowing me to run through. I have taken my gold medal out of my sock drawer and proudly mounted it on the wall, allowing it to shine brightly in every area of my existence.

For the first time in my life, I finally know what love means. I always thought that it was something unattainable, something that I didn't deserve and, certainly, a place that I had never been before. Now I know that it is the seed from which all great things grow.

Financially, I'm back on track, the president of 8634, Inc., a multimillion-dollar company involved in marketing/infomercials, corporate affiliations, food supplements, aircraft sales, personal appearances and speaking engagements. I am a representative of Visa, Anheuser-Busch and Coca-Cola, and a frequent motivational speaker, whose presentations center around a singular theme: how to awaken the power within.

I have discovered that our performance in life is a direct reflection of the image we have of ourselves. For a long time, I dressed as poorly as I felt deep inside. But one of the first things I did after my awakening was to trash my old clothes (and there weren't many), give away the van and start life all over again with the mantra, *"You only have one chance to make a first impression."*

Now I look as good as I feel. I get up every morning eager to tackle my day. From loving my wife to having a meaningful relationship with my kids to being totally fulfilled in business, life has never been better. A licensed pilot, I fly my own plane, drive a gorgeous new car and dress in a wardrobe that could grace the cover of any men's fashion magazine. I am in the best shape I've been in since I competed in the Games twenty years ago. But now I'm not merely in touch with my body but also my heart. And when those two feelings meet, a combustible reaction occurs, allowing me, at forty-six, to enter a realm I never thought possible.

My wife, Kris, and I recently bought a 103-acre ranch in Santa Barbara County. And best of all, as the most shining evidence of our enduring belief in the future, I became, at forty-six, the proud father of a beautiful baby girl, Kendall Nicole Jenner.

Now I am on a new mission, a mission to share my experiences and help people realize the potential that lies deep inside. In this way, my victory may become more than one note in the history books. It may become a victory that gives something back, allowing me to help others realize that no matter what their situation in life, they have the power to move forward and make life a great adventure. As Helen Keller once said, "Life is either a daring adventure or nothing."

Somewhere out there, your stadium is waiting, filled with all of the people you love. They are rooting for you as you struggle, and they'll be cheering as you finally come around the backstretch and blast through the finish line, not merely a competitor but a champion. Sports is but a metaphor for the bigger game of life, but it can also become a mirror. Through sports, you can find yourself and your capacity for victory and defeat. Through sports, you can find answers to help you compete in the greater challenges of life.

I used to think that sports was the most competitive field on earth—until I got into the business of living. We have to be good competitors in both. But the similarities go deeper, because in both sports and life the competition is not really other players. The real competition lies deep within our souls, where that champion lives. How do we bring it out? We begin with our dreams.

We all have dreams. We all believe we have something special to contribute. Most of us never fulfill our dreams, mainly because we're just trying to get through life, trying to deal with our daily tasks and personal commitments. Ninety-nine percent of the populace is "just trying to get by."

I am a living example that dreams do come true.

I'm here to tell you that it can happen to you.

I want to share my secrets with you, secrets to optimum living

that were literally right under my nose. The same power that propelled me to win the gold medal in the Olympic Games provided me
with a near-perfect template for awakening every area of my life.
Once again I competed in the decathlon. Only now I competed in the
ten events not as sport but as a mission in personal growth, each event
representing a specific area of my existence. Only after I'd conquered
each event and mastered its corresponding lesson for life would I
learn the secrets of the Champion Within.

> *"Only in something like running can finality be achieved,
> the sort of finality that is almost perfection. But it is not the
> kind of perfection that leaves you with nothing to live for.
> You are not your own executioner, because sport is not the
> main aim in life. Yet to achieve perfection in one thing,
> however small, makes it possible to face the uncertainties
> and more difficult problems of life."*
>
> —*OLYMPIAN ROGER BANNISTER,
> FROM HIS AUTOBIOGRAPHY* FIRST FOUR MINUTES

What elevated the original Olympics was not the sport but the
sacrifice. Sport was merely motion, but when coupled with sacrifice to
the point of exhaustion in the most competitive nation on earth, sport
became a holy rite worthy of the gods who presumably watched from
the mountains above. As the national religious festival of ancient
Greece, the Olympic Games were the destination of an athlete's journey of pain and sacrifice, the essence of the Greek Ideal as stated by
Socrates: "What a disgrace it is for a man to grow old without ever
seeing the beauty and the strength of which his body is capable."

Atop Olympia, in a meadow surrounded by snow-covered mountains and studded with shrines, altars, statues and the temple of the
Greek god Zeus, the wreath of wild olive symbolized life's greatest re-

ward, one man having conquered himself to become the definition of an athlete, who, wrote the great poet Pindar, "delights in the toil and cost." The Olympic champion was more than mere hero. In life, he was an idol; in death, he frequently assumed the role of a minor god.

Of all the ancient competitions, no contest tested an athlete's ability as thoroughly as the pentathlon, a five-event test that included the long jump, discus, javelin, sprinting and wrestling. It became a favorite at the Greek games seven centuries before the birth of Christ, eventually evolving into today's decathlon, the toughest contest in all sport. An almost masochistic two-day menu of ten almost contradictory athletic abilities, the decathlon, said Olympian Bill Toomey, requires a "super-schizophrenic," able to heave a shot like a wild beast, then turn around and sail over a high jump like a gazelle, then turn around to face eight more events that have nothing in common—except pain.

I've always compared the decathlon to a big, high, snow-shrouded mountain. It might allow you a visit, but never habitation. Like life, the decathlon demands not merely physical ability but, more important, *mental* agility. You have to achieve balance between mind and body and train in solitude until you can sail through each event in your sleep so that, when running the ten events, you can keep focused under the constantly escalating pressure. In this way, the decathlon tests your ability to see how far you can reach down inside yourself.

Just as our true competitors in life are our own inner fears and perceived shortcomings, in the decathlon the competition consists not of other decathletes but of the standardized international "tables," the Holy Grails that award points to individual performances in each event, providing an exact gauge of individual athletic ability in a way that team sports can never measure. Individual performances in each event—coming in first, second or tenth—don't matter. If you fall short in one event, you have to immediately forget failure and move on to the next.

It's the only standardized test throughout history of a person's athletic ability. What are the basics of athletics? Running, jumping and throwing. The decathlon tests those abilities in three ways of throwing (shot, discus, javelin), three ways of jumping (long jump, high jump, pole vault) and four ways of running (the 100-, 400-, 1,500-meter runs and the 110-meter high hurdles). Michael Jordan is a great athlete, but basketball is not a standardized test of athletic ability. Who's to say that Michael Jordan is better than Oscar Robinson was in his day? It's all subjective. Only in the decathlon can athletes test their abilities and compare their performances to the greats: Jim Thorpe, Bob Mathias, Rafer Johnson. . . .

"The decathlon is a struggle against time, distance, fatigue and one's inner fear of weakness and failure," said Olympian Ken Doherty. If you play the game well, it elevates it from sport to the grandest of missions, which Carl Gustav, King of Sweden, anointed when he presented the first gold medal in the decathlon to Jim Thorpe in 1912, saying, "You are the greatest athlete in the world."

Thorpe returned the compliment with a simple, "Thanks, King."

Real life is not only as tough as the decathlon, the world's most difficult game. It's *tougher* than the decathlon. The decathlete only has to accomplish ten events in two days, but each of us has ten, twenty, even thirty events to deal with daily over a lifetime. In the decathlon, the events are cut and dried: you run against an international score table; the better you do, the more points you get. But how do you judge your performances in the events of your life? How do you know your score as husband or wife, father or mother, son or daughter, grandfather or grandmother, entrepreneur, employee or boss? The events of life are endless. The competitor must be versatile, able to juggle a multitude of activities simultaneously.

You can easily access the methods I used to propel my performance, first in the Olympics and later in my life, in subsequent chapters of this book. But for now, I'd like to give you a brief glimpse into the decathlon of life. When I first put it all on paper, I was astounded. I knew the ancient Greeks were brilliant when they devised the Olympics. Now, after seeing how each of the decathlon's ten events imparts its own specific lesson for living, I feel like they were almost godlike.

Let's go briefly through the events that form the chapters of this book:

1. The 100-Meter Run: The gun fires now. Time is not your friend; every second represents an opportunity missed. The first event of the decathlon is the first event of your new life. You've got to come out of the blocks hard. How to get started. I want to show you how to take the first step toward your goal and gear up for the race ahead.

2. The Long Jump: It's the only event in the decathlon where you can see the finish line clearly. How to determine the long jumps of your life—your dreams and aspirations—and how to set goals that will enable you to reach them as you leap from plan to action.

3. The Shot Put: Of all of the ten events in the decathlon, the shot put requires the most brute strength. How to evaluate your weaknesses and go with your strengths.

4. The High Jump: Like the bar a decathlete continuously raises in the high jump, you've got to keep raising your

standards in life. How to start low but constantly improve, until you can scale heights you never thought possible before.

5. The 400-Meter Run: In this toughest of foot races, the demonic force racers call "the Bear" crawls on your back and tries to drag you down. How to deal with the bears in life, the obstacles that threaten your mission, and how to keep going when the world tries to drag you down.

6. The Hurdles: This is the event that's most like daily living: a line of hurdles, one after the other, which the decathlete must sail over with perfect symmetry of mind and body. How to take the hurdles of life one at a time—and win.

7. The Discus: The discus was my best event in the decathlon. When its turn came in the Games, I knew it was time to make my move, to pull ahead of my own personal records. How to know when it's time to make your move in life and how to "go for it" with all your heart and soul.

8. The Pole Vault: The decathlete keeps raising the bar on the pole vault until he reaches the height at which he can jump no higher, meaning that this event always ends in failure. How to break through failure in life and find greater heights.

9. The Javelin: An ancient weapon of war and chase, the javelin is a remnant of the days of warriors and knights.

To throw the javelin well, the decathlete must imagine an inch-round point in the air, then throw the javelin through the point, effectively putting blinders on all distractions. How to focus in on your mission in life and keep your eye on the point, amid the storms of change and distraction.

10. The 1,500-Meter Run: This is your longest footrace, the true test of a champion. The track stretches in front of your forever. How to run the race for all it's worth.

There is one condition. Like the ancient games, the essence of success is toil and cost. You've got to commit yourself to doing the work. No great war was ever won, no mountain climbed, no seemingly insurmountable obstacle conquered without the would-be conqueror becoming one with the mission. I made a commitment in 1972 to train six to eight hours a day, 365 days a year, for the next four years. Anything less would have guaranteed failure. You have to be willing to make an equally total commitment to do the work that can move your life forward. Because nothing in this life comes without it.

If you're willing to make the commitment, this book can show you how to awaken that power, that champion who lives within us all, as you compete in—and *win*—the Olympics of your life.

So let the Games begin!

CHAPTER ONE

UP FROM THE ORDINARY

Who am I?

I am the ordinary kid who becomes somebody through sheer struggle, the guy who fails and fails and finally, as if failure is sick of him, succeeds.

If you were around in 1976, you probably remember me. I was the big news of the Bicentennial Olympic Games, the bolt of red, white and blue who became an overnight sensation, who ran from field to screen, from athlete to pitchman and television personality. Everywhere I went there seemed to be an anthem playing and a crowd waiting. I was an All-American for an innocent time: President Ford sought national healing in the White House; "Charlie's Angels," the number-one television show, brought a hint of cleavage to the tube. I was the great white hope, the kind of guy who'd teach your son baseball and have your daughter home by ten P.M. "If there was anything he might worry about, it would be that people would consider him too perfect, perhaps contrived," wrote Frank Deford in an August 9, 1976, *Sports Illustrated* article titled "Heading for the 11th Event," adding that I was "completely in control" of myself.

But the perception was wrong.

Because I was ordinary. Absolutely ordinary.

Let me take you back to the morning after my victory at the Twenty-first Olympic Games, and you'll see just how incredibly ordinary my life has been.

"I don't remember Bruce being any different than any of the other kids."

—*WASHINGTON IRVING JUNIOR HIGH COACH JACK MCCLEARY*

I stood buck naked in front of the mirror on the morning after the '76 Olympic Games with my gold medal hung on a gold-link chain around my neck. I was all alone in a hotel room and, in my reflection, I could see the hard-won harvest of a dozen long years of slaving. I had scored a startling 8,634 points, breaking the records of my heroes—Jim Thorpe, Bob Mathias, Rafer Johnson, Milt Campbell, Bill Toomey and Nicolay Avilov—with a score so close to my own personal-best predictions it seemed almost psychic.

I swore I'd never do anything to tarnish the medal and all it stood for. But in my reflection I didn't see the new world-record holder. I didn't even recognize the Champion Within whom I had so resoundingly awakened before the world.

I saw an absolutely ordinary guy, who was, frankly, scared.

"What now?" I asked myself.

For four years, I didn't have to grow up. My only job in life was scoring points. I could dedicate everything to my sport to the exclusion of all else and live a sheltered existence. I was totally secure in that environment; I was in control. I was the best in the world. Now I was leaving the one arena where I felt comfortable—the decathlon—and was heading right back into the arena that I'd neglected so long for sports: myself.

I felt as if I'd learned to play the piano, practicing six to eight hours a day for twelve years of my life, and finally had the chance to play that piano in front of the world. I felt as if I'd played the most beautiful music the world had ever heard, but now that the song was over, I had to put my hands in my pockets and never play music again. I had walked the long road to Olympic glory, and now life was lifting me up and returning me right back to where I'd started, as if to say, "Now let's see how tough you are, big guy."

I was losing my cover, my shield, and being thrust right back into the world of insecurity. Once again, I was that dyslexic kid standing up to speak in front of the class. But now the classroom was a stadium and the whole world was watching.

The biggest race was yet to be run.

Now I had to grow up.

As I stood before the mirror, the telephone was ringing off the hook. The road to fame stretched before me, lined with rapacious agents and a ravenous press, everyone seeking to capitalize on my achievement, then chew me up and spit me out. Movie producers wanted to fly me to Rome to screen-test for the role of Superman, and countless other offers were anxiously being presented. ABC offered me a job as a sports commentator and special correspondent for *Good Morning America. Cosmopolitan* magazine editors were begging me to pose, naked or clothed, for a centerfold. Fashion photographer Francesco Scavullo was ready to take my picture. Ralph Lauren personally wanted to outfit me with a complete new wardrobe. Millions of dollars of advertising campaigns were being designed with me in mind, running from the ridiculous to the sublime: throwing Norelco fluorescent lightbulbs like javelins on television; popping out of a giant Wheaties box.

Two weeks before the Games, I had walked though New York City and nobody had even noticed. Now I couldn't even step out on a street without causing a traffic jam. Taxi cab drivers stopped their cars to run out and shake my hand. Office workers left their desks for autographs. Even my best friends called me to check whether I'd "changed." My face was on the front page of every newspaper (*Dieu du Stad!*—God of the Stadium—proclaimed a French front page) and a pack of reporters constantly waited outside my hotel room doors, all asking a single question: "Who is Bruce Jenner?"

All I could say was, "I'm no different than anybody else. I did one special thing with my life, which is sure exciting, but I'm no different than anybody else in this room."

It was the truth.

I was absolutely ordinary.

But achievement, whether it's a gold medal in the Olympics or in real life, always begins in the ordinary. To cite a few extreme examples: Thomas Edison's teachers thought he was too dumb to learn; the father of the great sculptor Rodin called his son "an idiot," and Rodin seemed to prove him right by becoming the worst pupil in his school; Walter Cronkite was turned down for his first radio job for "lack of a decent performance"; Henry Ford went broke five times before he produced the Model T.

And Bruce Jenner? Well . . .

I grew up solidly middle class in the suburbs of New York City and then Connecticut, where athletics was as much a part of my family tradition as going to church and getting a good education. My dad, Bill Jenner, had competed in the U.S. Army Olympics in Nuremberg, Germany, in 1945, winning a silver medal in the 100-yard dash, and his father had run the Boston Marathon for fifteen years. But for Dad, war won out over sports: he served in World War II, then returned home to upper New York State, where he traded in his combat gear for climbing boots and became a tree surgeon.

My mother, Esther Jenner, was an All-American mom and

housewife who worked when she could as a secretary to make extra money. Every five years, the family moved. But while the locations were different, the settings were always the same: tree-shaded streets in the middle-class towns of Ossining, then Yorktown Heights, then Tarrytown. We finally settled on the lakefront in Sandy Hook, Connecticut, always dependent on the growth of the trees overhead. Trees meant business for my dad, and his firm, a mom-and-pop operation called Jenner Tree Surgeon, would tackle any problem.

I was the second of four children—two sisters and a brother. By the time I turned two, I'd already developed a big chest, wide shoulders and boundless energy, prompting my dad to nickname me Bruiser. Trying to curb my wanderlust, my parents fenced in their yard. When that didn't help, they strapped me in a harness tied with a clothesline to a stake planted in the middle of the yard.

But when it came to school, I wasn't going anywhere. My older sister Pam, who was closest to my age, was a constant thorn in my side. She was the 4.0 student, named to the National Honor Society, and I was the slow kid, always struggling scholastically.

I would've surely followed in my family's middle-class footsteps, just another working stiff raising a family in the suburbs. But I soon faced something that would make me different, an obstacle that would make me try harder just to become like everybody else, a disability that would force me to develop my mind and, in doing so, dramatically alter the arc of my future.

I had difficulty reading.

From the beginning, I did not want to go to school. When my folks first took me to kindergarten, I screamed and yelled. It was total trauma. I just wanted to go home with Mom. All I wanted to do in school was sleep. I would sit in the back of the kindergarten classroom in an endless nap. Most of the time the teacher wouldn't even wake me. She thought I had a sleeping disorder. When she discovered that my problems persisted when I was awake, the teacher got more aggressive. I was put into the "slower" class, which, for a kid whose biggest fear is that his peers will think he's stupid, is like hanging a banner around his neck that screams DUMMY!

I wasn't a bad kid. I was always the teacher's pet, the little guy who needed shelter from the world. I never caused any problems. I just liked to sleep, to daydream. I wanted to be a million miles away from that classroom. I would sit there and look out the window and dream of escaping to a land where nobody ever had to read.

Yes, *read*.

That little four-letter word became the bane of my youth.

Not only did I have a perceptual problem when it came to reading, the problem spread to every area of my existence. Picture the young dyslexic in reading class, although to the lay public in the fifties the word "dyslexia" was largely unknown. The teacher, confident that a child's reading skills offered a glimpse into his or her brain, would go from desk to desk, asking each student to stand before the class and read. Frantic, I would count paragraphs, desperately trying to figure out which one was going to be mine so I could start practicing and be ready. It was a death sentence: counting kids and chunks of type until both whirled dizzily. Before I could even find my designated paragraph, I'd break out in a sweat, trying in vain to brace myself for the worst: looking like an idiot before my class.

"Please read the first paragraph in Chapter Four, Bruce," the teacher would say, the words assaulting my ears like a shotgun's blast.

I'd walk to the front of the class, open the book and stare down at the page. I could see the words, but they just wouldn't register. The fluid motion that most people take for granted, as words come off the page and register in your brain, just didn't happen for me. It was like a short circuit between my eyes and my mind, derailing the reading train every time it started down the tracks. My eyes would move forward, but the first word would come up slowly before it registered, then the next would register faster, then the process would repeat itself. So when I attempted to read a sentence, everything would come out backwards—if anything came out at all. My head would be spinning and I wouldn't even be thinking about what was on the page, only that everybody was looking at me and I was doing horribly.

When I flunked second grade and was forced to repeat it, my worst feelings were confirmed.

Dyslexia has since become an overused word. Every time a child has any problem with reading—reversing the digits in a phone number or inverting two words in a sentence—parents are ready to label the child dyslexic and spend a lot of money on doctors, therapists and special-education teachers. Each of us has reversed digits in a telephone number. But take that simple mistake and multiply it a hundred times and you can start to understand what life is like for a dyslexic. It can range from a kid not being able to read to an adult being unable to decipher signs on a highway. Today we know that 10 percent of the population is dyslexic, a percentage that at one time included Albert Einstein and Thomas Edison and now includes Tom Cruise and Cher. We know there is treatment and, eventually, redemption. But in the fifties, nobody even knew what the word meant.

From kindergarten through the sixth grade, school was absolute torture for me, simply because I was deathly afraid the teacher was going to call on me to read in front of the class. I was the only one who gave my reading disability much thought until junior high, when everyone guessed that I needed glasses. My parents took me to get some tests—which showed that my sight was 20/20.

Finally, I heard the word.

"Bruce is dyslexic," said the school doctor to my parents, as I sat beside them.

"What's that?" asked Mom.

"Is it a disease?" asked Dad.

"Am I going to die?" asked I.

The doctor smiled and said, "Go back to class, Bruce."

If you're dyslexic, you're always going to be dyslexic. You don't get around that. You can't take two aspirin, get plenty of rest and wake up cured. You're stuck with dyslexia for life. It's up to you to determine the extent of your problem. The biggest issue with dyslexic kids, however, goes deeper than reading difficulties. The most serious damage that dyslexia does to kids is to destroy their self-esteem, their sense of self-worth. We've put so much pressure on kids to do well in school, to be good students. Not being a good reader, and therefore not a good student, makes kids feel they're a failure in life.

That's how I felt.

Then something miraculous happened, something that lifted me up from the ordinary and showed me a first glimpse of a world grander than anyplace I could have imagined in my classroom daydreams. It was an experience that showed me that whatever shortcomings and hardships life imposes upon a person, it conversely bestows a blessing, almost as compensation, some sort of skill that, if recognized early enough and sharpened and honed, can evolve into true excellence.

One day in fifth grade, I discovered the extent of my reward. The coach had set up a long line of chairs around the gym and asked all the kids in school to race around them, scoring them for time. When my name was called, the fear of going before the class miraculously vanished; no more sweaty palms or pounding heartbeat. As the coach started the clock and told me to run, I took off in a white heat. I ran for all I was worth and, when I returned to the starting point, the coach wore the most beautiful smile I'd ever seen.

"*Great time!*" the coach exclaimed.

All the other kids ran the race and nobody could beat my time! Next thing I knew, I was being called the fastest kid in the entire school. For the first time in my life, I felt like "somebody," and that feeling felt good.

"Geez, I didn't know you were that fast," said one kid after another.

"Neither did I," I replied.

I was as surprised as anyone.

This accomplishment became a very big deal. I held my head up higher. School had always represented failure, but then, in the time it took to run around a line of chairs, kids were coming up and patting me on the back, shouting, "Great time!" For the first time in my life, I had a reason to feel good about myself. For the first time, I had people cheering me on! My self-esteem rocketed from zero into the stratosphere, all because of two little words of encouragement. Those two little words—"Great time!"—sparked a fire inside of me. Looking back now, if I could have held on to those words of approval, my gold medal would never have landed in my sock drawer. But thirty years later, I would still be seeking words of assurance and praise, just as I did on that day in fifth grade.

What a world of difference a few words of encouragement can make! Whenever you have a chance, pass out those words of encouragement freely. Because words really do have the power to change lives. Just look what two little words did to mine.

Sports quickly became my reason for living. I went out for basketball in the sixth grade and got further reinforcement merely by seeing my parents cheering for me in the grandstands. That meant I must be doing something right.

It became important for me to succeed in sports for several reasons. Primarily, growing up a dyslexic kid, I always thought that everybody was better than me because everybody was a better reader.

But when I discovered my athletic ability in the fifth grade, sports became the center of my universe. I could go onto the athletic field and take on a kid who was a good reader and a good student and, basically, clean his clock.

Soon, my dad was seeking a family sport, something we could do together. Midget racing cars? Too dangerous, decreed Mom. Waterskiing? Well, now, that might be perfect. Dad bought a boat and skis and we soon had a house on Lake Zoar in Connecticut. I took to the skis like I'd taken to those chairs in the classroom, eventually winning three East Coast waterskiing championships in the boy's division.

My school coaches, always on the lookout for able young men who might push their teams forward, closed in on me from all sides: "Gee, Bruce, maybe you should go out for track/football/baseball/basketball!"

Believe me, it was nice to be wanted. After years of scholastic disappointment, I had finally found something that I was good at, and, luckily, I didn't let it slip away.

Just as the coaches came recruiting, so did other kids. I quickly became the guy to beat, the measure against whom everybody could gauge their own talent. When fifth grade was over, I changed schools, from an all-white elementary to one that was racially mixed. The fastest boy in the new school, a black kid named Jim Everett, approached me on the schoolyard.

"I hear you're really fast," Everett said, more as a dare than a compliment.

Oh, man, what have I gotten myself into? I thought to myself.

I had invaded the "fast territory" merely by transferring to Everett's school, and now everybody wanted to see what I was made of.

We squared off on the playground, with Everett's buddies working the whistle, and ran a quick dash. When I looked up at the finish line, I had not only been trounced, I'd been left in the dust.

Soon after this drubbing, I learned a secret: the source of an athlete's or an individual's power resides not merely in the muscles but in the mind. This wisdom was driven home when I went out for wrestling in the seventh grade. Frankly, I got my butt kicked. I got pinned in the first five matches. I'll never forget staring up at the ceiling while some big kid slammed me to the canvas in a headlock.

Then something clicked in my mind. I simply *decided* to win, to reach deep into the core of my being and summon up a victory. Once I envisioned my goal—pinning my opponent—I could go out and make the vision a reality on the mat. "Oh, so that's the way this works," I said to myself. "His butt is supposed to be on the ground."

What changed? My attitude. I began to think like a winner. Whether you're talking about business, relationships or sports, attitude is everything. Studies of successful people have shown that attitude accounts for 80 percent of their success, aptitude only 20 percent.

When you think like a winner, you become one.

Even though I weighed many pounds less than most of my competitors, my attitude—my determination and belief that I could win—carried me through. I won because of the strength of what I began to recognize as my "athletic mind." From that point forward, I won practically every match, including the county championships.

I grew fast, headed toward six feet, a tall, lanky bundle of energy and determination. The rapid growth took its toll. My right knee was sore all the time. I went to the doctor and was diagnosed with Osgood-Schlatter syndrome, fairly common among teenagers, whose tendons don't grow as fast as their bones, especially in the knees. The irregular growth shifts the tibia—the support bone between the foot and the knee—a little bit forward, and the pain has to be endured until the tendons catch up with the bones.

Because of Osgood-Schlatter, the school doctor wouldn't let me play any sports. I couldn't even go to gym class. I started swimming and diving at the YMCA, but my newfound reason for living was suddenly gone. As I spent most of my last year of junior high school on the sidelines, riding my bike on the hills above the sports fields on my newspaper route, I could see the football team at practice. As I watched enviously, I was certain that the one thing I had found that I was good at—sports—was the one thing I'd never be able to do again.

For a full two and a half years, I was sidelined.

Once the doctors gave me permission to go back to sports, I became hell-bent. I had a sport for every season: I played football for three months, and when football season was over, I played basketball for three months, and when basketball season was over, I played at track for three months. Then, during the summer, I competitively water-skied. But most of all, I loved pole-vaulting. All it took was one glimpse of a kid racing down the track, planting that pole and soaring toward the clouds—and I was hooked.

I was a high school freshman with exactly two days of practice when I attempted my first competition. Issued one standard vaulter's pole, I walked to the pole-vaulting facility, where a sand pit, instead of a foam rubber pit, awaited. Sand is the cruelest sort of pit, a pit that can crack a vaulter's back if the landing is less than perfect. My opening height was eight feet, six inches, and I was psyched. I was ready to run down and split the sky. I had vaulted over something like nine feet, six inches the day before in practice, so I was confident that eight-six would be a snap.

I came flying down the runway, planted the pole and soared skyward. My feet crossed the bar, followed by my hips and then, in the awkward backward ballet that is pole-vaulting, the rest of my body followed, soaring high over the bar. Somewhere on the way down, my face slammed into the crossbar and I went crashing down on my back into the sand pit with a sickening *thud!* The wind was knocked out of my lungs, my lip was split almost to my nostril and a broken tooth hung pitifully onto my bloody lip.

This was my introduction to track and field!

But I didn't quit.

"I'll conquer this," I said to myself, and I went on to do exactly that. I couldn't read words off a page, but I could darn sure focus on a goal and bring it to fruition. When my focus kicked in, there was nothing I couldn't accomplish.

When it came to school, I was below average.

When it came to girls, I was afraid.

When it came to conversations, I was shy.

Sports was my only redemption.

By the time I got to high school, I still had no idea of what I was going to do with my life. But now, at least, I had reason to study. I had to get at least passing grades to stay eligible for sports. So I bought home a C in everything, except phys ed, in which I always made an A. Still, I never thought of athletics as a future. I didn't lift weights. I didn't seriously concentrate on any one sport. I played at sports, accent on the "play."

I made the all-county and all-state track teams. I won state championships in the high jump and the pole vault during my senior year. As a member of the Sleepy Hollow High School football team, I even got my picture on the front page of *The New York Times* Sports Section.

I was adept at every game, master of none.

In my senior year, we moved from Tarrytown to Newtown, Connecticut, and I enrolled in a smaller school, where I instantly became the big man on campus, the jock who could command respect in any sport. The football team started me as a running back and, occasionally, even as a quarterback. But I was a big fish in a little pond, such an ordinary commodity nationally that when graduation came—the season of sports scholarship offers—I didn't get a single bid. Average grades and below-average SAT scores, coupled with an average high school athletic program, exiled me to college scout disinterest.

No college wanted me, and that wasn't great news. It was 1968. Vietnam was raging; the draft was in full gear. If I didn't get my buns into school, my butt was heading into battle. I wanted to go to college, but I thought I was finished with school sports forever. So I made plans to enroll at the junior college near my home and go to work with my dad in the tree business, maybe eventually even taking it over. I was already working with Dad when a partial scholarship offer dropped from the heavens.

It was definitely not from Notre Dame.

One of my high school coaches knew L.D. Weldon, track coach at Graceland College in Lamoni, Iowa. Months before, Weldon had called, asking me to apply to Graceland. I had sent in my application and been accepted, but because Graceland didn't offer scholarships and I didn't have the 2,500 dollars tuition, I told them, "Thanks, but no thanks."

Now Weldon was on the phone, this time offering *cash*.

"Bruce? L.D. Weldon here. We've got a situation. . . ."

He explained that the school's soon-to-be-starting quarterback had transferred from a junior college to play for Graceland. But now the faculty discovered that he didn't have enough credits for admission. With football practice already in full swing, Graceland was stuck without their starting quarterback. They had a backup guy who could start, of course, but if the backup got injured, it could end their season.

"You played quarterback in high school, didn't you, Bruce?" Weldon asked.

"Well, I played running back and quarterback and all sorts of positions," I replied. "But I really wasn't a quarterback."

It didn't matter. Graceland was desperate, he said. Weldon was offering me 500 dollars to help defray the college's 2,500-dollar tuition, plus free room and board in his own basement.

"We want you out here quick—tomorrow," said Weldon.

My mind began racing. Man! I could be playing college football tomorrow! I thought. I had figured I'd never play again after high school, and now I'd gotten a scholarship offer!

I talked to my parents that night, signed a student loan at the bank the next morning, called L.D. Weldon and practically screamed into the phone: "I'll be on a flight tomorrow morning at nine A.M., and I'll be in Des Moines at one!"

I was eighteen years old, leaving home for the first time, never having ventured past Ohio, flying into Iowa to play for—what was the name of that college?—oh, yes, Graceland.

I had to look it up in the *Encyclopaedia Britannica*. Set in the cornfields of Iowa, the college is run by the Reorganized Church of Jesus Christ of the Latter Day Saints, a branch of the Mormon religion. Forget about sex, drugs and rock 'n' roll—Graceland didn't even allow dancing. At the height of the era of peace and love, I was headed to a cornfield college run by Mormons to be a backup quarterback for 500 dollars a year and a room in somebody's basement and the less-than-glorious major of . . . phys ed.

"Oh, my gosh, what have I done?" I moaned repeatedly to myself on the airplane. "Is the college full of guys with black hats and beards? Didn't I hear someone say the population of Lamoni, Iowa, is a thousand citizens and ten thousand hogs? Somebody's picking me up at the airport named L.D. Weldon. How the heck is he going to find me?"

The moment I got off the plane, a man with his hand extended came out of the crowd.

"L.D. Weldon here," he said. "You must be Bruce."

He was a big man, about sixty-five, in a plaid hat, with an eager grin and a rock-hard handshake.

"How did you know it was me?" I asked him, once we got into the car.

"I can spot an athlete anywhere," he said.

L.D. Weldon would quickly exert an enormous influence on my life, becoming almost like a second dad to me. He was the track coach, not even part of the football program, and he had recruited me merely as a favor to the football team. I didn't know that L.D. had his own plans for me as well. He had studied my athletic record and knew that during the football off-season I'd be looking for other sports to play.

"One of the high school coaches I knew told me this kid also ran track," L.D. would later reminisce. "He said the kid could high jump six-two, pole-vault about thirteen feet, do the triple jump and had even thrown the javelin a hundred and eighty feet. We got some money out of the football program for him, but I had him figured for the decathlon all along. I knew that he must be able to jump, and he had a good throwing arm if he could throw the javelin that well. Those two things, jumping and throwing, are the two most important abilities for the decathlon. Speed is important, too, but there are ways to get around that."

The decathlon. I had never even heard the word.

L.D. Weldon was obsessed with the decathlon, and, looking at my multisport record, he immediately saw something—a young kid with some athletic talent, perhaps. But even more importantly, I think he saw a good heart and a fire burning down deep inside to succeed. He was always on the lookout for what he called "multieventors," athletes who can compete in a lot of different events. He'd trained a decathlete named Jack Parker who took the bronze medal in the 1936

Olympic Games, and he was certain that I had the stuff of which champions are made.

He had much more confidence in my abilities than I had.

"You're a great athlete, Bruce, and I can see you competing in the decathlon," he'd say repeatedly during our nightly talks in his windowless basement apartment. "I'm going to coach you through it."

Three weeks after my arrival at Graceland, L.D. Weldon's investment blew up in his face.

It happened during the Graceland–Tarkeo College Game. I was playing linebacker. The coach had called a play in which I was expected to rush in and block the punt. I came flying through the line, and nobody touched me. I made a mad rush for the punter, and just as I bent down to block the punt, the safety hit me with a right to the knee and—*Bango!*—I heard my knee snap like one of my dad's tree limbs, tearing the tendons and sending me to the showers. I hopped off the field knowing something was catastrophically wrong.

Not only was I finished for the season; I was now absolutely certain that my athletic career was over. I returned to my parents' home in Newtown and had knee surgery on January 2, 1969, in Danbury, Connecticut. The surgeon put my knee back together as best he could, shook his head and said, "Good luck." With my leg in a cast for six weeks, I missed school for the first two months of 1969.

When I got back to Graceland, my leg was shriveled up to nothing and my knee was locked shut. L.D. immediately put me into physical therapy, appointing himself chief therapist. He would sit there and try to bend my knee. The motion was slowly returning, and, by the end of the school year, I could run a little and began to work out lightly, including, at L.D.'s insistence, throwing the javelin.

L.D. had big plans for me, he kept saying. He wanted me to run the decathlon the next year, when I was a sophomore; he even got me a decathlete as a roommate in that windowless basement, hoping his spirit might rub off on me.

But I was bummed. I felt that it had really been a wasted year, both athletically and scholastically. Because I had missed more than a month of school, my grades were just barely passable. I came home to work with my dad, climbing and pruning trees. My knee was getting better, so I could return to competitive waterskiing—even though L.D. had begged me to give it up, worried that I might get hurt, forever ending my chances to compete in the mythical decathlon he kept harping about. But I kept skiing. Even though I couldn't ski the jumps, I even won a few tournaments.

My future? I just didn't know. When the summer was ending and sophomore year beckoned, one question kept repeating itself in my mind: Do I really want to go back to school?

Sure, I thought about running L.D. Weldon's decathlon. But with my busted knee, what kind of decathlete could I make? The knee surgery had removed the specter of going to Vietnam; the military probably wouldn't take me.

I was free to do whatever I pleased, and what I loved most was waterskiing. I hated to leave it for school—especially when I was offered a job. A dream job! A friend and skiing buddy named Joe Poroznick from Richmond, Virginia, worked in the ski show at Cypress Gardens, the big, famous water-ski show in Winter Haven, Florida. Joe told me he could get me a spot in the show.

My eyes lit up. I was nineteen years old. Why not go to Florida, take a year off from college and become a professional water-skier, enjoy a life of beaches and bars and beautiful girls? I was already in Virginia at a water-ski tournament when Joe offered me the job. Halfway to Florida! All I had to do was hop into my 1956 Ford convertible and follow the sun to the good life at Cypress Gardens.

"You've got the job if you want it," Joe kept repeating.

I packed up my convertible with all my possessions, my water skis sticking out the back, and drove to the freeway, unsure of my destination. I knew a fork in the road was coming up ahead: one lane headed south to Florida, the other headed north toward home.

"Do I turn left and go south to Florida, or do I turn right and go north back home, make some money, then hop on a plane and go back to Iowa and my sophomore year, L.D. Weldon and this thing called the decathlon?" I kept asking myself.

As I approached the fork in the freeway, it was crunch time. I knew in my heart that going north was the "right" thing to do, the decision preferred by my parents and my coach. But that southbound route held the promise of fun, freedom and adventure.

I was still absolutely undecided when I reached the fork in the road. But then this big old station wagon suddenly pulled up on my left side, making it impossible to turn left and head south without dramatically slowing down or speeding up.

The fork heading north was wide open.

I felt it was an omen: to do the natural thing, the thing that I knew in my heart was right. So I turned north on the freeway, heading toward home, toward college, toward L.D. Weldon, toward the decathlon. As the miles sped by, I felt stronger and stronger about the wisdom of my decision.

I had made a commitment, however unwittingly, and I would never be ordinary again.

CHAPTER TWO

THE 100-METER RUN: THE RACE BEGINS WITH ONE STEP

You stand in the blocks like one raw nerve, anticipating the sound of the gun. It's the first event of the first day of the decathlon and the pressure is cranked up to a high boil. In the blocks, you don't await the gun, you anticipate *it. So when it fires, you're already one step off the blocks and pouring every piece of your existence into the run, opening your mind, body, heart and soul full throttle. Two-tenths of a second can mean a difference of fifty points. Although the 100-meter run is barely longer than a football field and the race is over in ten seconds, there is no discounting its importance. This is the beginning, the point from which everything else will spring. And so you rage: against the gun, against the clock, against your limits.*

Spring 1970: a kid and his coach are driving to a track meet. The coach is confident of his kid's abilities, although the kid has never before competed in the contest he's headed toward, the ten-event decathlon. He is an able athlete, but having never even successfully completed five of the ten events, things are not looking good. In practice, he'd stumbled in the hurdles, not even finishing the race. He had never competitively thrown the shot, never thrown the discus and had never done any long-distance training or even run 1,500 meters. But the coach has enough confidence for them both. "Don't worry about this kid," he tells all doubters. "His heart's ten times bigger than his stride."

They are headed to the Drake Relays in Des Moines, Iowa, a respectable decathlon where the competition can be fierce. The coach sits sideways on the seat, facing the kid instead of the road, barreling toward Des Moines at ninety miles an hour, talking a hundred miles a minute.

"The decathlon is a test," he says. "A test of your athletic ability. A test of your character. A test to gauge the toughness of your athletic mind. It's going to be the biggest physical challenge of your life, barring none. You're going to have to push yourself like you've never pushed yourself before, both mentally and physically. You're heading into completely unknown territory."

Then he smiles and turns his eyes back to the highway. "But this is just the first one," he says. "Just go in there, have some fun and see how good you can do. We'll take it from there."

The kid should be shaking in his track shoes. But youth bears the gift of innocence. You leap before you look. You bound off the blocks before you know the difficulties of the race, and that in itself is *power*. The kid isn't thinking about winning; he just wants to finish, to get through the ten events with his body and some semblance of pride intact.

"Here we go," he says to himself as the gun fires and the first event, the 100-meter race, begins. "Let's just try this."

He gets off the blocks strong in the 100 meters, receiving a respectable score. He's never long-jumped before, but his first and second jump far exceed his expectations and his third could compare to Olympic records. The sloppy style of his shot put reveals a severe lack of technique, but the distance says everything about his strength and will. He clears the high jump an inch higher than he'd ever jumped in practice. He runs the 400 meters like he's been doing it all his life. He effortlessly three-steps the hurdles, which he'd botched so badly the week before. His pole vault, discus and javelin all net good scores, and when he squares off for the 1,500 meters, he runs his guts out, for a time so swift it unleashes a mantra in his mind: *I'm doing it. I'm doing it!*

What is happening? The kid's power can't be attributed to practice. He has no idea of what he's doing! But when stares up into the stands, he sees his coach beaming, giving him the high sign, a single fist in the air, which means, "Way to go. That's my boy!"

His power lies merely in his ability to *begin*.

He sets a new school record of 6,991 points and finishes in sixth place.

That rookie kid was me at my first decathlon, and the story illustrates everything I'd like to impart in this chapter: the exhilaration of finding your place in life, your arena to play in; the significance of a strong start; the incredible influence of a mentor. From the moment of my first decathlon, I would have no doubt about my future. I didn't want to play football, I didn't want to play basketball, I didn't even want to water-ski. I had found my arena to play in—the decathlon.

Finding your place in the world is life's greatest achievement, the highest destination of every soul's journey. It's the playground of the Champion Within. Some search for this place forever; others sail into it as effortlessly as an expert sailor on a windless sea. Whether your field is business or athletic, technical or creative, no glory can be attained until the player steps on the playing field. The old adage is true: showing up really is half the game.

As citizens of the greatest country in the world, we're all entrepreneurs in the free enterprise system. We can be whoever we want to be. It's all up to us. But we chain ourselves: to bad jobs, bad relationships, bad habits. I want to tell you that we can break free. We can strip ourselves of the chains that bind us and break into a new world.

To paraphrase John Wooden, the great UCLA coach: "Things turn out best for the people who do the best with the way things turn out."

We choose our destiny.

But where do we begin?

We begin by finding an arena to play in. For me, it was the decathlon. Your challenge is to find your own arena. If you're already standing in it but not reaping its full rewards, you're halfway there. If you're in an arena that's less than fulfilling, then it's up to you to walk out of it and move into something else. Greatness lies deep inside you. Some pull it out. Others don't. But it's down there.

I know it's down there, because I found it in my life.

"Begin difficult things while they are easy.
Do great things when they are small.
The difficult things of the world
Must have once been easy.
The great things must have once been small.
A thousand-mile journey begins with one step."
—*LAO-TZU*, TAO TE CHING

What does the 100 meters, a short footrace, have in common with the long haul of one person's life? One very important thing: You've got to get started.

The 100 meters is the first event of the decathlon and the first event of your new life. You are standing on the blocks, anticipating the gun. The road to your future stretches before you in a maze of contradictory lanes and lines. But you do *not* concentrate on the finish line. Not yet. Dwelling on the long road ahead will make the race seem too overwhelming, too scary. If you try to do too much at once, you run the risk of doing nothing at all. The pressure of the 100 meters being the first event of the day only adds to the intensity. The runner who hesitates when the gun is fired, who comes off the blocks with anything less than maximum effort, is guaranteed defeat. Your mission is merely to get off the blocks as fast as you can and begin the race.

Remember, success is not measured by heights attained but by obstacles overcome. We're going to pass through many obstacles in our lives: good days, bad days. But the successful person will overcome those obstacles and constantly move forward.

It all begins with getting started.

The purpose of this chapter is to help you off the blocks and into the race, to begin the 100 meters, the first step toward your dreams. I am going to show you how I got started. But first let me give you three lessons, seen through the lives of the famous first beginnings of three once absolutely ordinary people. People who, just like you and me, started the race in the ordinary and ran into the extraordinary in an incredibly brief period of time.

> *"There is a tide in the affairs of men,*
> *Which, taken at the flood, leads on to fortune;*
> *Omitted, all the voyage of their life*
> *Is bound in shallows and in miseries . . .*
> *And we must take the current when it serves,*
> *Or lose our ventures."*
> —*WILLIAM SHAKESPEARE*, JULIUS CAESAR

BELIEVE IN THE POWER OF YOU.

Deep within each of us lies a power, a power forever begging to be awakened. One man felt this power with such intensity that he would allow nothing—not parents, pain, muscle limits, not even the threat of a stint in a military jail—to stop him from bringing that power to the forefront of his life. In my speeches, I refer to that strength as "The Power of You."

I remember meeting him in the early seventies in the YMCA weight room in San Jose, California. It was during a bodybuilding competition, and this guy was as big as a house. He could hardly speak English, except to say his name, and I thought to myself, This is Mr. Universe. Is he harming his body with such tremendous muscle mass? And secondly, what's he going to do with the rest of his life after his bodybuilding career is over?

I didn't know then that I was standing before a man who epitomized the power of getting started and never giving up, no matter the hardships.

His name means "black plowman," and when he was born in Graz, Austria, the son of a village cop, being a plowman would've represented a sizable step up the family career ladder. The house he lived in had neither indoor plumbing, a telephone nor a refrigerator until he was fourteen. Son of a stern disciplinarian, his chores began at six A.M. and continued throughout the day. He even had to do squats and sit-ups to "earn" his breakfast.

In his little house in his little town, the boy dreamed of strength, of size, of endless opportunity. His dreams carried him oceans away in his mind, far from the cold, hard Austrian earth and into America: a land of wide-open spaces and larger-than-life heroes. With dreams as big as these, he grew to despise "living in a little country" because he didn't want anything in his life to be little. "I wanted to be part of the big cause, the big dreams, the big skyscrapers, the big money, the big action," he would later recount in the 1991 *Current Biography* yearbook.

Graz was a "big" distance from the USA. But Arnold Schwarz-

enegger was determined to find a way to get off the blocks of his ordinary existence and race into the extraordinary world of his dreams.
What did Arnold have in his meager arsenal? No money, no property,
no relatives abroad. He had one thing and one thing only—his body.

That would be ticket enough.

Arnold began training for his own 100-meter race. He began lifting weights to train for the local soccer team, but what he encountered
in the gym—"animals climbing around snatching up 315 pounds in
one movement"—impressed him more than anything he'd seen on the
soccer field. He began a bodybuilding program and he kept lifting until it became an obsession. Hoping to dissuade him from what they
considered his strange conduct, Arnold's parents forbade him to work
out more than three times a week. But he sneaked into an unheated
room of the house and, with rudimentary weights, trained constantly.
He wrote down his weight-lifting goals and allowed nothing to ever
stop him from accomplishing them. "The last thing I ever wanted to
do is disappoint myself," he would later say.

"When I was fifteen, I had a clear vision of myself winning the
Mr. Universe contest and was driven by that thought," he would remember. "It was a very spiritual thing in a way, because I had such
faith in the route, the path, that it was never a question, in my mind,
that I would make it."

He joined the Austrian Army, but the call to bodybuilding competition was so strong that he went AWOL—to travel to Stuttgart, Germany, and compete in the Junior Mr. Europe competition. He won, of
course. He could bench-press 500 pounds! Propelled by his vision of
winning the Mr. Universe contest, he became "like Leonardo da
Vinci, a sculptor shaping the body," working out five hours a day, loving every minute of it, "because I felt that each time I went to the gym
I was one more step closer to winning the competition."

When he turned twenty, his dream came true. Arnold Schwarzenegger became the youngest man to ever win the Mr. Universe title. The next year, he landed in America. Within two years, he had won the unprecedented triple crown of bodybuilding—Mr. World, Mr. Universe and Mr. Olympia—eventually winning more bodybuilding contests than any competitor in the world. Two years after his arrival in America, he founded bricklaying and mail-order book-and-cassette businesses and invested in California real estate.

Along the way, he learned English and earned a bachelor's degree in business.

Today, Arnold Schwarzenegger, one of the world's most popular movie stars, never stops to rest on his laurels or even analyze his past. "I never start evaluating," he says. "For me, it's a waste of time. I don't want to analyze yesterday. Tomorrow. Period. Because that's what counts."

I presently serve on the board of the California Governor's Council of Physical Fitness, which is chaired by Arnold Schwarzenegger. As he stands before governors and presidents or sits at the controls of his 12.5-million-dollar G-III jet, he is no longer the young foreigner who couldn't speak English but one of America's leading citizens, a king in the land of BIG. All because he had a dream, and he got into the race to achieve it.

FIND SOMETHING IN YOUR PRESENT
TO JUMP-START YOUR FUTURE.

When I take my kids to Disneyland, I'm amazed at how huge a dream can grow. It's hard to believe that one man started what has become such a giant of entertainment, a source of joy for billions of people around the world. I often wonder how all of this could spring from a single human mind.

But when you study the man who started it all, the answer is simple: Walt Disney had the ability not merely to dream but to start the race to make his dream come true. I read about Disney's amazing journey in several volumes of *Current Biography*.

He never called himself an artist.

Art was for scholars and intellectuals, and he was a hard-working animator who barred the word "art" from his offices. Neither the word nor its accompanying location—school—had been a major influence on a boy who just loved to draw. He had drawn for as long as he could remember, probably starting when his family moved from Chicago to a Marcelene, Missouri, farm. The boy fell in love with animals and tried to bring them to eternal life on the page.

He didn't graduate from high school but enlisted as a Red Cross ambulance driver during World War I. When he returned home to Kansas City, he took a job in the field he loved most: as a commercial "artist" with the Gray Advertising Agency.

He wasn't an artist.

He was fired "for lack of ideas."

He went to work for another Kansas City advertising agency, sketching illustrations for farm journals, moonlighting in a studio he built above his father's garage, making his own cartoon slides for a film company. He called the cartoons "Laugh-o-Grams." He spent six months with a group of cartoonists, making his own series of short animated features, but the venture failed.

In 1923, with forty dollars to his name, he took a train to Hollywood, where he stayed with his brother, Roy. Pooling their life's savings—290 dollars—they borrowed 500 dollars from an uncle and produced a series of comedies, combining actual film footage with animation. They struck a deal with Universal Pictures to direct a cartoon of Walt's creation, *Oswald the Rabbit*. But the deal soured and Walt had to relinquish rights to his creation.

According to the biography *Walt Disney: An American Original* by Bob Thomas, the cartoonist eventually suffered a nervous break-down.

Dejected, he took a train to knock on doors in New York City. But a cartoonist without a character was like a gunslinger without a gun. During a sleepless night on the way back home to Hollywood, in an upper berth of the train, his thoughts shifted from his troubles to, oddly enough, a mouse. Such a tame mouse that it would scamper across his drawing board when he worked in the Kansas City advertising agency, a mouse that he named Mortimer, then Mickey.

Walt Disney had his new character.

Back in Hollywood, he began the race. Although the first two Mickey Mouse cartoons failed, the third, *Steamboat Willie*, struck a chord in the American consciousness and soon the world's. Mickey Mouse was soon anointed the King of Cartoons, and the cartoonist/ filmmaker/imagineer, Walt Disney, lived happily every after.

GO WITH WHAT YOU'VE GOT!

One of my favorite success stories is a real-life fable I read about in the 1973 *Current Biography* when I was training for the Games. Every time I came up against seemingly insurmountable obstacles, the story would flash through my mind. It's about a man who stands as proof of the galvanizing power of getting started and believing in yourself and your ideas.

He was an old man, sixty-five, retirement age, whose entire worldly possessions consisted of one old house, one old Ford and a Social Security check of 105 dollars a month.

There was no job in sight, no son or daughter to come to the rescue. But he was accustomed to misfortune. He'd been born into it, on a farm where his father died when he was six, forcing his mother to take a job peeling tomatoes by day and taking in sewing by night. Left alone for long periods of time, the boy and his two siblings were forced to forage for food and to learn to cook. When his mother remarried a cold, heartless man who hated her children, the kids were sent away.

The boy spent his life in every sort of labor: farmhand, buggy painter, railroad laborer, streetcar conductor, ferryboat operator, insurance salesman, lawyer, filling station owner and finally restaurateur, operating a moderately successful cafe on the side of a busy highway in Corbin, Kentucky. But when a new interstate was built in the mid-fifties, bypassing his cafe, the old man was forced to sell out at a price that barely covered his debts.

Life had come down to this: sitting in his little house and staring at a future on the government dole. Then, suddenly, he had a thought: Remember the Utah restaurant that had bought his "secret" fried chicken recipe, done well with it and encouraged others to pay four cents for every chicken fried in his secret spices? Maybe, the old man thought, others might be interested in his recipe.

So Harland "Colonel" Sanders packed up a pressure cooker and a bag of chicken seasoning and drove to restaurants, one by one, offering to cook his secret chicken first for each restaurant's managers and staff. If they liked it, he'd cook chicken for the customers. If the customers liked it, Sanders would strike a deal: four cents for every chicken served.

With one switch of his old Ford's ignition, Colonel Sanders had begun his 100-meter race, bounding off the blocks with one viable idea and, most important, extraordinary determination. The Colonel would not quit until he blasted through the finish line with the velocity of a chicken wing hitting a pan of hot grease.

Look at what grew from one old man's ability to begin!

In his first two years of hard traveling, according to *Current Biography,* Sanders had signed up only five restaurants—which, at four cents a bird, would have required sales of 100 chickens at each café a day to make him 20 dollars.

But he didn't let a slow start stop him. He believed in what he was doing and was certain that in time others would, too.

By 1960, 200 restaurants were serving his chicken.

By 1963, more than 600 had signed up, earning the old man with the white hair, white suit and Old South demeanor 300,000 dollars a year.

By 1964, he had sold his Kentucky Fried Chicken business to future Kentucky Governor John Brown for 2 million dollars, plus 75,000 dollars a year for life, retaining all rights to KFC franchises in Canada.

KFC went on to become a billion-dollar business, now operating around the world. A 5,000-dollar investment in the company in 1964 would've been worth 3.5 million in 1973; countless KFC franchisees have become millionaires. And millions of people around the world are licking their fingers over the Colonel's fried chicken—all because one man had the ability to get off the blocks and run the race.

Arnold Schwarzenegger's muscles.

Walt Disney's mouse.

Colonel Sanders's chicken.

What did these seemingly diverse individuals have in common? They each selected an arena to play and excel in, singling out the one thing that they had at their immediate disposal, the thing that set them apart from the multitudes. None of these men were born to privilege. If anything, they had less than much of the general populace. What set them apart was their ability to take whatever they had at their disposal and get off the blocks and *run* with it.

Do you remember the great Robin Williams movie *Dead Poets Society?* Williams plays John Keating, the teacher of a class of prep school boys who have been taught to follow in their fathers' successful, yet safe, footsteps. Keating, however, has other plans for his class. He teaches them poetry. He tells them to tear up their textbooks. He leads them on strange marches and lectures them about their dreams. A pivotal scene shows the boys standing around the school's trophy case, staring at class photos from long ago.

Keating tells the boys, "The young men you behold had the same fire in their eyes as you do. They planned to take the world by storm and make something magnificent of their lives. Now they are all pushing up daisies. How many of them really lived out their dreams? Did they do what they set out to accomplish?"

Keating leans in close, as the boys huddle around him.

"*Carpe diem*," he whispers. "Seize the day!"

Seize the day! Those three words should be emblazoned on the front door of every schoolhouse in the land. They should be part of the anthems of nations the world over, stamped upon every person's consciousness at birth. Instead, like John Keating's kids, we are tutored endlessly about history when it's the present and the future that count.

In *Dead Poets Society,* Keating's boys abandon their buttoned-down aspirations like butterflies abandoning a caterpillar's colorless shell, rushing forth to heed the calls buried deep within their hearts: creative pursuits, personal adventures, previously unattainable women!

All because a teacher showed them that they had power over their destinies and could be whatever they wanted to be.

As I've mentioned, I wasn't a very good student. But I can teach a few lessons for life. One of them is this: each of us has a calling, a calling that's either burning or buried deep inside, and it is our duty to ourselves and to our world to follow that calling wherever it leads.

But like Keating's kids, most of us ignore that calling. We plow the safe ground, the path of least resistance, the safe port in the storm. LIFE'S A BITCH, reads a popular bumper sticker of the disenchanted, AND THEN YOU DIE.

Believe it or not, the second part of that slogan—the part about dying—can become the key to finding your place in this world. If I learned one thing in my twenty-year "down time" between winning the Olympic gold medal and the start of my new life, it's that you have to die before being reborn.

The good news is this: you can do it in your mind.

Is your life a bitch? Well, then, try dying.

I'm serious about this. Imagine yourself at your own funeral. See yourself in the casket, study the faces of the mourners, listen to the eulogy, flash back on everything you did in your life. Most important, flash back on all the things you *didn't* do. Was there a great calling you heard but didn't heed? Did potentially pivotal days go unseized? Were there paths not taken, adventures not answered, treasures not dug?

This simple exercise will help you put your life into perspective. If your heart aches over something you passed up, if you focus immediately on one "could've" or "should've," then that's the very thing you should pursue.

Getting started is merely a matter of following a few very basic, simple rules:

1. Recognize the Champion Within. Realize that deep inside of you a champion is waiting, ready to rise and radically transform every aspect of your existence.

2. Find your arena to play in. Keep an open mind. Look at finding your life's purpose as an excavation; you might not find the answer the first time you dig. But keep digging. If you're having trouble, use Arnold's method: begin with your dreams. Visualize yourself as a cham-

pion—the ultimate peak performer—and ask yourself,
"Where would that champion play if he or she could
play anywhere in the world?" Look at your surroundings
and see if there is room for that champion to play where
you are. If not, where do you have to go for the champion
to reach full potential?

3. Once you've found your arena, enter it. Don't hesitate.
Take that first step. Like Walt Disney and his mouse, go
with what you've got at your disposal and give it your all.
If it doesn't work out, don't quit. Merely reframe your
mission and move on.

4. Rewire your brain regarding the word failure. As
Colonel Sanders proved, you can find something in your
present that can jump-start your future. Know that failure is but a temporary stumble in the race and that
every successful mission is the final result of endless
missteps and that no real victory is won without it. As
my friend motivational speaker Barry Farber writes in
his book *Diamond in the Rough,* "There is never a
straight line between where we are now and where we
want to be. But a mistake, a failure or a negative thought
is just another bend in the road. Go beyond that bend
and you're that much closer to your destination. Give up
when you hit a rocky patch and you'll never reach your
goal."

5. Cut off all lines of escape. Put yourself in a situation
where the only answer is action! Vow total commitment
to your cause.

Neither Schwarzenegger nor Disney nor Sanders had to rush out and search for the thing that would bring them such happiness. Their destinies were already inside themselves. So look inside yourself and evaluate your strengths and weaknesses. In countless stories I've studied, all many people had to do was close their eyes and think— and the answer to their life's mission practically appeared right in front of them. Try it. The answer will probably amaze you with its simplicity.

I think of the example of Will Rogers, perhaps the most famous philosopher-humorist of the first half of this century. Will Rogers, however, never spoke onstage for the first ten years of his career. He was a cowboy who specialized in rope tricks. Considering himself a country bumpkin, he didn't dare speak! But when forced to talk at one performance, Rogers said a few words and immediately had his audience howling. His career took a dramatic turn.

He started life over again as a public speaker.

His arena to play in was hidden deep inside of him. All he had to do was open his mouth and start.

Starting—that's the key. Once you recognize your power, your gift, you must be able to get off the blocks and run. So find your arena to play in. The first place to look? Wherever you are. "Bloom where you're planted," my wife, Kris, likes to say. When seeking your arena, look first at where you already are. What gold might you mine from your present situation? If you think about it hard enough, you'll be amazed at the number of directions in which you might bloom.

If you're thinking, It's easy for him to say that, forget about it. When I started the race that eventually led to the '76 Olympics, I was headed toward a third-rate college with a busted knee and a broken spirit. I didn't even realize that I'd found my arena to play in, my place to bloom—the decathlon.

In fact, I knew next to nothing about the game.

But like Arnold Schwarzenegger, Walt Disney and Colonel Sanders, I'd found the arena in which to play out my life's mission, the field of my dreams. It lay right in front of my windshield the moment I came to the fork in the highway and turned north toward home and my sophomore year at Graceland College.

I'd found a place to start, to get off the blocks and into the race, and that held all the power in the world.

"A good plan violently executed right now is far better than a perfect plan executed next week."
—GENERAL GEORGE PATTON

The call to action for the ancient Olympic Games was a supreme ceremony. Each Olympic year, the heralds would travel throughout Greece and, to crowds gathered in market squares, formally announce the date of the games and the conditions for eligibility. According to the 1966 book *Ancient Olympic Games* by Heinz Schobel, the heralds would proclaim: "Any freeborn Greek who has committed no deed of violence and has not incurred the wrath of the gods may take part in the Games. And may the world be free of murder and crime and the rattle of weapons silenced."

The participants would travel from far-flung villages, granted safe passage by a three-month sacred truce: all wars were suspended and all weapons holstered as the most powerful men in Greek civilization began the ten-month period of preparation before traveling to Olympia for a thirty-day training period with the world's greatest trainers, men so famous that sculptures were carved and songs written in their honor, all prelude to the battle before the gods.

Wouldn't it be wonderful to have heralds pass through our town squares and give us ten months to prepare ourselves for the biggest event of our lives? There would be no time for procrastination! Ten months would mean victory or defeat, honor or disgrace.

There is power in beginning! More power in one act than the cumulative strength of a billion thoughts. But since the days of the ancient Games, no competitor enters the arena alone. Look far enough into any success story and you'll find evidence of a mentor, who, like the men who trained the ancient Greeks, deserves the glory of sculptures and song. For Ray Charles, who grew up in the backwoods of Georgia, it was a boogie-woogie-piano-playing neighbor named "Mr. Willie" Pit, who put the young Charles on his lap and taught him how to play. For actor Sidney Poitier, who arrived in America from the Bahamas with less than two years of education and three dollars in his pocket, it was a waiter in a restaurant who tutored young Sidney, then a dishwasher, in reading.

But nobody personifies the power of a mentor more than the legendary boy wonder of the 1948 Olympic Games—Bob Mathias.

"We sent a boy to do a man's job and he did it far better than any man ever could."
—PAUL HELMS, HELMS ATHLETIC FOUNDATION,
QUOTED IN AN ILLUSTRATED HISTORY OF THE OLYMPICS
BY DICK SCHAAP

Four months before the 1948 Olympic Games, Mathias, who spent his youth as a sickly, anemic kid in Tulare, California, had never held a javelin, never pole-vaulted, never run 1,500 meters, never even *heard* of the decathlon. He was talented in local athletics but not a national standout. However, his high school coach, Virgil Thomas, believed in him so much that he predicted that if his student would begin immediately, he could somehow make it onto the

Olympic team in 1952, even though Mathias was only seventeen years old!

Bob Mathias—on the strength of a mentor's belief in his abilities and the innocence of his youth—began the race and beat his coach's prediction by four years.

One short month after he started training, Mathias entered his first decathlon. Amazingly, he won first place! Two weeks later, he won the U.S. decathlon championship. Six weeks later, he was representing the United States in the 1948 Olympic Games.

Most people would've been happy to have even gotten to the Games. Mathias wanted to *win*. After his first three events, he was solidly in third place, a boy behind men: the powerful Frenchman Ignace Heinrich was in second; the awesome Argentine Army officer Enrique Kistenmacher was in first.

Then they went to the fourth event, the high jump.

Mathias knew he had to jump at least six feet just to stay in the competition, much less win a medal. But the boy who had never high-jumped until four months before couldn't even clear five-nine on his first try; on his second, he once again crashed into the crossbar.

But instead of surrendering to, "It's nice just to be here," Mathias retired to the sidelines before attempting his third and last leap.

Writer Dick Schaap recalls what followed in his book, *An Illustrated History of the Olympics:*

> The air was heavy and the ground damp at the Wembley Stadium in London, and Mathias wrapped himself in a blanket to keep warm. As he waited before his final jump at 5' 9", he worried and thought and finally came to the decision. "Forget about form," he told himself. "Just get over the bar."
>
> Then, instead of approaching the bar on the side, as he normally did, he lined up almost directly in front of it, took

a deep breath and sprinted and jumped. He was awkward, was off-balance. But he was effective. He cleared the crossbar, then went on to leap 6'1.25".

One of the spectators at Wembley Stadium, Brutus Hamilton, the track coach at the University of California and a former decathlon man, nodded knowingly. "The kid's going to win it," Hamilton told a companion.

The kid won it.

The next morning, still stuck in third place with five events to go, Mathias ate a steak for breakfast, then went on to winning scores in the high hurdles, the discus, the pole vault, the javelin and, finally, the 1,500 meters, becoming the youngest decathlon gold-medalist in Olympic history before an ecstatic crowd of 70,000.

"What are you going to do after the Olympics?" someone asked the seventeen-year-old after his victory.

"Start shaving," replied Mathias.

By the time he returned home to his parents house in Tulare, 200 marriage proposals had been mailed to him, as well as a personal greeting from President Truman. Mathias then went on to equally auspicious victories in college football, later Olympic Games, movies and politics.

From the simple seed of *beginning*—without doubt, without restriction, without fear—a seventeen-year-old boy won the gold medal in the decathlon, becoming the World's Greatest Athlete.

What propelled him into the race? Merely that someone—a coach, a mentor—believed in him. Someone could see seeds of greatness within him, when all he could see was the ordinary.

"There are many people who could be Olympic champions, All Americans who have never tried. I'd estimate five million people could have beaten me in the pole vault the year

I won it, at least five million. Men who were stronger, big-ger and faster than I was could have done it, but they never picked up a pole, never made the feeble effort to pick their legs off the ground and get over the bar."
—OLYMPIAN BOB RICHARDS,
QUOTED IN CHICKEN SOUP FOR THE SOUL

When I returned for my sophomore year at Graceland College from my fork in the road, my coach and mentor L.D. Weldon was waiting.

"Good to have you back, big guy," he grinned, then gave me a hearty pat on the back. "Okay. This year we're going to run the de-cathlon."

The decathlon. I knew next to nothing about the sport. But that was okay. L.D. Weldon knew *everything*.

Listening to L.D. Weldon's tales of decathletes like Bob Mathias and Jim Thorpe, the self-proclaimed "dumb Indian kid" who won the first U.S. decathlon Gold, gave me the courage to try. I was going against the decathlon, the great snow-shrouded mountaintop, heading into a decathlon competition called the Drake Relays in the spring of 1970.

It was not only the first decathlon I'd ever run.

It was the first one I'd ever seen.

But I didn't hesitate about getting into the race for one very good reason. I didn't want to let my coach down.

Technically, as a track coach, L.D. was just "okay." He knew his stuff, but he wasn't cutting edge and really into technique. L.D. was a motivator. Down deep in his soul, L.D. was a wonderful person who loved working with young people, giving them guidance. He got more out of you because you didn't want to let him down.

I remember a shot-putter on Graceland's team, Dean Trugue. He was about six-five, maybe 260 pounds. We were at our conference championships, and it was pretty tight between us and another school, and Dean was in second place in the shot when he should have been leading. It came down to the final throw, and L.D. came over to Dean Trugue, and instead of lecturing him on technology— "Dean, you've got to get lower in the shot, you've got to get your body lower, you've got to get behind it more!"—he chose a more personal route.

"Hey, Dean, come over here," L.D. called from the sidelines.

Big old Dean Trugue lumbered over and L.D. flashed him a big grin. "Here's the deal; we need this shot," he said. "You've *got* to beat this guy. Here's my offer to you. I know this restaurant on the way home where the steaks are two inches thick, the juiciest, tastiest steaks I've ever put in my mouth. If you beat this guy, we'll stop there, and I'm buyin' you the biggest steak—the finest cut—they've got."

L.D. went on for about ten minutes, describing the steak, its marbling, how perfectly it sizzled on the plate, making the steak seem so tantalizing that Dean Trugue had saliva running down his chin. L.D. had triggered Trugue's passion. For Dean Trugue, technical jargon would've seemed like a back scratch compared to the promise of sizzling beefsteak! When Trugue stepped back onto that field, he was a different man. With the saliva glistening on his chin, he stepped up to the pit and, with every ounce of his mass behind the ball in his hand, screamed a thundering yell and beat the tar out of the competition.

That night, I watched him rip through a steak that could have fed a family of five, with L.D. Weldon patting him on the back with every bite.

Passion is a funny thing. It can't be taught in school. It can't be learned in books. It's like a virus; you contract it from others. Sometimes you will do for others what you will not do for yourself.

Seek out help in your mission. If you don't already have a mentor, find one. Find somebody—a coach, teacher, friend, spouse or colleague—who will propel you, push you, promise you the steak dinner of your dreams if you'll only get started. There is magic in beginning, but getting off the blocks requires help. Go out and find the L.D. Weldons in your life, the kind of people whom you don't want to let down.

Gravitate toward the people who light a fire in you. Conversely, as Mark Twain once said, as quoted in *Best of Success,* compiled by Wynn Davis: "Keep away from people who try to belittle your ambitions. Small people always do that, but the really great make you feel that you, too, can become great."

My wife, Kris, who became as powerful a mentor in my life as L.D. Weldon had been in my sport, taught me one important lesson: "Not everybody is your friend." Most people don't want to see you succeed! Why? Because "small" people are naturally insecure and afraid; success threatens them. People are either for you or against you. There is no in between. Recognize this reality, then surround yourself with those who truly believe in you and are excited about your endeavors.

Once you find your mentor, become a mentor to somebody else. Encourage others, whether a son or daughter, a business partner, a friend. One of the great things about being successful or learning something is the ability to give it back. Teach someone else how to do what you do best. As the great motivator Les Brown writes in his book *Live Your Dreams,* "You heighten your own life when you help others heighten theirs." There is incredible reward in that, which we will discuss in greater detail later in this book.

> *"I'll never reach my destination,*
> *If I never try."*
>
> —GARTH BROOKS, *"ROPIN' THE WIND"*

Finding your arena in life—that's the beginning. Next comes the race to unleash the Champion Within. By the time you finish this book, you will have learned the secrets of running this race, enabling you to summon up the most powerful part of yourself at any time of need. At this point, however, I can only say this: it all begins with your ability to persist through pain. When you suffer the storms that come along to knock you off your path, when you are running so hard you lose yourself in the race, then your future will open before you like a golden path through a rainbow.

A good example of this comes from a rough-and-tumble cowboy from Oklahoma named Troyal. His story is recounted in the 1992 *Current Biography Notebook*. He went to Oklahoma State University on a javelin-throwing scholarship, and he might have made a pretty decent track-and-fielder. But soon he felt the stirrings of different professional passions, and he judged his commitment level by asking himself a simple but perfect question: "If God came to earth with a box containing the reason for my life inside of it, what words would I most like to find in the box?"

He didn't have to think very long. The box would contain two words: "The Music."

He'd found his arena to play in. All he had to do was begin the race.

He could pick a little guitar and his voice wasn't half bad and he'd written some great songs. But Nashville wasn't knocking on his door. He got a singing gig in a place called Wild Willie's but had to moonlight as a bouncer in a beer joint, where his life took on all of the drama of a Country-and-Western song.

One night he met his future bride—not by the bar but in the ladies' restroom, where Troyal was summoned to break up a fistfight. A jealous ex had cornered a woman named Sandy Mahl, who'd dated her man. Sandy tried to throw a punch and got her fist stuck in the Sheetrock.

Troyal pulled her hand out of the wall, kicked her out of the club and offered her first a lift home and second a lift home to his place. "Drop dead," said Sandy. But the cowboy persevered and they married a few years later. Upon college graduation, the couple hooked it to Nashville, seeking success. "I thought the world was waiting for me," Troyal would later remember, "but there's nothing colder than reality."

They returned to Oklahoma City, but Troyal didn't forget his dream. Two years later, he and Sandy pooled their last 1,500 dollars and headed back to Nashville for a second attempt at the Big Time. During the day, Sandy worked for a dry cleaner and Troyal at a boot shop to make ends meet, then they hit the clubs at night. One night, he showed up at an "audition evening" at the famous Bluebird Cafe. In the audience, a Columbia Records scout caught Troyal's act and signed him to a record deal.

Troyal Garth Brooks, the best-selling C&W artist of all time, has sold more records than Michael Jackson or Madonna and is coming close to outselling the Beatles—all because he found his arena to play in, began the race and didn't quit until he had won.

Everybody has the potential to create a moment when their dreams gel, when they graduate into the big leagues and the Champion Within begins to perform. For Garth Brooks, it was a night in a Nashville nightclub. For me, it was the 1972 decathlon when, from a place so deep within me that I didn't know it existed, I went from contender to champion in the time it took to run a footrace.

"Nothing would be done at all if a man waited until he could do it so well that no one would find fault with it."
—*CARDINAL NEWMAN*

The kid who showed up to compete at the Olympic Trials in Eugene, Oregon, on the July Fourth weekend in 1972 should not have been there. I hadn't shown an ounce of Olympic destiny. After running my first decathlon, I began a string of respectable scores, from 6,808 in my second match to 7,330 in my third, working the decathlete's circuit—the Kansas Relays, the Drake Relays, All-Comers events. I was a flipper and a flopper and a wrong-legged pole-vaulter. I didn't even finish my fourth decathlon; when I failed an easy opening height three times in the pole vault, I stormed off the field, jumped in my car, drove to a deserted mountaintop and looked down into the valley. "To hell with the decathlon," I said. Later, I came in last at two national championships. But I kept at it, mostly for the sheer love of the game. When I won third place at the NAIA National Championships in Billings, Montana, and was named a small-college All-American, I was as surprised as anyone.

But the Olympics? No way! I was just another awestruck TV spectator. I'll never forget watching the closing ceremonies of the Games in Mexico City in 1968. With my knee in a cast from a football injury, I watched by myself in the TV room at Graceland while everybody else was on the athletic field. Awaiting surgery and thinking my athletic career was over, I had my injured leg propped up on a chair as the closing ceremonies concluded in an explosion of fireworks and pageantry. What I remembered most was this big electronic sign at the end of the stadium. When the fireworks went off, the sign lit up with the words, MEXICO '68, and then, as this flame diminished, the sign changed from MEXICO '68 to MUNICH '72, the site and year of the next Olympic Games.

I literally got tears in my eyes, like so many people do when watching the Games. At the time I had never even run a decathlon before. But watching that sign somehow meant something to me. And when my leg healed and, with L.D. Weldon's help, I broke 7,600 points in my 1972 season, which at that time won you a ticket to the Olympic Trials, that sign lit up once again in my memory: MUNICH '72.

I was going to go to the Trials.

I was an unknown, not even considered, much less mentioned, in *Track and Field*'s authoritative Top Ten list. I didn't know exactly what I was doing, which is good. When you get started in anything, you just do it and learn. You're in the arena and you're playing the game. Whether it's sports or business, you've gotten started. And that's enough.

I was a rank amateur who had never even traveled that far west before. But there I was, a skinny kid with shaggy hair, a Fu Manchu mustache, a bum knee wrapped tightly in an elastic bandage and the name GRACELAND slanted across my tank top.

I didn't think I had a snowball's chance in hell. Three people out of a field of thirty would represent the United States in the 1972 Olympics. I was there by sheer luck and I knew it. I didn't expect to win, place or even show. Was I oblivious to the potential that lay deep within me? Just as much as you probably are. The seeds of greatness are planted deep within us all, but it takes a test to bring that greatness out, a test of persistence and pain. Once awakened, it blooms, astounding us with the ferocity of its power.

I had arrived at my moment.

I was going to give it my best shot, but at the time I was thinking, Whatever happens, happens. If I didn't make it, everybody would have just said, "Hey, you gave it a great shot—way to go. Maybe four years from now will be your time."

The Olympic Trials began. I ran a decent 100 meters, decent long jump, decent shot, high jump went okay, a pretty good 400 meters. My first day has never been my strongest day. But I went through the first five events, and I was sitting firmly in eleventh place. I got a great night's sleep. The pressure was on everybody else, not on me.

Next morning, I was well rested, no aches or pains. I was ready for the hurdles, and *bang*, when the gun sounded, I ran the hurdles well, keeping myself solidly in eleventh place, with my best four events to go. We got to the discus, and I had the best throw of my life, moving me up to tenth place. Next came the pole vault, javelin and the 1,500 meters.

Still, I wasn't thinking about making the team, just doing the best I could. I jumped well enough in the pole vault to move from tenth to seventh place. I threw the javelin well enough to move from seventh to fifth place, with one event to go.

Whoa!

All of a sudden, Bruce Jenner, Unknown, is in freaking fifth place at the *Olympic Trials*, with the 1,500 meters, one of my best events, coming up next.

I began thinking, Maybe, just maybe I can sneak into third place.

Just as that little sign, MUNICH '72, started to burn brighter, my doubts began singing in a chorus: "Make it on the team? Are you kidding? Those things always happen to everybody else, never to you!"

Who was ahead of me? Two of the greatest decathletes in America. Jeff Bannister of New Hampshire and Jeff Bennett of Oklahoma Christian were going to take first and second place, no doubt about that. But who was in third? Steve Gough from Seattle Pacific. I knew one thing about Gough: the 1,500 meters wasn't his strongest event. I knew his best time versus my best time, and I had been running the 1,500 about fourteen seconds faster than he had. "What was the cutoff point?" I asked myself. What was Steve Gough's score? I figured that if he was running below 7,300 points, I still had a chance. If he was above 7,300 points, he was too far ahead to catch. But *below* 7,300 points, I knew I had a chance.

I remember it plain as day: lying there, belly on the grass, hands folded, as the scores thus far were announced over the P.A. system. I didn't care about Bennett or Bannister, but when they got to Gough, I listened intently.

The announcer said the magic words:

"Steve Gough from Seattle, Washington, in third place . . . *7,298 points!*"

I literally jumped up off the ground, my brain screaming, "I can do it! I can make it on this Olympic team!"

The MUNICH '72 sign burned brighter in my mind! The prize was right there, right in front of me. All I had to do now was reach out and grab it and pull it in, and I would be going to the 1972 Games. For the first time in my life, I realized that I had a chance to make it onto the team. All I had to do was beat Steve Gough's time in the 1,500 meters by eighteen seconds.

Eighteen seconds is an eternity in the 1,500 meters. But I knew that I had beaten his personal-best time by fourteen seconds. I figured Gough was going to run his best time, so I had to run at least four or five seconds faster than I had ever run before. But at least I had a chance.

For the next fifteen or twenty minutes before the race started, I went through every emotion that I could imagine. I went from laughing to crying, from wild exhilaration to teeth-chattering fear. I was an emotional basket case. My heartbeat went from 80 to 160 instantly, pounding so hard that I started hyperventilating. My head was literally spinning. The adrenaline was flowing so hard, I was getting dizzy. A pins-and-needles feeling spread through my fingers and my toes like they were going to sleep. Within a couple of minutes, my hands went totally numb. Minutes before the biggest race of my life, I was literally falling apart.

But if I said it once during those fifteen minutes before the race, I said it a thousand times: "If I have to *crawl* fast enough to beat this guy by eighteen seconds, I will crawl. I don't care how bad it hurts, how tired I get, how bad I burn, *I'm going to do it.* I'm not going to let it slip through my fingers."

The gun blasted.

My strategy? Follow the winner. Jeff Bennett was a great 1,500-meter man. I had never beaten his personal best in a race, so I decided to line up right behind him, stare at the small of his back and just let him pull me to a fast time merely by never letting him out of my sight. I stared, running as easy and relaxed as I possibly could, thinking, Don't use any muscles that you don't need to keep up with him, because you're going to need it all at the end.

Halfway through the race, I thought I'd better check to see where Gough was running. I took my eyes off the small of Bennett's back and looked over my left shoulder, and a cold chill shot up my spine. Gough was right behind me, looking at the small of *my* back, trying to run just as easy and relaxed as *he* possibly could.

I yelled to Bennett, "Jeff, pick up the pace!" and, immediately, Bennett took off, with me being pulled right behind him and Gough being pulled right behind me.

We came around the next turn, headed toward what I thought would be the finish line. Only I wasn't sure. I'd lost track of where I was in the race. I felt so good that I thought maybe there were two laps to go, instead of one. So I said to myself, "If I hear that bell, signifying one lap to go, I'm gone."

Boom! The bell blasts, and *varoooooom*—MUNICH '72 lit up in my brain. I sprinted past Bennett like he was standing still. I remember running the turn down the backstretch, and taking off—but then my mind went blank. Everything became a blur. I was just running as hard as I possibly could, giving it everything—physically, mentally, emotionally. I vaguely remember being incredibly tired, and my butt muscles were burning, but the legs kept churning faster and faster. I had no idea where Gough was; at this point, the competition didn't matter. At this point, the competition was a place somewhere deep within myself.

The next thing I remember, I was twenty yards from the finish line and I heard the announcer saying, "It looks like Jenner is going to be our third man."

I leaned into the finish line like a sprinter would lean in the 100 meters, trying to wring out every second I could, and for the next twenty or thirty seconds I literally almost died. . . . I collapsed on the ground, then, reviving myself, I stared up at the scoreboard.

It said: JENNER, 4.16.

I had run the race *eight seconds faster* than I had ever run before and beat Gough by twenty-one seconds—three seconds faster than I needed to win.

I was going to the Games!

It was a miracle, the most monumental event of my athletic career. In the last lap of that race, I discovered that my seemingly ordinary body housed a champion, a champion who astonished me with his capacity for action and accomplishment under enormous pressure, a champion who was the essence of all I could hope to become as a human being. Before this moment, I had never reached down that deep to come up with a performance in either life or sports. But in four minutes and sixteen seconds, I was reborn as someone who knew that greatness resided within him and, through hard work, preparation and determination, that greatness could take me to heights still unimagined.

With a beginner's confidence, I had accessed the force that exists within us all, and that force was now propelling me toward the Olympic Games.

The next day, an Oregon newspaper headline screamed: BANNIS-TER, BENNETT MAKE TEAM. BUT WHO'S JENNER?

Jenner was now an Olympian, headed to his first Olympic Games, and he would never be the same again.

CHAPTER THREE

THE LONG JUMP: GOALS FOR GOLD

You stand at the starting point and stare down 120 feet to the takeoff board, then fifteen feet more to a sand landing pit. Your destination is the longest distance you can possibly travel, so you set your sights on the back of the pit, to a distance greater than anyone has ever traveled. You'll always fall short of your target, but this is no time for doubt. You'll need all the speed you gathered in the 100-meter footrace, plus height, distance and the velocity of a bullet. The run has to be absolutely perfect. You've got to hit the takeoff board with your right foot, never the left, to properly launch your leap. If you go over the board, the jump doesn't count. If you're short of the board, you're just giving up precious distance. Therefore, takeoff is critical. Once you've hit the takeoff board, the results are etched in stone. In the long jump, preparation is everything. *When you land it's too late for planning; when you land, you immediately know whether you've won or lost the game.*

The Shadow stalked me for four long years

He winked hello as I stood on the sidelines of the Olympic Stadium in Montreal in 1972 and watched Nicolay Avilov of the USSR receive the gold medal, and he mocked me as I committed myself to victory in '76. He swirled around me as I lay sleepless in my hotel bed on the night after the Games, starting the stopwatch that began screaming in my brain, forcing me to bolt upright in my bed, throw on my running clothes and begin my midnight run through the streets of Munich. He followed me home to the cornfields of Lamoni, where he began haunting every aspect of my existence, whispering in my ear of fear and failure and inadequacy, making me leave home and hit the road, no longer a young man but an athlete obsessed.

The Shadow wasn't merely Avilov, a wonderful Olympian, a decent human being and a friend. The Shadow was my doubts, my fears, the million things that could and would try to stop me as I attempted to make the long jump from wanting to achieving. The Shadow jumped on my back as soon as I found my arena to play in and chased me as I began the race.

I could clearly see my major goal right there in front of me. Now all I had to do was evade the Shadow and run the long jump toward my dream. I quickly discovered that wanting is never enough; wanting is an empty promise, a half-truth that lies somewhere on the edge of fantasy. When not accompanied by specific goals, a want is a welcome mat, inviting the Shadow to invade your life and destroy your dreams.

The long jumps of your life are the big things, the things that are lasting: success in work, relationships, health, finances. To get the most out of the leap, you have to plan your steps, and the best way to play your steps is to set specific goals.

Athletically, the long jump was my weakest event. I wasn't a natural sprinter. I didn't have the natural "knee lift" that propels the great long-jumpers off the takeoff board and to longer and higher distances. Enormous inner strength and precise goal-setting techniques allowed me to wring the most out of what I had. My goals became a lever; little steps, well plotted and taken in a daily fashion, lifting whatever I lacked in personal strength.

"If you don't know where you are going, how can you expect to get there?"

—BASIL S. WALSH

Success sets conditions. The first? Know where you're going. The second? Know how you're going to get there.

Sylvester Stallone knew his direction when, according to the 1994 *Current Biography Yearbook,* as a financially bankrupt aspiring actor and screenwriter, he turned down 250,000 dollars for his script of *Rocky* to wait for a producer who would cast him in the leading role.

Comedian Jim Carrey knew where he was headed when he wrote himself a postdated check for 10 million dollars "for acting services rendered," even though he had absolutely zilch in the bank, and carried the check around in his wallet until he could cash it.

Thomas Edison, who said success is "one percent inspiration and ninety-nine percent perspiration," exemplified the spirit of direction when he invented the lightbulb by applying electric current to every substance onto which he could string filament between two electrodes, until he found the one substance that worked.

In his book *See You at the Top,* Zig Ziglar explained how postwar Japan exemplified the power of goals and direction. In 1950, with its young men lost to war, its cities bombed and without natural resources, the leaders of Japan began three decades of perhaps the best example of goal setting and achievement that the world has ever known. First, in 1950, the leaders of Japanese government, business and industry set the goal of becoming the number-one producer of textiles before the fifties were over. When that goal was achieved by 1960, the leaders set the goal of becoming the number one producer of steel by 1969, even though they didn't have one steel mill in the entire county at the time. When that goal was accomplished, they set the goal of becoming the number one nation in the world in the seventies in auto production. When that goal was accomplished by 1980, they set the goal of becoming number one in the production of electronics and computers by 1989.

What did these individuals and this tiny nation share? Inner strength, talent and perseverance. All of these things are important, but the most vital force when headed toward achievement is the power of *direction.*

We all know people who have no time in their lives, who work endless hours but get absolutely nowhere, who confuse activity with progress and drift through life as aimlessly as a balloon. I've learned that lack of action isn't their downfall—it's lack of direction.

In *See You at the Top,* Zig Ziglar tells the story of John Henry Fabray, the great French naturalist, who conducted a series of experiments with a group of processionary caterpillars, insects that follow each other around in an orderly procession. Fabray lined a few of the bugs around the lip of a flowerpot, with their favorite food—pine needles—down in the center of the pot. For seven days and seven nights, the caterpillars went round and round the flowerpot until they literally died from starvation! As Zig stresses in his famous motivational speeches: "With an abundance of their favorite food less than six inches away they starved to death, because they confused activity with accomplishment."

Unless you win the lottery, success is impossible—as an individual, a sports team, a family or a nation—without knowing where you're going and how you're going to get there.

Motivational speaker Dennis Waitley once said, "Successful in-

dividuals have game plans and purposes that are clearly defined and
to which they constantly refer. They know where they are going every
day, every month and every year. They make life happen."

Life is an accumulation of how we spend our seconds. If we don't
account for those seconds, if we don't know in advance how we will
spend our time—which Ben Franklin called the stuff which life is
made of—how can we expect victory?

We plan our vacations down to the hour.

We balance our checkbooks to the penny.

We even feed our dogs according to a schedule.

But most of us do not plan our lives.

According to Keith Ellis's book *The Magic Lamp,* Yale University surveyed its graduating class in 1953 and discovered that only 3
percent had written goals. Twenty years later, Yale surveyed the class
again: the 3 percent who had written down their goals had amassed a
net worth greater than the other 97 percent combined!

More recent surveys have shown that 75 percent of the population has no idea of what they want to do in life; 20 percent have some
inkling of their desired destination but no understanding of how to get
there. Only 5 percent know what they want to do and have a plan to
make it happen. As master motivator Napoleon Hill said, "The world
has a habit of making room for the man whose words and actions show
that he knows where he is going."

Christopher Columbus did not sail into the New World on
the strength of a dream. He did not sing "Que Sera Sera"—whatever will be will be—as he crossed uncharted oceans and pushed
a surly crew toward an uncertain fate. He kept a daily log, created
his own maps and set and kept specific daily sailing schedules to
accomplish his mission. His log quoted in *The Log of Christopher
Columbus,* as translated by Robert H. Fuson, reads like a manual for
goal setting:

Also, Sovereign Princess besides describing each night what takes place during the day, and during the day the sailings of the night, I propose to make a new chart for navigation, on which I will set down all the sea and the lands of the Ocean Sea, in their correct locations and their correct bearings. Further, I shall compile a book and shall map everything by latitude and longitude. And above all, it is fitting that I forget about sleeping and devote much attention to navigation in order to accomplish this. And these things will be a great task.

What new worlds are you headed toward in your goals? Are you ready to stay your course through rough seas and possible doom?

As songwriter Don Henley asked in a song, "How bad do you want it?"

To succeed, you have to want it badly enough to risk everything for your goals. First step? Know your destination. This is the essence of a long-range goal. Whether you're starting a business, improving your relationship with your spouse or kids, losing weight or getting physically fit . . . you must first know where you're going before you begin the trek to get there.

I love the "Backward Thinking for Forward Motion" goal-setting technique of Hollywood personal manager and producer Ken Kragen, who guided the careers of eighties superstars Lionel Richie, Kenny Rogers and Travis Tritt, advised the Clinton presidential campaign and produced the "Hands Across America" project. Kragan's "Backward Thinking for Forward Motion" is an amazingly simple yet perfectly functional approach, as explained in his book *Life Is a Contact Sport:* "By thinking backward from your ultimate goal, you can create a road map to travel forward to get you there," says Kragen. "This method can be used to achieve almost any professional or personal goal, whether it's to feed the hungry, design a car, or move into a new position."

Everybody arrives at their destination differently. Every athlete trains differently for the decathlon. But nobody gets anywhere without first knowing where they're going. Keep an open mind, and find out how other people do it. Then keep trying things until you find out what works best for you. I always kept changing workouts. My motto became "Whatever works." Whatever I had to do to score points, that's what I did. I knew my direction. I knew what I wanted and knew what I would sacrifice for achievement.

And the Shadow, invading every aspect of my existence, was there to push me toward a definite direction. He shoved me out of my little town and my limited aspirations toward a place where I could race toward the long jump of my dreams.

"The first step toward getting somewhere is to decide that you are not going to stay where you are."
—JOHN J.B. MORGAN AND EWING T. WEBB

I packed up my ten-year-old Volkswagen with everything I owned—javelin, shot, wardrobe and phys ed degree crammed in the backseat, vaulting poles strapped onto the roof—and drove like a bat out of hell for two days straight until I reached what was, in the spring of 1973, the Mecca of track and field, San Jose, California.

I had dreamed of moving to California since I first landed in the state for a short layover on my way to the Olympic Trials the year before. In my mind, California had everything: the weather, the training facilities and, most important, the winners.

My little college town of Lamoni, the village of 900 people and 10,000 hogs, wasn't exactly building Olympic champions. I was the big fish in the little pond. I had to find a place where I could spend four years devoting myself to the Games. "You've gone about as far as you can go here," advised my coach, L.D. Weldon. "You need to move to the next level."

I needed a place where the best athletes in the world were training, a place where I would be able to learn and grow from a circle of champions.

If I wanted to build a car, I'd go to Detroit.

If I wanted to become a stockbroker, I'd go to Wall Street.

If I wanted to become a surfer, I'd head to Hawaii.

In 1973, the great spawning ground for future Olympic champions was sixty miles south of San Francisco, in San Jose.

Track-and-field city.

San Jose State University had churned out sprinting champions John Carlos, Lee Evans and Tommy Smith. One of the world's best shot-putters, Al Feuerbach, lived and trained there.

On the drive out, visions of training with the greats kept me awake. Throwing the shot with Al Feuerbach! Hurling the discus with world champions Mac Wilkins and John Powell, who worked out in the local YMCA weight room! Nine athletes from San Jose would make the 1976 Olympic team, bringing home three gold medals, one silver and a bronze. A San Jose sports columnist calculated that if the Santa Clara Valley was a separate nation, it would have finished fifth in the '76 Games, trailing only the USSR, East Germany, the United States and West Germany.

Without realizing it, I was following the mastermind principle: *Find out what you want to do in life and go and associate with those who are already doing it.* Your duty to yourself and your mission is to be absolutely the best you can be. To do this, you've got to associate with those who are better than you, who can push you, who can help you take your game to a new level.

If you're a golfer, it's playing with the best foursome you can find, people who have played in the championships, who have brought home the trophies. If you're a salesperson, it's going from a small market to a larger market, where your competition is tougher but the numbers are bigger. If you're a college student, it's pushing yourself to get into the Harvards, the Stanfords, the Princetons of the world or, barring that, to associate with the leaders at the college you end up attending.

You've got to go to the mountain; the mountain will not come to you.

I found a tiny apartment in a three-story building right next to the track at San Jose City College, where I would run my daily laps. The apartment was on the second floor and, down below, like an adjunct of my living room, lay the track; so close I could toss a discus off my back porch and it would land on the backstretch. I didn't look at the track; the track looked at me, peering into my windows and screaming, "Get your buns out here!"

All I had to do was hop off my balcony and I was in my arena, ready to play.

I decorated my abode in the style of my obsession. I used a sixteen-pound shot for a doorstop, stacked my vaulting poles behind the couch, put my wardrobe—nylon sweatsuits, running shoes, shorts and T-shirts—in the closet and placed my barbells on the porch where the barbecue grill was supposed to go. In the middle of the living room, in the spot reserved for the La-Z-Boy, I placed a hurdle, so I could not pass an idle moment without being reminded of my goal.

I had found my home. Now I had to go out and meet my community. I headed to the YMCA weight room, where the cream of San Jose track-and-field society worked out.

I didn't know a soul.

It was a hot and musty gym, full of cold steel and colder attitudes. I walked inside with the confidence of the cocky new kid, the Big Thing from the Iowa corn fields, the kid who could go against anybody in Lamoni and win. I walked into this YMCA weight room full of stellar athletes and there—right there in the corner!—stood one of my heroes, Mac Wilkins, who would win the 1976 gold medal in the discus. He was doing squats with 700 pounds on his back. The bar was bending in half, but he was doing sets of ten!

Suddenly, I didn't feel so strong anymore.

I looked around the room for a lifting partner. I wasn't going near Mac Wilkins! Finally, off to the side of the gym, I saw someone lifting a weight that I judged closer to my level. Upon closer inspection, I discovered that this wasn't one of my heroes—at least, not yet. This wasn't even a man, but a woman—a girl!—Maren Seidler, a noted shot-putter on the '72 team.

I walked over, introduced myself and asked, "Mind if I lift with you?"

"Not at all," she said, smiling.

We began with squats. We stacked up the weights and slowly added more and, within a few minutes, the truth became painfully clear: this woman could outlift me!

I had to admit weakness before I could discover my strength.

It's the same in life. We have to start realistically and constantly raise our standards. And the only way to raise our standard is to set goals. In 1974, I made up a little slogan. Everybody likes a slogan! When I began selling insurance part-time to make ends meet in San Jose, I could see the salesmen in their offices beneath banners that proclaimed SELL OR DIE!

I followed their lead when I wrote down my longtime goals, my "macro-purpose," for the decathlon:

85 IN '75!—meaning scoring 8,500 points in the 1975 domestic decathlons, which were a year away.

86 IN '76!—meaning scoring 8,600 points in the 1976 Olympic Games.

Those scores would become my sales quota. Those scores represented the business I wanted to build. I'd taken my dream, found my arena and gotten started in the race. Now I was running the long jump of my life, focusing on the takeoff board and breaking the approach down to specific steps, the "micro-goals" that would take me down the runway and propel me toward my destination.

First, I developed a clear vision of where I wanted to be. Whether you write your goals down on a piece of paper or write them down in your mind, as I did, you've got to know where you're going— daily, weekly and especially, in my case, over a four-year period.

Second, I put myself in a place where I could learn from the best in my business, who were literally my neighbors.

Third, I had to begin building myself physically, mentally and emotionally. I had to learn *everything* about my competition: not the other players but myself. I had to know when I could push myself and when I had to rest. Just like a businessman has to know how far he can push himself in his career before it begins to take its toll on his physical and mental well-being, a decathlete needs to know his limits.

Like the long jump, I wanted to hit that farthest point at the back of the pit, that point that would represent my wildest dreams of victory. Beginner's luck wasn't going to help me now. I had to do the work.

All I had to do was walk through my apartment's sliding-glass window, hop off my balcony, then step onto the track that lay right beyond and begin the run.

There, waiting for me, was the Shadow.

"Come to the edge, He said.
They said, 'We are afraid.'
Come to the edge, He said.
They came.
He pushed them . . . and they flew."
—GUILLAUME APOLLINAIRE

If you are afraid, welcome to the club. Fear is the force that has both driven and destroyed many a pioneer on the journey from one land to another, both on the actual frontier and the endless inner roads of the soul. I always put fear three feet behind me, never allowing it to get in front of me. Fear can push you. It can make you run faster and think smarter. It's a great motivator. But you have to learn how to use it wisely. Fear, to me, is like fire. Fire, out of control, can burn your house down. But controlled, fire will heat your home and cook your food. If you allow fear to get in front of you, it can stop you cold; put it three feet behind you and it can propel you in your mission.

You can talk about the goal-setting systems of the master motivators: of Wayne Dyer's idea of "seasoning," the idle times in a person's life when the time comes for reexamination, plotting a new course and setting new goals for a new spring; of Tony Robbins's Ultimate Success Formula, the practice of first knowing your outcome and then taking the types of actions that will produce the desired results; of Zig Ziglar's practice of writing down one goal on an index card, keeping that card in front of you until you achieve the goal, then writing another, then another until your stack of cards grows as large as your accomplishments.

I've found that the Shadow works just fine for me.

Put your fears behind you and literally race them, using your goals as a road map to guide you to where you're going and as a checklist to gauge how far you've come.

Shortly after I arrived in San Jose in 1973, I discovered that setting goals involves more than running from fear. I developed a lower-back problem that was so painful I couldn't even bend down to wash my feet. My goals immediately changed. Before I could do anything else, I had to get rid of the back problem. I had to do just the opposite of what I wanted to do: I had to rest.

The situation gave me plenty of time for reflection, which turned out to be a blessing in disguise. With time on my hands, I discovered that the science of successful goal setting has several components.

Every quest begins with a vision, a vision so strong that we will risk everything to achieve it. Perhaps the best story illustrating this is told in *The Continuum Dictionary of Women's Biography* by Jennifer S. Uglow. It is the tale of the young girl born into the peasant family in Lorraine, France, an altogether ordinary girl until, at thirteen, she had a vision which she would later describe as "a voice from God." It came to her through the faces of saints—St. Michael, St. Catherine and St. Margaret—a vision so preposterous in scope that even an adult would have been deemed crazy to speak of actually following its order. The voices advised her that her life's mission was to free France from the English and ensure the coronation of Charles VII.

Imagine! A thirteen-year-old told to rescue her country.

But the little girl believed! Her vision was so deeply embedded she would not let it pass unheeded. She suffered numerous failed attempts to visit Charles and was subjected to several psychological evaluations by priests. But the girl's belief in her vision was so contagious that she convinced the citizens of her town to give her men's clothing to wear and a horse for her journey.

Eventually, she reached the first goal in her mission: an audience before the would-be monarch, Charles of Chinon. She was so persuasive that he made her a captain of an army of men. And Jeanne, soon to be known the world over as Joan of Arc, went forth to win the siege at Orleans and watch Charles crowned shortly afterward.

Joan of Arc didn't say, "Maybe." She didn't allow happenstance to guide her. She had a vision and followed it into history. Is the importance of your vision in life any less than that of this thirteen-year-old? Like Joan, we have to consider our vision a gift from the gods, an order from on high, and follow it to wherever it leads. As author Erica

Jong says, "Everyone has talent. What is rare is the courage to follow that talent to the dark place where it leads."

For a goal to become ingrained it must move from the realm of dreams into the realm of reality. The best way to achieve that is to write your goals down and keep them with you until they're achieved.

This is the true currency of champions.

When Lee Iaccoca began his career in the auto industry, he wrote down his entire career plan on a small card. He carried the card with him constantly, until almost every goal—down to the exact dates he expected to receive the promotions—was reached. By then, he had revolutionized the auto industry. "Writing something down is the first step toward making it happen," Lee Iacocca told *Forbes* magazine in 1996.

In the book *Believe and Achieve* by Samuel A. Cypert, the goal-setting techniques of several business leaders, including Domino's Pizza founder Tom Monaghan and Minneapolis business leader Curtis L. Carlson, are examined in detail. Domino's Monaghan, who rose from poverty to running a pizza empire to buying the Detroit Tigers baseball team, carries a legal pad on which he writes his goals, thoughts and aspirations. When one pad is full, he begins another, but not for later reflection; Monaghan believes that merely writing down his goals leads him to act upon them. His empire is proof that this method works.

Curtis L. Carlson, chairman of a Minneapolis conglomerate that includes TGI Friday's and Radisson Hotels, guides his days by writing down one single, ultimate goal on a piece of paper, then keeping that piece of paper in his pocket, even when it becomes frayed and dog-eared, until the goal is reached. That mission accomplished, he writes a new goal on a piece of paper, which he keeps in his pocket until that goal is reached. Many pieces of paper later, Carlson, whose companies are worth well over a billion dollars, continues his "One

Page at a Time" goal-setting technique. "All we have to do," he tells managers, "is keep our eye on the target."

I discovered that there is one more ingredient to successful achievement: a deadline. Without a deadline, a goal can remain still-born as a dream. A great example is the story of a good friend of mine, diet guru Richard Simmons, who started life as a famous fat kid from New Orleans. He tells his story in his book *Never Say Diet*:

> *I quickly grew from a smiling chubby baby to a smiling chubby toddler to the fattest kid on the block. I was the last chosen for an athletic event and the first in line for lunch. I was dressed in clothes purchased in the Husky Department and was never allowed to wear T-shirts with horizontal stripes. I discovered I was really fat when I was eight years old and my mother took me to the "I'm Afraid to Admit My Size" sale.*

For twenty years, the kid grew fatter, breaking diet after diet, deadline after deadline, goal after goal. He read, he exercised, he even prayed. He just couldn't lose weight! Having gained fame on local television ads as a fat man promoting everything from husky jeans to candy bars ("I even dressed as a human meatball!"), he was leaving a supermarket, where he'd signed boxes of spaghetti for a special in-store promotion, when he found a note in an envelope underneath his windshield wiper. The anonymous note read: "Fat people die young. Please don't die."

"Everybody who loses weight is triggered off by something, and that was the something for me," he would later write. "Die . . . I kept thinking. 'Fat people die young. Please don't die.' I didn't want to die."

His goal finally had a deadline! The next week, he checked himself into a hospital in Rome, where the doctors informed him he was a walking time bomb, ready to explode. He quit eating and dropped 112 pounds in two and a half months. The reckless starvation diet practically killed him, but the weight loss phenomenon named Richard Simmons was born, teaching Dustin Hoffman, Paul Newman, Diana Ross, Barbra Streisand and millions of other Americans the importance of putting a deadline on their diet goals.

Every goal reaches a moment of fruition, when it becomes time to *act*, to seize the moment and make the goal real. I love the story of Michelangelo, as told by author Irving Stone in his biography *The Agony and the Ecstasy,* who for ten years had labored with a set of detailed plans, specific goals and exacting schedules to build St. Peter's Cathedral—all without success, much less completion. Bedridden at eighty-two with a severe attack of kidney stones, he returned to his project to discover that the contractor had misread his plans, requiring that one chapel be torn down, rendering his previous designs for the Sistine Chapel useless.

Michelangelo knew that he and only he could complete the dome. No other person could imagine his grandiose vision, much less complete it. Aspiring to "create a work of art that would transcend the age through which he had lived," writes Irving Stone, Michelangelo abandoned his previous goals and discarded his drawings, models and plans.

He would complete the design of the Sistine Chapel in a single night!

Stone writes:

After eleven years of thinking, drawing, praying, hoping and despairing, experimenting and rejecting: a creature of his imagination, compounded of all his arts, staggering in size, yet as fragile as a bird's egg in a nest, soaring, lilting heavenward, constructed of gossamer which carried effort- lessly and musically upward its three-hundred-and-thirty- five-foot height, pear-shaped, as was the breast of the Medici Madonna. . . . It was a dome unlike any other.

"From which magic did such a wonder of design arrive?" asked Michelangelo's friend Tommaso in *The Agony and the Ecstasy.*

"Where do ideas come from?" the master artist replied. "Sebas- tiano asked that same question when he was young. I can only give you the same answer I gave him, for I am no wiser at eighty-two than I was at thirty-nine: ideas are a natural function of the mind, as breathing is of the lungs. Perhaps they come from God."

In one blinding night of absolute clarity, the human equivalent of a nuclear reaction occurred. Preparation, talent and perseverance collided in the mind of one man, propelling Michelangelo Buonarroti into the realm of magic and miracle, into the realm of the Champion Within. He knew where he was going. He'd set specific goals to get there. But it took that extra push of panic and pain for him to enter the zone where the intangibles take over, that altered state much later de- scribed in *The New York Times* as a moment "in which the mind func- tions at its peak, time is often distorted, and a sense of happiness seems to pervade the moment."

If you have any doubt that this extraordinary force exists, all the proof you need spreads across the ceiling of the Sistine Chapel, one of the true wonders of the world.

"I had always set short-term goals. As I look back, one of those steps or successes led to the next one. When I got cut from the varsity team as a sophomore in high school, I

learned something. I never wanted to have that taste in my mouth, that hole in my stomach. So I set a goal of becoming a starter on the varsity. . . . When it happened, I set another goal, a reasonable, manageable goal that I could realistically achieve if I worked hard enough."

—MICHAEL JORDAN

You must devise a formula for your dream.

Or as a high school football coach in Escambia, Florida, used to tell his star player, "It's a dream until you write it down. Then it's a goal."

That player's name was Emmitt Smith, and his story was recounted in the July 1, 1996, issue of *Sports Illustrated.* Now the star of the Dallas Cowboys, Emmitt obviously took his coach's advice to heart. One night in 1993, Smith, already the leading rusher in the NFL, sat down to write out new goals. A picture began to form in his mind: that of Walter Payton, the leading rusher in NFL history. Emmitt could see Payton so clearly it seemed like he was in the same room, evading tacklers, eating up yardage, smashing records and leaving a pile of numbers in his wake.

Emmitt wrote those numbers down: Payton had rushed 17,000 yards in his career. Emmitt had rushed 9,000 thus far in his own. He wanted to know how many more yards he'd have to rush to break Payton's record, so he did the math, figuring that by the time he turned thirty-three he could enter the history books at the leading rusher in the NFL. "I can be there," Emmitt told *Sports Illustrated,* "but I've got to hit one helluva pace. I've got to get ahead of the curve . . . and I can do that. There's time, there's time."

He had written down his dreams. But to truly turn them into achievable one-page goals, he had to break them down into a formula, which he did, writing out fourteen separate goals for the 1993–1994 season on a single sheet of paper, a piece of paper studded with his Cowboys number in a star and "Personal Goals" written across the top:

Keep Jesus Christ #1 in my life.
Stay healthy.
Average 125 yards rushing/game.
Lead team and league in rushing for third year in a row.
Lead league in scoring.
Over 1,000 yards in rushing by eighth game.
Catch 70 passes.
No fumbles!
Be named to the 1st Team All Pro.
Go to the ProBowl for 4th Year.
Be named MVP of the NFL.
Go to Super Bowl and win again (with 225 yards rushing
     and 3 TD)!
Be named Super Bowl MVP.
Go to Disneyland.

This is the process by which a dream becomes a goal.

It can be boiled down into two words: getting specific.

After I became absolutely clear of my major, "long-jump" goal—winning Olympic Gold—I broke it down into a subgoal, "85 in '75, 86 in '76," which I broke down to an even more concise formula: to work out eight hours a day, seven days a week, 365 days a year. This simple process made a seemingly impossible dream achievable, merely by giving me a formula that, if followed, would assure my success.

The formula consisted of five realistic goals that took my daily life into account. Listing them here, I've written the goals first, followed by an italicized section on how you can make the this goal-setting formula work for you.

1. Live in the Champion's Domain. I accomplished this by moving to San Jose and making my surroundings a laboratory for my success. *Surround yourself with people who assist you in bringing out your best. Just like I put the hurdle in my living room, surround yourself in both your home and office with icons that will constantly remind you of your mission.*

2. Discipline Myself to Do the Daily Work. I knew that the key to Olympic success is the minute-by-minute, day-by-day preparation. So I devised a training routine that began daily with running, then segued to weight training, then specific event training, before returning to running in the evening. *Give yourself a list of daily goals in your field of endeavor, activities that, taken collectively, will train you to best achieve your goals.*

3. Use Food as Fuel. I began feeding myself the proper foods and started a food supplement regimen that would empower my body in my race. *Take your health seriously; make it a major goal. Remember, your body is the vehicle that's going to drive you to success.*

4. Visualize Victory. I exercised my mind as hard as I exercised my body by visualizing all the things I had to do

to put myself in a position to win. *Your mind is the computer that can access your dreams. Where does it begin? Visualization. See the meeting, the sale, the advancement before it actually happens. Your mind goes through the process of success hundreds of times before you get into the heat of the battle. Win in the mind first, then win in the boardroom or on the battlefield.*

5. Make Myself My Biggest Competitor. My goal was to compete against myself daily, to push myself hard enough so that when my moment arrived in the Games, I would be prepared, both mentally and physically, to win. *Realize that the reason most people fail isn't because of the competition but because of the limits they place upon themselves, allowing defeat to take over. Take responsibility for your own destiny. You can come up with a performance, if you can reach down and dig deep enough into your competitive soul. You can overcome tremendous obstacles.*

My goals looked great in the free-flowing paper of my mind.

Just as I'd upped the ante on my arena by moving from Lamoni to San Jose, now I was devising goals that would up the ante on my abilities. Would my formula of personal goals put both my mind and my body to the ultimate test? Only time would tell.

I was out to build a champion, step by step, goal by goal. If I succeeded, I was be rewarded with Olympic Gold. Anything short of that, and the Shadow would surely arrive to celebrate my failure.

CHAPTER FOUR

THE SHOT PUT: PLAY TO YOUR STRENGTHS

When you have sixteen pounds of steel on your shoulder, there is no time for weakness. The shot is a graceless and ponderous ball; throwing it is all about strength. Shot-putters call their stance a "power position," and 70 percent of it is in the legs, the body's natural foundation of power. You relax in the back of the circle with the shot tucked almost to your left ear. The best throw out of three determines your points for the event. You turn your body in a pivot, swinging your front foot ahead while simultaneously sliding the back foot across the circle. You don't throw the shot, you push it, driving with your legs, so when it explodes it's not merely a bullet fired from your arms but a cannonball blasted from the center of your entire body.

I know a lot about you. You are just like I once was. If you haven't discovered your strengths and identified your weaknesses, you're not really living. You're coasting, waiting for the bell to ring to start your real life. You're the sleepy kid in the back of the classroom, the student barely squeaking by, the lonely adult suffering from the plague of wasted potential. The "has been," "could've been," or "would've been" kid, always putting off until tomorrow what you could do today.

I know something else about you. You were born a champion. Your very birth was as improbable as the twinkling of a star. As Pablo Casals writes, as quoted in *Chicken Soup for the Soul,* "You are a marvel. You are unique. In all the years that have passed, there has never been another child like you. You may become a Shakespeare, a Michelangelo, a Beethoven. You have the capacity for anything."

You have infinite capabilities.

But you can just as easily become a candidate for doom.

In life, as in the shot put, you have to play to your strengths and downplay your weaknesses. This is the obvious law of sports, business, relationships and health. Yet it's amazing how many of us do exactly the opposite.

In employment agencies across our land, applicants who have made—or more likely unmade—careers by going with their weaknesses are legion.

Consider a few of the more glaring examples:

The unmotivated salesman
The unspirited athlete
The unorganized boss
The unenergetic laborer
The unfriendly manager
The unempowered motivational speaker

Is there a word with an "un" prefix before your present course in life? Are you unlucky, uninspired or unfulfilled? If so, you're likely playing to your weaknesses and downplaying your strengths.

The world is full of examples of people who dramatically turned their lives around, merely by recognizing their strengths and going with them.

As a child, jazz great Herbie Hancock could see his own weaknesses through his older brother. He was quoted in the 1993 book *Hindsights* by Guy Kawasaki:

When he could shoot marbles, I could only mess up the game. When he could first throw a football, my hand couldn't get around it. I wound up being the mascot of the team, so sports was kind of a nightmare for me. Being a mascot for a team, you feel like a pet—like some subhuman dog or something. To this day, I have no interest in sports. When I was seven and my brother was ten, we all started taking piano lessons. For the first time, I was on an even keel with my brother. We started taking lessons, and he wasn't better than me—I wasn't better than him, either. I would practice and play the piano all the time, and he would divide his time between practicing and playing sports or playing with the guys.

Susan Butcher struggled through school. According to a pamphlet called *Color Me Successful* by the Lab School of Washington, she felt caged in a classroom and dreamed of being outdoors, running wild with her dog. Learning disabilities made schoolwork so difficult that when she graduated from high school Susan vowed that she'd never set foot in a classroom again. Why should she stay locked into the source of her weaknesses when all she had to do was walk out the door into the frontier of her strength—the great outdoors? She heard about the Alaska Iditarod Dog Sled Race, the longest race in the world, a grueling test of perseverance against the elements. By escaping the source of her weaknesses and going with her strengths, Susan Butcher became the first person to win three Iditarods in a row.

We all have strengths! We all have one or more powers that, once discovered, understood and put into action, can propel us past mere expectations and into the realm of dreams. It is your duty to discover what is good about yourself, and, once discovered, turn what you do well into what you have the power to do best by putting it at the center of your existence.

The moment I crossed the finish line at the Olympic Trials, somehow pulling an extra eight seconds from someplace deep inside me in the 1,500-meter race, I got my first glimpse into the most majestic part of my being. I instantly knew I'd discovered my strength—my athletic mind—and I relied on that knowledge for the rest of my career.

I didn't need a flash of revelation to show me my weaknesses. I knew I didn't have great speed; I had to rely on endurance. My natural-born athletic talent was marginal; only through extremely hard work and training had I risen above the pack. I was weak in business, in negotiation, in trusting people to a fault and, of course, I still had that dyslexic kid inside of me.

But now none of that mattered. From the moment I turned down that backstretch, bolting toward the finish line, I was never the same person again. I knew I could reach down and bring greatness out of myself any time I needed it. It was like being told that I had a computer chip hidden deep inside me, a chip designed to instantly turn me from man into machine—and all I had to do was switch that sucker on.

I am here to tell you that the analogy is true!

Find your strength and you have found the switch.

In my case, I discovered that my biggest strength was what I had previously thought my biggest weakness: my *mind.* In training, the athletic body does 80 percent of the work; the mind, 20 percent. But in competition, the ratio flips. Now it's an 80 percent mental challenge, 20 percent physical. Think about it. Everybody at the Olympic level has the physical ability to win. But not everybody has the mental toughness required to bring a winning performance out of themselves at a specific time on a specific day.

You see it every day in sports. Joe Montana didn't have the greatest arm in the NFL. But when there were two minutes left and you were down by three points, who did you want to have the ball? Joe Montana. Why? Because, as an outstanding football player, he had the *will to win*, another way of saying he was able to bring greatness out of himself when he needed it. I never thought Magic Johnson had great physical strength. He just didn't jump that high or rebound that fast. Mental toughness is what made Magic . . . well, magic. Larry Bird wasn't born with incredible physical talent. But with ten seconds on the clock, who do you want to throw the ball to? Not the guy who can jump the highest or the one with the most muscle mass. You want to throw it to the Larry Birds of the world, the people who have realized that they can reach down deep within themselves and pull out a winning performance.

This ability is reserved for the winners in life, but not because it is a force that is doled out to a select few. We all have this power. But it is only the winners who know how to pull it out of themselves when they need it most. It all boils down to confidence, one of the highest forms of knowledge. Confidence is knowledge with tangible power, a power that can be turned into action and accomplishment. The adage "You can because you *think* you can" hits the essence of confidence on the nose. It's that internal fire, that subconscious pat on the back, the smile on the face, the shine on the shoe, the infinite pieces that empower the whole. It's the inner strength that comes from being the best you can be that gives birth to the Champion Within.

Not everybody has someone to pat them on the back and tell them, "You can do it!" Champions know how to do this for themselves. Carry yourself as if you're a champion—make your clothing, surroundings and attitude reflect your inner fire—and you will be on your way to becoming one. Feed your own confidence; it's the fuel that can blast you into brave new realms of accomplishment. Harness your highest potential once and you'll have the confidence to do it for the rest of your life.

After running that 1,500-meter race and making it onto the 1972 Olympic team, I knew that I had something special. I knew that I, too, could reach down into the core of my being and pull out the champion.

Now let me help you soar with your strengths and come up with the performance of a lifetime.

"You will become as small as your controlling desire; or as great as your dominant aspiration."
  —*JAMES ALLEN, AUTHOR OF* As a Man Thinketh

In his book *Chicken Soup for the Soul,* Jack Canfield wrote about Roger Crawford, who was born without developed hands; his thumbs were nubs jutting out of his forearms. His arms and legs were severely stunted and he only had three toes on his shortened right leg. His left leg was amputated immediately after his birth. The doctors said he suffered from a rare birth defect called ectrodactylism and would never walk or be able to care for himself.

But Roger Crawford had two important allies: his parents, who taught him to believe that he was only as handicapped as he allowed himself to be.

His dad taught him to throw a football and volleyball, and Roger, at twelve, astonished his class by winning a spot on the varsity football team. His method of play? Visualize victory! So when the football sailed into his forearms during one game, he ran for all he was worth through several tacklers, including one who, grabbing Roger's artificial leg, found himself on the ground holding a leg and watching Roger hopping through the goalposts for a touchdown.

His self-confidence grew. But Roger met his Waterloo in typing class. You can't operate a typewriter without fingers! "I learned a good lesson," Roger later remembered. "You can't do everything. It's better to concentrate on what you *can* do."

Roger could play tennis. He found an offbeat tennis racquet that allowed him to grip it by wedging part of his hand into its supports. He became obsessed with the game, eventually going on to a college tennis and teaching career.

"The only difference between me and you is that you can see my handicap, but I can't see yours," he says. "We *all* have them. When people ask how I've been able to overcome my physical handicaps, I tell them that I've simply learned what I can't do—such as play the piano or eat with chopsticks—but, more importantly, I've learned what I *can* do. Then I do what I can with all of my heart and soul."

He found his strengths and he ran with them.

The book *Athletics of the Ancient World* by E. N. Gardiner tells of how the ancient Olympic Games were the essence of strength. They were born in a period called the Age of Strength, writes Gardiner, a period which offers many lessons for contemporary life. In those days, strength was muscle mass. The boxer and wrestler were kings for good reason: athletics was a training ground for warfare. Running and jumping did the warrior little good—except in retreat. The object of the early Olympic Games was to build strength in men, and it succeeded handily. The athletes trained so hard that many of them maintained their power through eight Olympics—or thirty-two years.

Tales of strength in ancient Olympians have become legend. One contender, Glaucus, was discovered when his father found him hammering in a plowshare with his bare hand. Another, Theogenes, heaved a huge bronze statue onto his shoulder and carried it through the marketplace. The young Olympian, Milo, trained for weight lifting by doing sets of ten with a bull calf until it was grown—at which point he carried the bull into the stadium, roasted it and ate it, to prove the strength of his appetite. Milo was eventually beaten by a shepherd named Titormus, who lifted a huge boulder that Milo couldn't even move, carried it sixteen yards and heaved it away.

The physical ideal of the day was the mighty Hercules, celebrated in marble and hailed in poetry by Pindar who called him "short of stature but unbending of soul."

Strength was everything.

Weakness, like defeat, was shunned.

Today, after centuries of advancement and enlightenment, we have somehow reversed the order of things.

We fret over our insecurities to the detriment of our strengths.

We concentrate on our enemies to the exclusion of our friends.

We endure elaborate analyses and instruction, striving to improve on the things we do worst.

We use our weaknesses as excuses not to improve on the strengths we have at our fingertips.

We all could be Hercules, but we are so worried about our lack of stature that we neglect the iron in our souls.

In their book, *Soar with Your Strengths,* Donald Clifton and Paula Nelson have set up a science for accentuating strengths and downplaying weaknesses. They cite a Gallup poll of more than 250,000 successful professionals in diverse fields that proves that high achievers are those who use their strengths to further their careers.

"While the principle may sound obvious, it is rarely applied," they write. "Instead of spending time trying to correct your weaknesses—as many of us do—our experience suggests that you should focus on your special talents. For every strength you have, you also possess a multitude of non-strengths. It would be a huge waste of energy to try and fix all of your weaknesses."

Here is a paraphrase of the authors' list of tips for developing strengths:

Pick One Strength to Pursue. We all are blessed with a variety of talents. There are millions of wonderful mothers who are exceptional cooks, able hostesses, stylish dressers and incredible wives. But there is only one Martha Stewart. Why? Because Martha, whose only marriage ended in divorce, didn't dwell on the things that she couldn't do (and, yes, there *are* things that Martha can't do); she pursued her strength—entertaining—and the rest, of course, is history. "Being a Renaissance man is in vogue nowadays, yet most people pursuing multiple strengths will achieve only mediocrity in the long run," write Clifton and Nelson.

Exercise Your Strength Daily. When Garth Brooks was bouncing drunks from Oklahoma beer joints or selling boots in a Nashville boot shop, he didn't go home and practice drunk bouncing or boot fitting. He exercised his strength—singing and songwriting—so that when opportunity knocked, he'd be ready. "World class sports figures, musicians and writers have learned that talent alone doesn't guarantee success. Ultimate excellence is a product of total commitment, hard work over the long term and heeding the message: if it doesn't feel good you're not practicing a strength," write Clifton and Nelson.

You Don't Have to Fix the Things That Don't Hinder You. Write this down as a new law of your life: you don't have to fix the things you do worst to develop what you do best. If I'd had to learn to read perfectly before I could graduate to the athletic field, I'd still be in that second grade classroom. Manage your weaknesses but concentrate on your strengths. Vince Lombardi, the legendary Green Bay Packers football coach, made a science of accentuating the positive. As Michael O'Brien writes in his 1989 biography, *Vince:*

On the Thursday before the contest with Detroit in 1962 . . . he showed the team films of running plays that had succeeded against the Lions. As he taught the film lesson, he reflected, "I want them to envision [the plays] working. They must take the field with confidence." The following afternoon, he showed a film of a recent Packer victory over Detroit. "We'll see no more films," he thought. "This is the picture I want to leave in their mind."

Fill your head with your own films of your successes and play them in your mind constantly.

Look for Complementary Partners. This point is best illustrated through the comedy partnership of Jerry Lewis and Dean Martin, say the authors Clifton and Nelson. Jerry Lewis began his show business career as slapstick comedian. But he had only moderate success as a stand-up comic, a one-note clown with a grating rasp and an over-the-top delivery, all of which could be seen as weaknesses. Lewis turned them all to strengths, however, with one simple strategy. He recommended that a nightclub owner re-place his opening act with a friend named Dean Martin, whose strengths were in the precise area of Lewis's weaknesses. Within days, Martin and Lewis were playing to sell-out crowds. Within the year, they were filming their first movie.

This is the essence of a perfect partnership: one person's strengths complementing the other person's weaknesses. What would Fred Astaire—whose first casting director scrawled in a memo, "Can't act! Slightly bald! Can dance a little!"—have been without Ginger Rogers? In my own case, my wife Kris's strengths helped me cast off the weaknesses that had consumed me—insecurity, blind trust in others, willingness to subsist in meager surroundings—and returned me to the strength I had long neglected, my athletic mind. I'm not a negotiator; that's Kris's strength. I'm not super-organized; Kris is. Conversely, Kris can't speak before a crowd of 15,000 or motivate a sales and business force to victory—two of my strengths.

Develop a Support System. My friend television writer and producer Stephen Cannell runs a studio that has produced more than two dozen prime-time television series, from *Wise Guy* to *The A-Team,* since it was founded in 1980. Stephen's strength is writing. His weakness? He's dyslexic. He has a hard time reading. Had Stephen concentrated on his weakness, he'd be spending his time watching television, not writing television shows.

All he needed was help in the form of a writing assistant and his weakness was vanquished.

Think of the example of a handicapped businessman. Does he abandon his ambitions and stay at home merely because he cannot drive himself to the office? Of course not. I know a dozen salespeople who absolutely love interacting with customers but hate paperwork. Imagine if these salespeople refused to hire help. Every time they'd have to file a report, their enthusiasm would wane and their sales would certainly eventually be affected. All they have to do is hire help, and they can push aside their weakness and allow their strength to take them onward.

Life is very simple. We are all blessed with different gifts. Know what yours are, then go out and seek help with your weaknesses.

Cast Out the Negative! I have one additional piece of advice to add to Clifton and Nelson's list above. It's about a weakness that can bring you down as fast as the Hindenberg, a weakness as poisonous as alcoholism or drug addiction, and just as dangerous to your success.

A weakness for negative people.

Nothing can derail a successful spirit faster than living, working or playing with negative opinions. People with negative opinions poison your spirit, and thus your life, in the same way cyanide poisons your body. Having endured more than my share of negative people, I can speak from firsthand experience. The adage "We are who we associate with" is absolutely true. Realize two things: first, the world is full of negative souls; second, that doesn't mean you have to live with one! Cast negative people out of your life and seek out those who quest for the best in themselves and others.

Positive people are all around you! I know because I found one in my wife, Kris, and we have consciously surrounded ourselves with other positive friends and associates, creating a tangible community of constant empowerment to work, live and play in. Surround yourself with those who not only want to see you succeed but are eager to help you get there, and you will have built a house for your success to grow.

"Follow your bliss."

—JOSEPH CAMPBELL

In the parlance of the shot put, going with your strengths means putting yourself in the "power position," where your best talents can shine. Politics is full of candidates who understood and then utilized their power position. The best example comes from the American presidential campaign of 1896, as recounted in a June 1996 *Time* magazine article written by Peggy Noonan. It concerns the underdog, William McKinley, the down-home, folksy governor from Canton, Ohio, who faced the great, stem-winding orator, Congressman William Jennings Bryant.

McKinley knew his strengths. He was pure heartland of America, a down-to-earth, stable guy next door, more at home on his front porch than the campaign trail. He also knew his weaknesses: lack of personal magnetism and a dearth of oratorical talents.

So instead of plodding forth into his opponent's area of strength—the campaign trail—McKinley stayed at home where he could play to his strengths and downplay his weaknesses, launching the first "front porch campaign" in American history. He literally sat on his front porch in Canton, Ohio, and invited America to visit him one by one.

America came.

They came in delegations and were met at the train depot by a team of horsemen who led the citizens in a parade to McKinley's house, where the candidate sat waiting on his front porch or in his living room.

"If you want to see a presidential candidate, you ring the bell and walk in to see him," Noonan quotes English journalist George Stevens as writing. "That is what he is there for. I rang and walked in. Mr. McKinley was sitting in a rocking chair not ten feet from the door. He is gifted with a kindly courtesy that is plainly genuine and completely winning."

William McKinley went with his strengths and not his weaknesses.

He became the twenty-fifth president of the United States.

Of course, McKinley had a team of advisors to point out his strengths and weaknesses. We have to analyze ourselves. How? Begin by making a detailed accounting.

Start with your strengths. Ask yourself simple questions:

1. When do you feel strongest?

2. What event in your life brought you the most joy and happiness? What strength created this event for you?

3. What do you find easiest to do in your life?

4. What are your special gifts?

Now consider your weaknesses:

1. When do you feel weakest?

2. When have you felt like a failure? What weaknesses contributed to this feeling?

3. What do you dislike most about yourself?

Still having trouble? Follow the self-analyses of several successful individuals who discussed their strengths and weaknesses with author B. Eugene Griessman in his book *The Achievement Factors*.

Comedian Steve Allen is a very successful musical composer—despite a glaring weakness: he swears he cannot read music.

"From the start, I had the ability to create my own things, and that ability soon outdistanced my halting ability to read [music], so I got impatient and I didn't have a piano for a few years, so I lost the ability to read altogether," he told Griessman.

Imagine! A rare talent going to waste merely because he couldn't write his creations on paper. Allen found a way to go with his strengths: he began composing his songs with a tape recorder. He'd tape the song and send the tape to be written out by one of the millions of people who can read music but not compose it.

He found a support system to handle his weaknesses, enabling him to soar with his strengths.

Andy Rooney of CBS's *Sixty Minutes* told Griessman:

"I'm quite creative. I do not tend towards clichés with words. I have a quick flair for occasional humor. I work quite hard. . . . That's one of the things I didn't know about myself until later in life. . . . Because a lot of the things I do, I don't have much ability to stick at and finish properly. But when it comes to writing, I work hard. I get in here early every morning and I stick to it."

Rooney's weaknesses?

"I'm not as intellectual as I'd like to be. I think my brain capacity is limited," he told Griessman. "I'm better at starting something than finishing. My hobby is woodworking. I'll get an idea for a piece of furniture and get some great wood and really work on the hard part of it, and get it almost done, then not bother to sand it properly."

By getting into a creative field with a deadline, Andy Rooney has been able to play to his strengths (hard work, "a quick flair for occasional humor" and creativity), and the weekly deadline pushes him to downplay his weaknesses (an inability to finish things).

"Peanuts" cartoonist Charles M. Schulz, creator of Snoopy and Charlie Brown, is the king of the comics pages. But even Schulz has weaknesses that forced him to define and go with his strengths.

"I don't know how good I am at drawing a comic strip, but I think I know as much about drawing a comic strip, if not more, than anybody else," he told Griessman. "I think I'm really an expert on the comic strip as a medium. . . . I'm very proud of what I've done, and I think I've created some of the best comic strip characters that have ever existed. But this does not mean I'm the best. Nobody is the best at anything. That is a foolish, modern thought."

Schulz knows his weaknesses:

"I feel inferior in a lot of areas. I feel inferior that I can't draw better than I can, that I don't have a wider, broader knowledge, which I would love to have. I feel I don't have the extensive vocabulary I think it would be nice to have. I suppose this is why I've been able to function so well with Charlie Brown. I can caricature all of these faults, realizing as I've grown older that these are common feelings and you'll meet almost no one who down deep really does not have feelings of inferiority. That is why, I guess, the readers can identify so completely with Charlie Brown."

By drawing a simple, easy-to-read comic strip full of characters with the simplest vocabulary and motives, Charles Schulz has capitalized on his strengths and cast off his weaknesses. Would he have been a better cartoonist if he had more skills? Probably not. By creating a masterpiece with the tools he had at his disposal, Charles Schulz made the most of what he had and didn't worry about what he lacked.

This is the true definition of genius.

Once you know your strengths, run with them, heave them like a shot into the arena where they can begin to propel you toward your goals. Fight whatever weaknesses pull you down, never allowing them to limit the velocity of your throw.

You have been blessed with powers that can literally make your dreams come true.

Discover them.

CHAPTER FIVE

THE HIGH JUMP: CONSTANTLY RAISING THE BAR ON YOUR ASPIRATIONS AND ABILITIES

In the high jump, where the head goes the body follows. You take an eleven-step approach in the form of the letter J, eyes on the bar, but never obsessing on it. If you even think about the improbability of leaping six feet backwards, you would never even try. At the end of the curve in the J, you plant your takeoff leg, draw up your knee almost to where it touches your chest, and you're airborne. Head first, then shoulders, arms, hands, hips and legs, you fly over the bar, body rotating backwards, like an astronaut going weightless. You land in the pit flat on your back, staring up at the height you've scaled, preparing to do it all over again, raising the bar each time you succeed. Three attempts are allowed at each height, until you reach the elevation where you can jump no higher.

What a perfect metaphor for life: where the head goes, the body follows; don't obsess over the mountain you're climbing—just climb it; and, finally, constantly raise the bar on your aspirations.

Citius, altius, fortius! Faster, higher, stronger!

The Latin motto of the modern Olympic Games can become the motto of your new life.

Once I got a glimpse of the Champion Within at the center of my being at the end of the 1,500-meter run at the Olympic Trials, I wanted to find a way to access it whenever I needed it most. So I vowed total commitment: I would train 365 days a year, seven days a week, twenty-four hours a day. If physical and mental preparation was the price to access this incredible power, I would gladly pay. So that, ideally, it would explode within me on the precise date of July 29, 1976, the date of the Twenty-first Olympiad in Montreal.

Just as I trained for the Olympic Games—sacrificing mind, body and soul for one shot at victory—so must you train for the Game of Life, for that moment when everything gels and perfection emerges. To the golfer, it's the hole in one. To the bowler, it's the perfect strike. To the salesman, it's the record year. To me, it was clearing a seemingly impossible height in the high jump—and every other event in the decathlon. We all have different ideas of perfection, but the various visions have one thing in common.

Preparation precedes excellence.

To be a winner, you have to train.

Taking a cue from the Latin motto of the modern Olympics, I have broken down the crucial period of raising the bar on your expectations and abilities into a more contemporary triad: visualize, train, compete.

Visualize yourself at the apex of your abilities, constantly filling your mind with visions of victory, never defeat.

Train yourself with constant challenges, systematically raising the bar on your abilities and aspirations.

Compete against yourself by striving for constant improvement, elevated expectations, higher goals.

Remember, the road to optimum performance in both sports and life is like the high jump. You start out at an opening height, a relatively low level that you can easily handle. Then you begin gradually raising the bar, just as in life you begin gradually raising your standards. Raising the bar in life all comes down to this: you have to be willing to do the hour-by-hour, day-by-day work to prepare yourself for the moment.

Faster, higher, stronger.

This is not an idea to contemplate; this is law.

If you don't raise the bar on yourself and your abilities, life is going to raise the bar on you. Life does not do this kindly. I'm talking about failure: unemployment, bad relationships, disease, death. Realize that complacency is not merely the enemy of your dreams, it's the cancer of the soul. Just as acting on your dreams can propel you to heights unimagined, dreams left unfulfilled can and will destroy you. Evidence of this is everywhere. One look into the faces of the legions of men and women who have let their dreams pass them by and you'll have all the proof you'll ever need.

The dream was born on a Nazi death march in his homeland. It endured months of grueling drudgery in a labor camp, marching for days without food and water. It hid in the shadows where invading armies sought him out, guns drawn, and barked in his consciousness like a mongrel dog as he entered the university, received a degree in philosophy and became a stage director—all which came to naught when, in 1956, the Soviet Army entered Hungary, imposing harsh military rule, killing thousands and taking many more prisoner.

Andrew Lanyi didn't defer his dream, his vision of becoming a success in America, and his story, told in the book *Sales Superstars* by David C. Forward, is nothing short of an inspiration.

Lanyi started out at an opening height—begging spare change from Austrian border guards, then boarding a steamer, then arriving with forty-five cents in his pocket in New York City—where he gradually began raising the bar.

Since there was absolutely no demand for non-English-speaking Hungarian stage directors in Manhattan, Lanyi took a menial sixty-four-dollar-a-week job as a file clerk and moved with his wife into a low-income housing project in Harlem.

With a child on the way, Lanyi immediately began raising the bar one tiny, almost imperceptible, yet crucial, notch at a time. Every day he tried to interpret the want ads, where one phrase soon became perfectly clear: "Previous experience required." Finally, he found one that said "No experience needed."

It was an ad for a part-time mutual fund salesman. Lanyi had never sold anything in his life. He could hardly speak English. He didn't even know what a mutual fund was. He had one thing going for him: mutual fund firms needed salespeople badly. "If you could move your lips, they hired you," Lanyi later remembered.

Enrolling in a training class, he began learning about mutual funds, then started seeking customers who could understand what he was trying to sell. Not an easy task for a foreigner whose English was so bad he had to mimic other customers to get food in a coffee shop. But Lanyi found a way: he studied the Budapest telephone book at the New York Public Library, writing down the hundred most popular Hungarian surnames, then seeking identical names in the New York directory. He had his first client call list.

He'd raised the bar another notch.

His sales grew. He made appointments with nine New York brokerage firms. He knew that recruits were paid a cost-of-living stipend for three years while they built up their business. Lanyi told his new bosses that if he wasn't self-sufficient within six months, he'd expect to be fired. Eight firms offered him a job. He chose the blue-chip Kidder Peabody, where he began working twice the hours of anyone on the staff.

He'd raised the bar again.

Within four years he was the top mutual fund salesperson in an office of forty. He began expanding his client base and eventually joined the stellar firm of Eastman Dillon, where he became the top salesperson on a staff of 900. While the other brokers worked in a "bull pen," Lanyi, who spent more time at the office than anyone else and brought in more business, asked for a private office. When his boss told the national sales manager of his star broker's request, the sales manager, terrified that Lanyi could jump ship, gave up his own office so Lanyi could have a proper place to work. "The next day, an interior decorator showed up and asked me how I wanted my new office to look," Lanyi later told author David Forward.

Once more, he'd raised the bar.

New roads beckoned. Convinced that even the best investment firms had weak research departments, he began specializing in research. A century-old investment banking house made him an irresistible offer. Six months after he arrived, he had new business cards: Senior Vice President. Five years later, he moved again to a firm that gave him his own division. Within the year, the Lanyi Research Division grew from eleven to twenty-five employees. Soon he was running his own firm.

Up and up and up—Lanyi raised the bar on his abilities and expectations.

Thirty-nine years after arriving in America, Andrew Lanyi is a millionaire many times over, one of the top two producers in Wall Street history, a highly respected motivational speaker and author. He lives in a penthouse in Manhattan and spends his summers in a second house in the Hamptons.

From a labor camp to a vagabond steamship to a low-income Harlem housing project, the Andrew Lanyi story is the essence of someone taking the high jump of life one level at a time. Could your opening height be any lower than Andrew Lanyi's? Chances are, you're starting out much higher. But whatever the level of your present, all you have to do to launch your future is take one jump at the comfort zone of your opening height, and you'll be on your way.

The first jump is easy; the first jump occurs in your mind.

"Dream lofty dreams, and as you dream, so shall you become. Your vision is the promise of what you shall one day be; your ideal is the prophecy of what you shall at last unveil."

—*JAMES ALLEN*

"Where there is no vision, the people perish."

—*PROVERBS 29:18*

In the twenty years since the Twenty-first Games, I've learned to follow new coaches in life, the master motivators, who do for my mind and spirit what the best coaches can do for an athlete's body: drive them to be the best that they can be. Zig Ziglar, Tony Robbins, Les Brown, Dennis Waitley, Barry Farber, Steven Covey . . . these are the new prophets of human potential, and their disciplines have helped me to unleash the champion in every aspect of my life.

One thing they all seem to agree upon is the importance of visualization; you have to first see your dream before you can accomplish it.

Thinking back, I heartily concur. I won the decathlon at the 1976 Olympic Games a million times in my mind. It was the one arena where I could be assured victory. In my mind, I set the rules and the supreme rule was: *Bruce always wins.* The 100 meters, the long jump, the shot put, the high jump . . . event after event, I would emerge not merely victorious but having smashed previous records to smithereens. From a technical standpoint, I saw my every movement synchronized in a dance of ultimate perfection. In my mind, I stood atop the victory platform a dozen times daily, with the gold medal slung around my neck, awash in accomplishment, anthems and applause.

When I took my mind to the track twice a day, I imagined someone chasing me, not like the smiling crowd of Philadelphians who chased Rocky Balboa in a victory run in the movie *Rocky.* This was a snarling, hungry beast stalking its prey; a cougar after a snake, a hawk after a mouse, the reigning gold medal decathlete, Nicolay Avilov, out to destroy his major competition: me. He wouldn't stop for a handshake; his mission was to beat my butt, to leave me in the dust. He chased me daily in my imagination, pushing me, forcing me to run faster, harder, smarter. Even though the real Nicolay Avilov was training on the other side of the world, he was never too tired to chase me in my mind. When my legs wouldn't pump and my arms were exhausted, when days dawned and nights fell in lonely silences, at the times when even my dog was too tired to run alongside me, Avilov was there. One slip-up and, *wham!*—he would sprint past me as fast as a Ferrari passes up a hitchhiker, leaving me and my dreams in the dust. That vision spurred me on. The adrenal glands would begin to pump, the heart would beat like a jackhammer, the mind and body would scream and I'd push forward.

At home in my tiny 145-dollar-a-month San Jose apartment, with the track looming outside my windows, I never allowed myself to dwell on the television but focused instead on something I'd borrowed from the City College athletic department: a hurdle. An artifact from the Olympic arena that awaited me four years in the future, the hurdle was a constant reminder of two things: first, it represented an event in which I needed to improve; second, it reminded me of how close we are to constantly tripping, stumbling and falling. Late at night, I'd spend hours pitting myself against that hurdle. The apartment was too tiny to take even a half-leap, of course, but in the alley of my mind I jumped it a thousand times: one foot at a time, in slow motion, working on the act of driving myself over the hurdle, ten hurdles in each race, clearing each one by only hundredths of an inch. Even when I shopped for groceries, I'd practice throwing an imaginary discus, visualizing victory amid the cold cuts and the magazine racks.

When I'd finally drift off to sleep, my mind would take me to the Olympics in my dreams, a neverland of running, jumping and throwing. I'd dream of throwing the discus and awaken with my arm literally striking the bed in a throwing motion. I'd dream of running and jolt awake from the thrashing of my legs. I was totally consumed. But the race that haunted me most was the final 1,500 meters, the last event of the decathlon. I would be coming around the backstretch, with 300 meters to go, and that force, that inner fire that had ignited within me during the 1,500-meter run at the Olympic Trials, would suddenly kick in again. The crowd would roar and the ground would tremble beneath me like a six-point earthquake, and I'd reach down and grab that fire from deep inside. Rocketing through that final turn, I'd come around the corner toward the finish line, far ahead of the pack with only 100 meters to go and . . . I'd hear a noise! A faint jingling from my back pocket. *The gold medal!* It was like a tambourine serenading my dream. I'd blast across the finish line in a dance of power and grace: perfect stride, head back, arms in the air, mouth open in a scream—breaking the world record. Then I'd be standing before the victory platform, listening to the announcer bellow, "Bruce Jenner, Olympic champion!" and I'd place my hands on my knees for balance, then rise and walk the three steps to the top of the platform and the sound of the jingling medal would segue to a booming version of our National Anthem.

Crazy? Delusional? Not at all! I am convinced that my mental training—raising the bar constantly on the achievements in my mind—was as vital to my Olympic success as raising the bar on my physical abilities.

"You are a mind with a body," wrote the original motivational master Napoleon Hill, in his book *Success Through Positive Mental Attitude*, cowritten with Clement Stone. "Because you are a mind, you possess mystical powers—powers known and unknown. Dare to explore the powers of your mind!"

I've learned that the mind powers the body in several ways: through autosuggestion, which turns messages planted in the subconscious into actions; through constant affirmations, which spur us on to improved performances; and finally, by blocking out harmful negative suggestions. "What your mind can conceive and believe, your mind can achieve," wrote Hill and Stone.

This is the essence of creative visualization. Before we can win on the fields of our endeavors, we have to first win in the arenas of our minds.

Visualization is nothing new.

In their book, *Beyond Strength,* Steven Ungerleider and Jacqueline Golding tell a story from the year before the 1976 Summer Olympics in Montreal, when representatives from the Soviet Union were busy taking photographs of the Olympic stadium. They were not doing this as some sort of cloak-and-dagger espionage. Their mission was competitive, but not in the way you might imagine. The Soviets took the pictures back to Russia for their athletes to study. They weren't studying the photographs to learn about the terrain but to visualize themselves in the heat of the battle, in the exact stadium where the battle would be held, to create specific mental images of themselves winning.

On the American team, imagination was equally important. All of the male finalists for the 1976 Olympic team reported using visualization extensively in training, and those who visualized themselves from the "inside" of their bodies, as if they were actually competing, were more successful than those who visualized themselves as observers. "Basically it boils down to the fact that if you're trying to accomplish something, a particular athletic movement, if you can't visualize it then it's pure chance you will be able to perform the movement," my good friend and '76 teammate Mac Wilkins, who won Olympic Gold in the discus, told the authors of *Beyond Strength.* "If you visualize it and can really see it . . . you have a clear target to aim for and a much better chance of realizing the target."

Where the mind leads, the body follows.

Before Steven Spielberg could direct his first film, he had to become a director in his mind. Since he was thirteen, he had known that making movies was his destiny. One day, at seventeen, he dressed in a suit, put a sandwich in his father' s briefcase and strode proudly through the gates at Universal Pictures, a vagabond visualizing himself as a celluloid prince. Undetected by the guards, who figured he worked there, Spielberg found an abandoned trailer, put his name (STEVE SPIELBERG, DIRECTOR) on the door and spent the summer meeting the people in the business he visualized for himself. Three years later, the twenty-year-old Spielberg signed a seven-year deal with Universal.

He imagined himself a director and then he became one.

The golfer Jack Nicklaus employs an even more direct method of visualization. "First I 'see' the ball where I want it to finish, nice and white and sitting up high on the bright green grass," he writes in his book *Golf My Way.* "Then the scene quickly changes, and I 'see' the ball going there: its path, trajectory, and shape, even its behavior on landing. Then there's a sort of fade-out, and the next scene shows me making the kind of swing that will turn the previous pages into reality."

Think about it. The technique is not so far-fetched. Every action begins with a thought. So every accomplishment begins with creative visualization. You have to see your goal before you can achieve it. The problem is, most of us have been taught to visualize the worst possible scenario instead of the best. According to one survey, before a child reaches ten he has been told "No" and "You can't do that" more than 100,000 times.

Underachievers are unconsciously committing psychic suicide by repeatedly sending negative messages from their subconscious to their conscious minds. They speak in the language of loss:

"I can't."

"I'm not."

"I'll never."

"I won't."

How do you break the cycle of negativity?

By visualizing victory. Try a few simple exercises:

1. Relax. Sit in a comfortable chair in a quiet room and visualize where you want to be: in your career, relationships, health, finances. Make the picture come alive in your mind. See yourself on the victory platform of your dream. When negative thoughts arise, flash back to this scene.

2. Use empowering language. Resist the words "can't" and "won't." Avoid cynical comments and feelings of resignation. Make your every thought and word a statement of empowerment.

3. Set up life-bolstering affirmations that will both encompass your dream and guide you in your direction. For

example, in the Olympics, I repeated the phrase referring to my goals, "85 in '75, 86 in '76," which would immediately force my mind back onto my aspirations.

4. Allow your mind to use tricks to propel you in the direction of your dream. Imagine yourself running, selling, earning, loving, succeeding in whatever picture works best for you.

5. Before dozing off at night, make your last thought a winning thought. Make it the first thing you think of in the morning and the last thing to consider at night.

6. Raise the bar on your aspirations and abilities in your dreams, just as you do in your life.

In his popular motivational book *Peak Performers,* author Charles Garfield writes, "Peak performers, particularly in business, sports and the arts, report a highly developed ability to imprint images of successful actions in the mind. They practice, mentally, specific skills and behaviors leading to those outcomes and achievements which they ultimately attain."

Brandon Hall, a salesman at Wilson Learning Corporation, is the epitome of preparation through visualization. Writes Garfield:

Brandon Hall told me about a graph he kept on his office wall, depicting his sale goal. Its ascending line conveyed the direction he wanted to go in selling corporate training programs. His production in 1982 had been $175,000. Even in the recession of that early part of the decade, he decided to *set his goal for 1984 at $1 million—a peak that was talked about but never scaled at Wilson Learning Corporation. Hall would envision himself topping it. He envisioned himself trouble-shooting each customer's training needs. He envisioned himself deciding which Wilson products were right for each situation. This was not mere wishful thinking. As he learned the ropes in his early, less lucrative days, and as he used the . . . process of mental rehearsal and effective follow-through, he acquired expertise and confidence. The result? He was the first Wilson Learning account executive to pass the $1 million mark.*

Visualizing is a start. But, of course, visualization without action equals nothing. Once your mind is focusing on positive thoughts, it's time to get your body to follow, raising the bar in reality, just as your mind raised the bar in your dreams.

"The fight is won or lost far away from witnesses. It is won behind the lines, in the gym and out there on the road, long before I dance under those lights."

—MUHAMMAD ALI

The mind connects to the body through the belly.

The gut, the stomach, the abdomen—this is the cradle of the Champion Within, the source of hunger, both for food and accomplishment. Make one important delineation: hunger is not want. Want is a wish, a mere coin tossed in a fountain, compared to the ferocity of hunger. Hunger is a force that *demands* action.

Just as you have to eat to live, you have to accomplish to survive.

I love the story Les Brown tells in his book *Live Your Dreams*. The author/politician/motivational speaker started life as the adopted son of a kitchen worker and a maid on the poorest side of Miami. He spent most of his school years in special-education classes for the learning disabled. But Les was the essence of *hunger*. Although he became a city sanitation worker and a lawn mower when he graduated high school, he dreamed of being a radio deejay.

At night, he learned the jive by listening to a transistor radio under his pillow. He used a hairbrush for a microphone and hosted his own imaginary show deep into the night. One day, Les Brown walked defiantly into the local radio station, entered the office of the station manager—a Mr. Sugar Bear Washington—and told him of his dream.

"Do you have any background?" asked the manager.

"No, sir," answered Les Brown.

There were no openings, then. But that didn't sate Les Brown's hunger. He returned the next day and the next day and the next, each time acting as if he were meeting the station manager for the first time. Finally, the station manager relented. "Get me some coffee!" he barked, and Les got a job—first as an all-around gofer and coffee fetcher, then as a limousine driver, picking up visiting celebrities like the Temptations and the Supremes, even though Les Brown didn't have a driver's license.

His hunger grew. During his down time at the station, he watched the disc jockeys, learning how they worked the control panels and introduced songs and commercials. Back home at night, he practiced, practiced and practiced some more, constantly raising his standards in his dreams.

His big chance came one Saturday afternoon when a disc jockey named Rock began slurring his words on the air. Les Brown was the only person in the building and he paced before the control booth window nervously repeating, "Drink, Rock, drink." As he expected, the telephone rang; the radio station's general manager was on the line.

"Les, I don't think Rock can finish his program," he said. "Would you call one of the other deejays to come in and take over?"

Les said he would. But, of course, he didn't. He called his mother, then his girlfriend, telling them to turn their radios up loud. He was about to make his radio debut. He called the general manager and told him he couldn't find any deejays at home to sub for the drunken Rock.

"Young man, do you know how to work the controls in the studio?" asked the general manager.

"Yessir!" shouted Les Brown.

He entered the booth, moved Rock aside and sat down at the controls. He flicked the microphone on and bellowed, "Look out! This is me, LB, triple P—Les Brown, Your Platter Playing Poppa. There were none before me and there will be none after me. Therefore, that makes me the one and only. Young and single and love to mingle. Certified, bona fide, indubitably qualified to bring you satisfaction, a whole lot of action. Look out, baby, I'm your lo-o-ove man!"

When telling this story to audiences, Les concludes with the line, "I was *hungry!*"

Hunger—that's the key to success. Are you hungry? I know I was. I was so hungry to be the best decathlete I could be, to win the Olympic Gold, that I dedicated every second of my existence to my goal.

But hunger without action leads to starvation. You've got to train, to raise the bar on your standards daily, so when the time is right you'll strike with everything you've got to give. The ancient Greeks epitomized hunger. They transformed that hunger into victory through training. Boy, did they train! And not necessarily in ways I could recommend or condone. Even the Greek name of their games became the English word "agony." Training was grueling, a regimen administered by trainers who were celebrated as near deities with tempers to be feared. Physical training began in earnest in each future Olympian's youth, in a two-year regimen called the *Epheboi,* whose slogan was "Rods and toils unmeasured." The toils increased day after day, year after year, until arriving at a virtual apex of aching: the ten-day training period before the Olympic Games. Runners were paced by riders on horseback. Wrestlers sparred with partners called "statues," in reference to their iron wills and bronzelike bodies. Boxers were bashed on the head with a punching bag to toughen both their strengths and their skulls.

Centuries later, you've still got to pay the price for success. Preparation is key. The old saying "The harder I train, the luckier I get" is true. We are in control of our destiny. But the law is clear: each day, you must take your commitment to the next level. This gradual, step-by-step progression is the key to unleashing the Champion Within, no matter what your field of endeavor.

To show you how training in both sports and life involves the same step-by-step, hour-by-hour, day-by-day progression of raising the bar, I'd like to present my own training discipline, followed by the training disciplines of individuals who have found success in radically different fields:

START EARLY AND BEGIN RAISING
THE BAR THROUGHOUT THE DAY.

Every morning I awoke with a sense of mission, with the attitude that life had handed me a gift of that particular day—and my job was to make the most of every second. My typical training day began before the sun rose over San Jose, when the track was quiet and even Olympic champions were slumbering. If I hesitated even one morning, I'd be stuck running on a crowded track. If I thought about what I had looming ahead in the day, the work would become a chore and my passion would be punctured. Whenever I even thought about skipping a workout—when the weather was nasty or I was dog tired—I'd make myself think a singular thought: after the Games are over—and they'll be over pretty quickly—I don't ever want to say the words "I could've won, *if* . . ."

"I could have won, *if* I'd run those extra miles."

"I could have won, *if* I'd lifted more weights."

"I could have won, *if* I would've prepared myself better mentally."

Exorcise the *if*s from your life by answering them every day. Use them as motivational tools—*or they will use you!* Let your *if*s jump-start your enthusiasm. Victory is a minute-by-minute process. You must be committed to winning twenty-four hours a day. The clock has to be constantly ticking in your brain, because every second is an opportunity that will never come again.

To borrow a slogan from Nike: "Just do it." The training period is not the time to rely on the mind; this is the time to push the physical. As I ran, the pain would start as a pressure in the chest or a rawness in the larynx, then intensify as I pushed my body beyond its physical limits toward the point where I knew the pain would be like a knife in the side. I'd run forward, pumping my arms to push my legs onward, four laps to the mile, five miles a morning. To stop would be surrender. So I welcomed the pain. It was the best signal that I was doing something right. From this threshold of pain, I began upping the ante: adding one mile for each year to the day's workout, until I progressed from three miles twice a day in '73 to four miles twice a day in '74 and five miles twice a day in '76. So it was five miles at a six-minute-mile pace, followed by a half-hour of stretching.

In his book *Everyone's a Coach,* cowritten with Ken Blanchard, former Miami Dolphins football coach Don Shula writes that his secret to victory is something he calls "over-learning":

"The essence of over-learning is that the players, through intense practice, have the skill and confidence to make the Big Play," says Shula. "Constant practice, constant attention to getting the details right every time produces a hunger to be in the middle of the action. When players have absolutely no doubt about what they're supposed to do, and how to do it, they thrive on pressure. If the heat's on, they want it coming their way."

Shula hits the concept right on the head. You don't merely train for your missions in life. You *over-learn.* You train so long and so hard and know your game so well that when the pressure's on you switch into overdrive, that place where preparation meets pressure and the Champion Within begins to perform.

Writes Shula:

I want our players to be so familiar with assignments that when the game starts they don't have to worry about what they're supposed to be doing. They can simply turn themselves loose physically to do whatever it takes to win the game. . . . They should be so familiar with their assignments that when the game starts they're operating on auto-pilot. The way you do when you're driving a car. You're not thinking about what your hands and feet are supposed to be doing. You're just doing it.

Shula cites the training programs at Disneyland and Disney World as examples of the "over-learning" concept. Employees at the parks have trained so exhaustively that when they see a piece of litter on the premises, they automatically bend down and pick it up, frequently not even realizing what they're doing. It becomes second nature.

"If you don't seek perfection," says Shula, "you'll never reach excellence."

The road to both begins in daily preparation. So when the moment of truth arrives, whether it's a major sales meeting, a crucial contact, or an Olympic Game, you will have built the foundation for victory.

Everything begins with a foundation. Build a foundation of strength, pride and optimism and the life you build from that base will reflect these values. Build a foundation of weakness, sloth and negativity and your foundation will crumble beneath you. Whether you're an employee at Disneyland or competing in the Olympic Games, whether you're focusing on your relationships, health or finances, your performance comes from a bedrock of core beliefs and values. If you want to create an atmosphere for personal growth and fulfillment, build from the bottom up. Analyze your core values. Are they limiting you or driving you forward? If it's the latter, consciously reshuffle your values to reflect your life plan. Once you know yourself as thoroughly as Don Shula's players knew their assignments, then you can begin to act on autopilot and the Champion Within can emerge. Begin with a sturdy foundation. This is the only way to begin building skyward.

THE CREED OF MORE.

Every day of Olympic training involved constant improvement, and there was no better place to gauge this than the weight room at the San Jose YMCA. I'd strap on a wide leather belt and wear my favorite tank top, the red one with the Soviet hammer and sickle on the front, a gift from a Soviet athlete and a constant reminder of the competition whose record I was trying to break. The red of the shirt would provoke me, also a constant reminder of the threat that haunted me ahead. It was a cheap trick, but it worked. For two and a half hours, I'd lift, starting low with the manageable, then bumping up the weight with each lift. Every exercise would involve constant and never-ending improvement: more weight, more reps, more sets. There was no slacking;

tougher and stronger men and women constantly surrounded me. My only route was the path of more resistance: bench press, curls, leg work, military press, two sets at 230, then 280, then 310, never going backwards, not even to gain momentum.

Sam Walton built the 50-billion-dollar Wal-Mart company one store at a time around one of the clearest concepts in American business: provide value to customers. But when considering the secret to his own personal success in his 1992 autobiography, *Made in America: My Story*, Walton stated the high-jump theory: "I've always held the bar pretty high for myself. I've set extremely high personal goals," he wrote.

Sam Walton's childhood was a testament to constant training. He played football, baseball and basketball, swam in the summers and was so competitive in the Boy Scouts that he made a bet with his troopmates that he'd be the first to make Eagle Scout. Through intense practice and training, Walton won his bet at the audaciously early age of thirteen, becoming the youngest Eagle Scout in the state of Missouri.

In the summer of 1932, his Boy Scout training paid off. From a 1932 issue of *The Shelbina Democrat*:

> *Because of his training in Boy Scout work, Sammy Walton, 14-year-old son of Mr. and Mrs. Tom Walton of Shelbina, rescued Donald Peterson, little son of Prof. and Mrs. K.R. Peterson, from drowning in Salt River Thursday afternoon. . . .*
>
> *Donald got into water too deep for him and called for help. Loy Jones, who had accompanied the boys, made an effort to get him out, but Donald's struggles pulled Mr. Jones down several times. Young Walton, who was some distance away, got to the pair just as Donald went down a fifth time.*

He grasped him from behind, as he had been taught to do,
pulled him to shore and applied artificial respiration that
the scouts must become proficient in.

    Donald was unconscious and his whole body had
turned blue. It took quite a while to bring him around.

Take a tip from Sam Walton and the Boy Scout motto: Be prepared!

FEED THE CHAMPION WITHIN.

When the champion emerges, the body becomes its vehicle. Strength is a crucial prerequisite. My daily breakfast was a bowl of good old Wheaties, but it was the desert gave me power: a morning's dosage of a day's regimen of fifty-seven pills . . . vitamins, protein, Vitamin C, B-complex, lecithin, potassium, bonemeal and more. The pills were taken in four different stages, each ration packed neatly in Baggies: one for morning, one for noon, one for evening and one for the protein shake before bedtime.

In his landmark 1920 motivational book, *I Dare You!*, William Danforth, founder of the Ralston Purina Company, dared readers to develop their full potential. The book has been reprinted thirty-two times and has sold almost 2 million copies. "Life is a glorious adventure," wrote Danforth. "Face problems aggressively —opportunities do not come to those who wait. They are captured by those who attack. I am daring you to think bigger, to act bigger, and to be bigger. And I am promising you a richer life and more exciting life if you do. I am showing you a world teeming with opportunity."

I dare you to unleash the Champion Within.

I dare you to live like a person in whom a champion already lives by performing and looking your absolute best. Even if it's only for a thirty-day trial, I dare you to try: make your diet, exercise regimen and wardrobe reflective of how you would live if you had already achieved your goals. I think you'll be amazed at the transformation that will occur. Appearance isn't everything, but it's one of the main nonverbal clues others have to who we are and where we're going.

I dare you to build a foundation of positive energy, to cast the negative from your life, whether it's negative people, negative surroundings or life's other myriad negative forces. I dare you to surround yourself with positive energy, people, foods and exercise.

I dare you to take control over your destiny, to realize that you are the master of your fate and the captain of your ship, and that your life is a voyage that you alone will steer to either victory or defeat. Your ship is your body and mind; your mental and physical health is what will either empower your mission or cause your downfall.

I dare you to read the empowering books of motivators like William Danforth, who writes in *I Dare You:* "Life is a bigger game than football or basketball, but the same rules maintain. If you keep strong, physically fit, full of energy and enthusiasm, you are the man whom life's coach is going to pick when the winning touchdown is needed. . . . Every day is a crucial test in the game of life. The longer you live the better you will understand that fact. Every time you take liberties with your physical strength . . . you will pay the price."

As Danforth wrote, "I dare you to be strong!"

BE YOUR OWN COACH.

With no coach to guide me and no trainer to push me in those innocent days of Olympian training, I had to push myself, practicing the events that I seemed weak in on each particular day. Discus, pole vault, hurdles—these are tests of gravity and steel in which success is obtained only by hard work and perseverance. If I'd done three hard days in a row of leg work and there was no bounce left in my legs, I'd forsake the leg-intensive high-jumping to throw the shot or the discus. I trained smart, but I always trained. Two and a half hours daily, from one to three-thirty. I would practice specific events; no excuses would be accepted. I practiced in San Jose with the best: throwing the discus with Mac Wilkins, tossing the shot with Al Feurbach, running with the San Jose City College cross-country team. But when I stepped up to the line, I knew I'd always be alone. So I knew I'd best get accustomed to the loneliness. Although we can learn from others, individual performance is not a group sport. Some days, I'd spend a couple of hours at my part-time insurance job, but it was a joke: I'd spend as much time selling insurance as the average insurance man spends training for the decathlon. As the Games grew closer, I spent less and less time thinking about things not directly connected to my performance, with the goal being that by two weeks before the Games, my mind would be 100 percent on the mission ahead.

The prolific Michael Crichton, the seemingly superhuman former physician, screenwriter, director and author of more than twenty books, including *Jurassic Park, Disclosure, Rising Sun* and *The Andromeda Strain*, is no Superman.

He has merely mastered the concept of raising the bar on his abilities.

Crichton has told interviewers that he writes his books through a process he calls "the thirty-five-day first draft." For thirty-five days, he wears the same clothes and eats the same lunch, acting as if he's writing the book in one long day. Each day, he adds time to his daily workload by getting up earlier and earlier to begin work, until, finally, he's rising at three A.M.

To ensure that he's constantly raising the bar on his output, he tracks it by computer.

Proof that Crichton's method succeeds is written across the bestseller lists. Champions like Crichton have one thing in common: they can work extremely hard when no one is watching. They don't require someone standing over them to push themselves forward. They are willing to do the work required to win. So in the heat of battle, when everyone *is* watching, they're mentally and physically tougher than anyone else.

PERSISTENCE MAKES PERFECT.

By seven P.M., I'd be whipped and hungry. But the kitchen and bedroom could not lure me from the daily duty. I'd climb the chain-link fence and hit the track, running to the light of a California moon. Ten laps to the mile, five miles before dinner, running full bore, imagining each step as taking me that much closer to the gold medal, until, as the pages flew off the calendar, I could feel the cold metal against my palm and hear it jingling musically in my back pocket.

The sense of having a medal jingling in one's back pocket is not reserved for Olympians. Champions in any field of endeavor hear it, too. It's the sound that keeps them training, selling, moving forward. In her book *Secrets of the World's Top Sales Performers,* author Christine Harvey tells the story of Michael Camp. He heard a medal jingling in his pocket at twenty-one, when he left a civil service job to become a potato chip salesman in Great Britain. While his colleagues were happy to merely meet their company's sales quota by selling one case of chips, Camp continuously raised the stakes on his abilities, becoming the top salesman during his first four consecutive months on the job. "I always set my own targets," he says.

Promoted to special accounts, where he would be selling 3,000 cases at a time instead of amounts in single digits, Camp began building his career around a holy grail involving seven steps, beginning with planning and preparation.

"Raising standards," Camp calls it.

At twenty-three, he was teaching his raising standards systems to sales personnel twice his age with twice his experience.

Six month later, at twenty-four, he became his company's youngest area sales manager, the boss of a team of nine, a team ranked thirteenth in the company. Camp vowed to make the team number one in a year, and he beat his prediction by six months.

At twenty-six, he became regional sales manager of a food brokerage company; at twenty-nine, he had risen through seven positions, from field sales to management; at thirty-one, he was made national account manager for one of Great Britain's largest and most prestigious grocery chains.

"Sales tools are no different than other tools," writes author Christine Harvey. "If you use an electric saw wrong, you might meet with disaster. You won't get the results you were looking for. If you use sales tools wrong, you don't get the result you were looking for either. Therefore, detail matters. Preparation matters.

"It brings up an age-old question: 'Are good salespeople made or born that way?' Camp taught himself to use the tools meticulously. He made himself a number one salesman. He made himself give attention to details."

As Camp told Christine Harvey, "Use persistence when all else fails."

Training separates the pros from the amateurs. If you need further proof, just consider these statistics from the May 1996 *Reader's Digest* article "If You Really Want to Succeed" by John E. Anderson. The article describes a 1988 Florida State University study of two groups of musicians. The musicians were separated into a "good" group and a "potential world-class" group. Each group kept exhaustive diaries of their practice schedules. The study showed that the "good" group of musicians practiced 7,500 hours in the course of the study, while potential "world-class" group practiced 10,000 hours.

Talent isn't everything; talent combined with training, however, is the force that makes the difference between being good and being truly great.

*"For me, winning isn't something that happens suddenly
on the field when the whistle blows and the crowds roar.
Winning is something that builds physically and mentally
every day that you train and every night that you dream."*
—EMMITT SMITH, DALLAS COWBOYS

I arrived in San Jose in 1973 a contender. I'd shocked the track-and-field world by even making it onto the team at the Trials and coming in tenth place at the Olympic Games. *Track and Field News,* in their annual list of those who fell short of and exceeded expectations, listed me as one of those who had done better than expected. Now I had to prove that I wasn't a fluke, a flash in the pan, the recipient of a lucky moment.

My hunger for victory never subsided, even when I broke a foot and had to miss two months of training, even when I injured my back throwing the javelin. I was hungry for points, the best measure of my accomplishment, and I vowed to increase my point total in each meet and break Avilov's world record—8,454 points—by the end of 1975.

I got off to a great start in 1974, scoring 8,240 in my first meet, the highest score in the world since Avilov's record two years before. At the AAU National Relays that summer, I had a score of 4,146 points after the first day. Just as I was preparing to run the hurdles, an old man hopped down from the grandstands and sprinted onto the track, fast as a leprechaun. He handed me a slip of paper and ran away as quickly as he'd arrived. On the paper, he'd written down all the marks I'd have to make that day to break the world record.

I froze.

I was hungry, but I hadn't expected to show up so early for the feast! Just one year before, I'd been laid up with a broken foot, not entirely sure I'd ever be able to run competitively again. Now I was bumping my dream—a world record!—and a full year earlier than my goal! I was about to raise the bar considerably and, frankly, that can be a scary proposition. You have to be ready for greatness; sometimes, it's more comfortable just to keep climbing, stay hungry and be average. Being average is easy. Being average allows you to run with the pack. Greatness—being a front-runner—makes you dig deep inside yourself and ask, "How bad do I want it?"

If the answer is anything less than 100 percent, then you don't want it bad enough, and life will pass you by.

I ran the second day hard, scoring 8,308—not enough to break my goal of 85 in '75, but good enough to be the highest score in the world in 1974, a score that entitled me to compete with the U.S. team against West Germany and the USSR in Tallinn, Estonia, across the bay from Helsinki, Finland.

I had done the work; now I was ready to raise the bar.

I had decided beforehand that I was going to run the 1,500 meters in 4.05 seconds, so fast I would break the world record. If I sat there and obsessed over that number—a pace that nobody who had set foot on this planet had ever run before—I never would have tried. So what did I do? To be honest, I obsessed over it! For fifteen minutes, I ran the gamut of emotions: absolute fear, panic, dread. I was headed into uncharted territory, like in *Star Trek*, "where no man has ever gone." I jogged around the track, warming up and wondering, Why am I so scared?

I didn't have an answer.

I didn't break the world record that day.

Later in the winter of 1974, *Track and Field News* issued its annual rankings for the past season. In the number one spot, with a 500-point, 20 percent improvement over 1973, was my name. I was raising the bar with an astonishing velocity and everything was going my way: four consecutive victories and an undefeated season in 1974. In 1975, I continued the climb: winning at the New Zealand Games, the Drake Relays and the French Championships.

But then at the U.S. National Championships in Santa Barbara, everything came to a screeching halt. The Champion Within, the force that I had used to continually raise the bar, suddenly failed me miserably.

It all fell apart.

CHAPTER SIX

THE 400-METER RUN: CONQUERING FEAR OF THE UNKNOWN

The Bear. Every runner knows about the Bear. He's that invisible animal that waits for you about 100 yards from the finish line in the 400-meter run. He jumps on your back and starts clawing and scratching, and he seems so heavy that you want to stop running so he'll get off your back and leave you alone. If you haven't met the Bear, you've never run the 400 meters. It's a less-than-50-second race that pushes every muscle in your body, a full-bore fight against slowing down, the only truly physically demanding event of the decathlon's first day. You accelerate out of the blocks fast as you'd run a short sprint race. You keep accelerating through the turn, then bolt down the backstretch, conserving energy for the last 200 meters. That's when the Bear attacks. By the finish line, you're completely spent, having battled the track, the tables and, if you've survived, the Bear.

You bolt out of the blocks in the 400-meter race of life a perfect creature, a singular individual with big dreams and high ambitions, a person who is going to take on the world and *win*. Fast, confident and strong, you bolt down the straightaway toward the first turn, with everyone cheering you onward. But there, at the 200-meter mark in the race, a force takes over and attempts to drag you down. At first you resist, but suddenly you're short of breath, then coughing, then wheezing, then doubting yourself. By the time you're on the back-stretch, the finish line looks like a distant shore across a wide ocean, victory has become a fuzzy memory and you feel that you'll be lucky to even finish the race alive.

You have met the Bear.

The Bear is your fears, both fear of failure and, even more im-portant, fear of success. Fighting this force, I discovered the answer to one of life's greatest riddles, a riddle whose answer propelled me to win the gold medal at the Olympic Games. It's a riddle about all the things we to do sabotage ourselves on the road to achievement.

If you encounter a bear in the wilderness, you're supposed to stay very still and pray that the beast moves on. Your fate is out of your hands and in the bear's. If a grizzly wants you badly enough, he's going to get you every time. But when you encounter the Bear in your subconscious—and, trust me, you will—hiding compounds the threat. You've got to stand your ground and fight, and the Bear does not fight fair. The Bear rips you apart with feelings of doubt, weakness and inadequacy, until you find it easier to sabotage your best chances instead of continuing the fight to the finish.

It was only when I stopped to face the Bear head-on that I dis-covered that the Bear was not an outside force.

The Bear was me.

"To venture is to risk anxiety, but not to venture is to lose yourself."

—*KIERKEGAARD*

Everything had started out so perfectly. Since 1974, I'd had two undefeated seasons. I was ranked the number one decathlete in the world. I'd had two full years of training outdoors; I'd stayed injury free, and I seemed to be headed toward my mission of raising the bar toward my goal of 8,500 points in 1975. I'd scored 8,308 in late '74, not quite meeting my goal of 8,400 in '74 but still bumping Nicolay Avilov's world record of 8,454 points.

I started training for the 1975 season, doing everything by the book. I lifted the weights, I ran the miles, I worked on the technique. I was in the best shape of my life. But when I went to the first competition of the 1975 season, the New Zealand Games in Christchurch, confident of breaking my goal of 8,500 points, I wound up scoring a measly 7,665 points. I went to the next event, the Drake Relays in Des Moines, Iowa, and walked away with a barely better 8,120. At the third event, the French Championships in Colombes, I scored an even lower 8,058. Scores in the 8,000 range are not considered bad scores. In most cases, I even won the meet, sometimes beating everyone else's scores by 400 or 500 points.

I stayed undefeated. But, for me, 8,000 points was no cause for celebration.

I knew something was wrong. I was stuck at one level and it seemed that I could rise no higher. An entire year of training and competing and I had not improved—my scores were in rapid reversal, substantially lower than they'd been at the end of 1974! That's bad news for anyone in any field, but for an Olympian it's a death sentence.

"How can I get to the next level?" I kept asking myself, until the question became an obsession.

What was wrong? I couldn't put my finger on it. I felt lost and confused. I went to the next meet, our National Championship decathlon in Santa Barbara, California. I got on the starting line of the first event, the 100 meters, and, of course, I wanted to do well, just like anybody who goes into a room trying to build a business or make a sale wants to do well. But I knew down deep inside that something was terribly wrong. Something was missing.

I remembered a story my good friend, the great boxing champion Sugar Ray Leonard, told me. Before he won the Olympic gold medal in boxing in 1976, he suffered what he thought was the end of his career, a disastrous loss in the '72 Trials. "I didn't even make the team," he said. "I looked in the mirror at my battered face and thought my boxing days were over. What a joke I was! I was a failure. I was ready to quit. My dream had turned into a nightmare. I had to wait four years to try again! I had sacrificed all my time—for what? To ruin a pretty face? Later, I learned a valuable lesson. I lost because of my fears; my fears descended on me and I lost the most crucial fight of my life. It was a revelation that changed my life. I felt like a heavy weight had been lifted off of my shoulders. I was like an arrow headed for the bull's-eye and nothing was going to get in my way."

I never thought Sugar Ray's story would have any lessons for me. Failure, setbacks, thoughts of quitting—those things happened to others, not me. I used fear as a motivational force; fear didn't use me! I put fear three feet behind me and raced it, beating its butt every time.

Then, seemingly overnight, I discovered that fear had become a major force in my life. I was in a spiral, and it wasn't merely due to fear of failing but also fear of success, which is a far more insidious force, a fear that wears a hundred disguises, each one capable of stopping you cold. If I'd had the opportunity to read *Go for It!* by Dr. Irene Kassorla, who has done extensive research into the reasons why we fail, I might have been able to understand and stop the spiral. In her 1984 book, Dr. Kassorla suggests that we "follow the frightening arrow" when we arrive at a crossroads. Instead of going down the familiar path, take the road into the unfamiliar, the path of your worst fears and weaknesses. Because that's the direction of growth and expansion. Risk, not security, is the force that creates winners.

Ironically, I discovered that winning, not losing, is the force that creates the most stress. Everybody thinks the opposite, of course. "But the reality is that winners experience problems and a great deal of fear," says Dr. Kassorla. "They seriously sabotage themselves."

She cites the cases of several clients:

A prima ballerina who would fly into a rage on the day of a big performance, rip off her ballet slippers and refuse to eat. Although the ballerina's dressing room was stocked with 250 pairs of slippers, she could never find a suitable pair.

An opera singer whose throat would mysteriously close shut before going onstage, after which his heart would pound and his clothes would become soaked in perspiration.

An athlete whose ability to perform was constantly hampered by back problems, even though X rays revealed no physical irregularities.

A beautiful actress who suffered a recurring acne flare-up whenever she'd get a big assignment.

What was happening? Why were the best and the brightest sabotaging themselves in the very area that was crucial for their success: the dancer's slippers, the singer's throat, the athlete's back, the actress's face? Dr. Kassorla discovered that her patients were merely acting out feelings of inadequacy from childhood, destroying themselves with the same pain they'd suffered at the hands of their elders. Now, as adults, they had become both parent and child, guard and inmate in the prison of their fears. "Because you overdose on negatives as a child, the resulting feelings of inadequacy and low self-esteem will keep you struggling and unconsciously seeking out pain for the rest of your life," Dr. Kassorla writes.

What did any of this have to do with me?

Everything.

So much that Dr. Kassorla featured my struggle against fear in a chapter of one of her books.

"Once Bruce Jenner decided to follow his frightening arrow . . . to embrace his goal of winning the Olympics despite his dread of failure . . . he could literally feel new power surging through him."

—DR. IRENE KASSORLA, GO FOR IT!

When the gun sounded on the 1975 National Championships, I came out of the blocks strong.

I ran the 100 meters and the long jump, threw the shot, ran the high jump and the 400 meters . . . all the events of the first day of competition. I was doing very well, headed toward a respectable 8,300 points—a score that should've won the meet for me easily. But winning was then a given. At this point in my career, nobody came even close to beating my score. Winning had almost become a bore. *I always won.*

But now I didn't just have to win; I had to beat a world record to achieve my goal of 8,500 points in '75. Something was still wrong, and it seemed worse than ever before. The fire deep within me seemed extinguished.

The question *How do I get to the next level?* had become a mantra by this time, haunting me constantly.

I got a good night's sleep after the first day's events and awoke the next morning ready to run the rest of the decathlon. I ran the hurdles well, threw the discus admirably, and then got to the pole vault, the eighth event in the competition, always my personal-best event. The pole vault is sort of the last question mark in the decathlon, because you have to make the opening height—and whenever you *have* to do something, when one act becomes the difference between do or die, pass or fail, you've created a prime spot for the Bear to rage.

When it came to the opening height, I practiced overcaution. You get three attempts at each height. But if you miss the opening height after three tries, you don't get any points in the pole vault—a disaster that virtually throws you out of contention.

I always warmed up with the bar at the extremely easy height of fifteen feet. That way, I'd be certain that everything was going right with my approach. I could pole-vault fifteen feet in my sleep. But at this particular track meet, because of my sudden insecurity and anxiety over not understanding why I seemed stuck at one level, I set the bar even lower, at fourteen feet. My plan was to just get one fourteen-foot jump in. Then, once the pressure of the opening height was out of the way, I'd start raising the bar.

Pole in hand, I came barreling down the runway for my first attempt. The fourteen-foot bar seemed ludicrously low, a height I'd made time after time in high school. But as I charged down the runway and planted the pole, I realized something was terribly wrong. My steps were off and I didn't even get off the ground.

One miss!

Suddenly, I felt very afraid. But why? Why was cold fear running through my veins? I had already won the competition; the question was merely how many points I was going to score. I guessed it was the pressure of facing a world record. I was headed toward a score that nobody—not even Nicolay Avilov—had ever achieved before. No human being had ever scored that many points, so deep in the recesses of my mind I was wondering why it should be me. The responsibilities that go along with winning, with being a world-record holder, are intense. I'd be favored in every meet for the rest of my life.

Was I ready to handle that responsibility?

Was I ready to become a champion?

Maybe the responsibility that goes along with those things was just too much for me to handle at the time. Something was wrong—that much I knew for sure. And I didn't know what it was. I just couldn't put my finger on it. I was missing something major, and no amount of wishing or praying could conjure up the Champion Within. Not only was he not racing in for a rescue, it seemed he was mocking me, belittling me, putting me back in my place as that sleepy kid in the back of the class.

Wait a second! I thought. I've done the same steps for the past five or six years. My steps were fine when I was warming up at higher heights! Now, all of a sudden, at a foot lower they're off. Maybe somebody moved my mark; maybe I started at the wrong place.

I remeasured my steps, but sure enough, I had started correctly. Now my blood pressure was starting to rise, my heart was pounding harder, and I decided to take this opening height a little more seriously. I hadn't lost a meet in about three years. Every aspect of my performance over the past two years had been perfect, beyond my expectations. But now I was choking on an opening height I could make in my sleep.

Second attempt: once again at the incredibly easy height of fourteen feet. I came flying down the runway, but, once again, my steps were off and I couldn't even get off the ground.

Two misses!

Whoa, now. What's happening here?

Having blown two jumps, I now had only one chance left to either make the opening height or lose the meet. Now my blood pressure was *really* soaring, my heart was *really* pounding. Everybody was watching. I hadn't lost a meet in two and a half years. I was supposed to be the best decathlete in the world, and I couldn't even get off the ground!

Third attempt: I ran the opposite direction. That's the rule: If your steps are off, run the opposite direction and set your mark at the other end of the field.

I stood at the end of the runway with my front foot on the line. I stood on the line for my third attempt—my last attempt!—planning to charge the box, to fly down there as hard as I could, ready to graze, grovel or grunt my way over the bar. I took a deep breath, cleared my mind, leveled the pole and came charging down the runway, thinking, Whatever you do, big fella, just get down and muscle yourself over this thing. *Just get over the damn bar!*

I was just about to jam the pole into the box, the first step in the acrobatic movement that rockets you over the mountain, but then my steps were even *farther* off the mark. I sailed beneath the bar and crashed into the pit with a sickening flop, still holding the pole, looking and feeling like an absolute dunce. Pain shot up my spine and humiliation reddened my face. My veins bulged. My throat opened . . . and what came roaring out was definitely not poetry. I used words I shouldn't have used but ones that seemed perfectly appropriate at the time. Then I heaved the pole across the field like a javelin and just missed a camera crew—antics all filmed in living color for national television.

I ran off the track, stomped out of the stadium, ran across a field and collapsed in a big clump of trees—and I cried. I literally bawled my eyes out.

I had lost it. Not just the meet—I had lost my confidence. The feeling that something was missing from down deep inside me had now totally consumed my body and my mind.

I didn't make mistakes like that, not in my best event, not in the pole vault. I was so totally humiliated and devastated, not completely comprehending what had just happened. It was more than simply missing the opening height. It was the death of a dream. It was the extinguishing of a spark. I desperately needed to get to the next level in my game and I had absolutely no idea of how to get there.

I had consistently raised the bar to a score of 8,300 points in the decathlon. Was that as far as I could go? Had I reached my limit? One thing was for sure: I had reached the crossroads of that gulf that separates ordinary from extraordinary, contender from champion, a crossroads that exists in every field of endeavor. Maybe you're a salesman who can't rise above a certain quota or a manager who can only motivate your team just so far or a craftsman who rises to a certain ability and can take your talents no further. Maybe you're on a diet and you've hit a plateau or you're racing a deadline and just can't get through to the end.

Whatever your work may be, when you can't find a way to the next level, you've discovered the Bear. It has jumped on your back and is snarling and biting and digging its claws into your skin, using all its considerable strength to drag you down.

The Bear had me firmly in its grip.

Finally, after about an emotional half-hour or so, I regained my composure and returned to the stadium. I did not throw the javelin or run the 1,500 meters. At this point, I just wanted to get out of there as quickly as possible. I tossed all my gear into my Volkswagen and sped back to San Jose. I spent the next week getting back into my workouts, preparing myself for the next decathlon, a triangular competition between the U.S., the USSR and Poland about a month away in Eugene, Oregon. It would be the first time Nicolay Avilov and I would compete head-to-head since the '72 Olympic Games. He was the Olympic champion. I was ranked number one in the world. It was going to be a great competition.

But now I was spiraling out of control in my first major crisis of the spirit. The Bear had me firmly in its grasp, and before I could compete in the decathlon, I had to compete against him in another Olympics.

I had to compete in the Olympics of my fears.

"Fear always springs from ignorance."
—RALPH WALDO EMERSON

In her 1980 book, *Overcoming the Fear of Success,* author Martha Friedman discusses examples of several seemingly successful people who go to incredible lengths—illness, blindness, even near-death—to sabotage their best chances for great success. "For some of us the achievement of a long-desired goal is tantamount to getting the death penalty," Ms. Friedman writes.

Let's study a couple of the examples from Martha Friedman's book:

Zoe, a well-known young artist, felt she would die if she completed a set of paintings she considered her masterpiece, a series about human suffering in World War II. She worked furiously on the paintings, frequently working so deep into the night she would awaken the next morning with her arm literally immobilized. But when she came close to completion, Zoe panicked: she began experiencing crushing migraine headaches and hypoglycemia that forced her to cease work. During her illness, she bought herself a marble Victorian angel to place in her studio—not as decoration. She fully expected it would soon serve as her tombstone.

Zoe was not a lunatic. She didn't really want to die. But death would come, she had convinced herself, when she finished the painting.

Why wouldn't a successful artist want to complete her masterpiece? The author suggests that the seeds of Zoe's fear of success lay in something called "Family Olympics," the childhood roles we are given in each of our families. In Zoe's Family Olympics, she was expected to become a full-time wife and mother, nothing more and nothing less; she was expected to never exceed the abilities or success of her brother, which she had already done many times over. Zoe should have been free of this past but, like many of us, she was not merely controlled by her history, she was severely limited by it. Even though she had twice married, she kept her father's surname, not because of any feminist sentiments but because of her intensely close feelings toward her dad.

Can you see the traps that had snared her? She loved her family, but her success would serve as a betrayal of her family's expectations for her. So she found ways not to succeed.

In another example, a successful writer named Lily got a substantial book advance from a major publisher and, burdened by guilt, was soon hospitalized with symptoms of blindness. Investigating Lily's Family Olympics, the author discovered that she was the child of a self-styled beauty queen who insisted that Lily and her brother worship her above all else. Because of her mother's need for constant attention, Lily's early life was guided by one central commandment: Never exceed the accomplishments or abilities of Mom. So Lily feigned blindness rather than work toward her success.

Both Zoe and Lily eventually finished their work—and neither died nor was permanently blind. Let their stories serve as caution signs, warnings that the road to victory is lined with deception and mirage; it's a carnival arcade of mirrors, all seeking to distract and confuse you on the long road toward your goals.

"To overcome the fear of success, we first have to recognize that we have it, and for this we must get in touch with what and who we genuinely are rather than what and who we perceive ourselves to be," writes Ms. Friedman in *Overcoming the Fear of Success.* "Our next step is to discover why we have such low self-esteem and that necessitates a trip into our Family Olympics."

In this process of self-discovery, the author says, behavior patterns that you may consider minor may be actually sabotaging your success.

If I had had the foresight to consider my own at the time, I might have been better equipped to handle my own meltdown. My Family Olympics were strewn with plenty of seeds for sabotage: a dyslexic youth who was the slow reader, the slow learner, the slow bloomer in the family.

And now I was preparing to run the world's fastest footrace.

I was forced to confront my fears on the Stanford University golf course shortly after my failure at the National Championships. I was running my usual path up and down the fairways with my dog, Bertha, and my old buddy and training partner, Vince Stryker. When we finally stopped to do a little stretching, Vince started talking about what had happened to me a few days earlier in Santa Barbara. He was a year younger than me and had sought me out as a mentor for the decathlon. But looking back now, I realize that Vince became an important teacher to me that afternoon, forcing me to answer one of the most important questions of my life.

"Do you mind if I ask you a few questions?" he asked.

"Not at all," I replied. "Fire away."

"All right, first thing," said Vince. "The Games are a year away. Do you want to win?"

I stared at Vince as if he'd asked me if I wanted to keep on breathing. *Did I want to win the gold medal?* I'd spent half my life preparing myself to win at the Games!

"Of course I want to win the gold medal!" I practically shrieked.

Vince motioned for me to calm down.

"All right, let me rephrase the question," he said. "Is winning the Gold the most important thing in your life?"

Now, that was something different. Winning was important of course. But was it the most important thing in my life? For the first time, I didn't have an answer. The more I thought about it, the more confused I got—so confused I had to leave Vince and run down the golf course alone. I found a shady tree and sat beneath it to seriously consider the question. The more I thought about it, the more afraid I got. One fear led to another, then another, until my fears began multiplying, as if the Bear had mated and given birth to a litter.

I couldn't get to the next level. The spark was gone from my game. I was working as a part-time insurance salesman for New England Life and, looking back on it now, I had sold myself a bill of goods. I had sold myself insurance against my own abilities. The policies of precaution will do you no good in a race, whether you're running against a clock or against a career. And on that day on the golf course, the fruits of my fears—negative thoughts—began replicating themselves furiously in my mind:

You don't deserve to win.

Don't put all your eggs in one basket.

You've worked so hard. What will you have to show if you lose?

Better keep the insurance business going.

Be a well-rounded human being.

Why should you be the one to break the world record?

PROTECT YOURSELF, IN CASE YOU FAIL!

I was thinking backup route, contingency plan, escape hatch, alternatives. By trying to protect myself against the worst possible scenarios, I was inviting disaster to my door. Why? Because of fear. I was terrified by the responsibility of being successful. Olympic champions become leaders, expected to stand proudly before the world. Why was I, of all people, worthy of such respect?

"Is winning the gold medal the most important thing in your life?"

I kept coming back to that question. I knew I had to answer it with a yes or a no. There could be no in-between.

It's a question we all have to answer at some point in our lives. Think about it. Is building your business the most important thing in your life? Is your major goal—whether it centers around your career, your relationships or your health—the most important thing in your life?

What is your commitment level?

In my case, suppose I said, "No. Winning the Games isn't the most important thing in my life." Suppose I was so caught up in thinking about being the well-rounded human being, the guy without his eggs in one basket, the guy with escape routes and contingency plans and insurance policies, that I answered, *"No!"*

Don't laugh. It may sound ludicrous. But this is answer most of us give when facing the truly important decisions in our lives. Think about the path you're following. What are the reasons you have for not putting everything on the line for your dream? Chances are, you'll answer with something like, "Oh, I'd go for it, but . . ." Those "buts" are what you need to study closely. Those "buts" are what can, and will, kill your dreams.

The more I considered answering Vince's question with a resounding "No," the more ridiculous it seemed. The food I ate every day was food for energy, so I could get out there and train at peak levels for the Games, to get stronger, jump higher, run faster. I trained six to eight hours a day every day, 365 days a year. When I wasn't physically on the track, I was thinking about what I needed to do once I got back onto the track. At night, when I tried to sleep, I dreamt about the Games, about technique, about strategy, about victory.

So if I answered "No," it would've been a lie. Because at that moment there wasn't much in my life but winning at the Games.

Sound familiar? You work at a job that consumes you, and when you're not working you're thinking about working. But is—fill in your major aspiration here—the most important thing in your life? Or are you holding a little something back, stashing away a few eggs for the future?

I considered the alternative answer. Suppose my answer to Vince was "Yes." Suppose I dug down deep, where the Champion Within lives, and said, "Winning is the most important thing in my life."

What if I said, "Yes," and then went to the Games and *lost?*

Would I die?

Would my life be finished because I'd put my entire life into this thing and lost?

Either way, I knew I had to answer, "Yes." Winning the Gold was the most important thing in my life. But before I could truly say *"Yes!"* I had to dig down into that place where the Champion Within lives, and I had to talk to myself for a moment, just as you have to talk to yourself before you go to bat for your dreams. I had to say to myself, "I have to have enough confidence in myself as a human being that I can accept failure. I have a support group of family and friends around me. If I fail, I'll recover. It's going to hurt, but I will survive. It might take me a day, it might take me a week, it might take me ten years. But I can recover and life will be good again. But what I have to do right now is to commit myself a hundred percent to winning, because anything less is a sentence to lose."

Saying these exact words to myself on that golf course, I immediately realized what was missing: that final, total commitment that I had to make to myself.

It was like the storm clouds opened and the sun shone through. My attitude changed—*just like that!*

We all have to look at the depth of our commitment level. For me, to be the best in the world in the decathlon, my commitment had to be a life-or-death proposition. I had to prepare myself mentally to win, to deal with failure if it happened, and to cut off all routes of escape. Your commitment level has to be equally intense, because if your mission isn't absolutely, positively the most important thing in your life, then it's going to be nothing.

If your mission isn't do or die, you're going to lose.

I ran back to Vince, who was still sitting on the golf course, and sat down beside him. "Hey!" I said. "To answer your question: *Yeah!* Winning the gold medal is the most important thing in my life."

As soon as those words left my mouth, something incredible happened. My stomach turned over and my adrenal glands started pumping. I was sitting there on that golf course in the middle of nowhere and I felt like I was ready to run the decathlon right then. Why? Because I had made a greater commitment to myself—not to anybody else, to *myself.* By putting all my energy into one goal, I was able to tap into an extraordinary resource. That single decision changed everything. Suddenly, the stress and anxiety disappeared. My mental attitude changed completely. By making a decision and choosing a direction, I felt as if I had come three-fourths of the way toward my goal.

I learned a great lesson that day, about commitment and about fear. I learned the many ways that I was fearful of success. I learned about the reasons I felt unworthy. I learned about how we sabotage our own best game. I learned that I couldn't advance to the next level unless I was ready to risk *everything.* Every cell of my body had to go with me onto that track before I could perform at my peak. At the instant of that commitment, I flicked on the switch that jump-starts the Champion Within who lives inside us all.

No matter your field of endeavor, anything less than 100 percent commitment to your cause is not going to be enough. Make a decision *right now* that your mission is the most important thing in your life, and when you return to face the race, everything will have changed. The current shifts. The falls subside. And life opens its arms to carry you down the river toward your dreams.

A month later, I went to the next competition in Oregon and put my hands on the starting line for the 100-meter run, and the new power pumping through my veins was palpable. Lining up beside me was Nicolay Avilov, the Olympic gold-medalist I had seen only in my dreams since I'd watched him atop the victory platform three years earlier. All eyes were upon us: Avilov, the world-record holder; Jenner the number-one-ranked contender.

The moment I got off the blocks, I was a different human being. It was like living my dreams. One event after the next, everything began ticking like clockwork. By the time I got to the final event, the 1,500 meters, I was close enough to reach out and grab the world record.

I grabbed it.

I scored 8,524 points that day. I broke the world record and achieved my personal goal of 85 in '75. I wasn't in any better shape physically, but mentally I had made a tremendous leap.

If you want to take your mission in life to the next level, if you're stuck and you don't know how to rise, don't look outside yourself. *Look inside.* Don't let your fears keep you mired in the crowd. Abolish your fears and raise your commitment level to the point of no return, and I guarantee you that the Champion Within will burst forth to propel you toward victory.

> *"He who conquers himself is the mightiest warrior."*
> —CONFUCIUS

In his landmark 1937 motivational book *Think and Grow Rich,* the great Napoleon Hill discusses the "Six Ghosts of Fear," which he identifies as poverty, criticism, ill health, lost love, old age and death. Hill describes these fears as a general describes an enemy, warning readers: "Before we can master an enemy, we must know its name, its habits, and its place of abode. As you read, analyze yourself carefully and determine which, if any, of these six common fears have attached themselves to you. Do not be deceived by the habits of these subtle enemies. Sometimes they remain hidden in the subconscious mind, where they are difficult to locate and even more difficult to elim-inate."

Hill came to the same conclusion that I had on that golf course with my buddy Vince: the only way to fight fear is with the mind. "You have absolute control over but one thing, and that is your mind," Hill writes. "This is the most significant and inspiring of all facts known to man! This divine prerogative is the sole means by which you may con-trol your own destiny. If you fail to control your own mind, you may be sure you will control nothing else. If you must be careless with your possessions, let it be in connection with material things. *Your mind is your spiritual estate!* Protect and use it with the care to which divine royalty is entitled."

I challenge you to grow! I challenge you to feel that same exhil-arating power that I felt when I pledged myself totally to my mission, lined up for my next decathlon and smashed that record to smithereens. I want to help you to climb up the ladder onto the next empowering level of your life . . . and then the next, and the next.

The only way to begin is to undertake a thorough analysis of your fears. As Hill writes in *Think and Grow Rich:* "The majority of people, if asked what they fear most, would reply, 'I fear nothing.' The reply would be inaccurate because few people realize they are bound, handicapped, whipped spiritually and physically by some form of fear. So subtle and deeply seated is the emotion of fear that one may go through life burdened with it, never recognizing its presence. Only a courageous analysis will disclose the presence of this universal enemy. When you begin such an analysis, search deeply into your character."

Hill lists six symptoms under which subconscious fears may hide: indifferences, indecision, doubt, worry, overcaution and pro-crastination. Take an inventory of each in your own mind. Pick up the rocks of these symptoms and see if you have fears hiding beneath them. Then, before you proceed to the next chapter, take a moment to complete the following exercise:

Analyze Your Fears. Take a week to concentrate on studying them. Understand when and why certain fears arise. Make a list of them, from mild to major. Are they fears of success or fears of failure? If they're fears of success, face them. As Dr. Irene Kassorla writes in her book *Go for It!*, "The way to get out of your fears is to first get into them!" When you feel afraid, stay with the feeling, investigate the root causes for it, think of it like a roller-coaster ride: it's going to be terrifying for a while, but then, once the ride is coasting peacefully to a stop, you feel exhilarated. You are either chained by your fears or you're free of them. It's your duty to yourself, and to your abilities, to get free.

Study Your Family Olympics, Then Put Them Behind You. Understand the causes of your fears. Look at your role in your family, write it out on a piece of paper and then tear the paper up. Chances are, the family members who are still controlling your subconscious have gone on with their lives. You should, too. Give yourself permission to escape the past, to break free from its grip. Breathe deeply and exhale. Free yourself from the burdens that bind you.

Follow the Frightening Arrow. When life places you at the crossroads of the well-trod path and a path into unknown yet limitless potentialities, plunge down the new road! Get out of the old patterns and run toward the new. Stop being your own worst enemy! Remember, it wasn't until I faced my fears head-on and vowed total commitment to my game that I found the fuel that empowered me toward victory. Unleashing your anxiety creates a chemical reaction in your soul, allowing you to discover your own boundless potential. As Will Rogers said, "Climb out on the limb. That's where the fruit is!"

Face the Bears in Your Life Head-On. Remember the words of the American author Orison Swett Marden, who wrote, "Obstacles are like wild animals. They are cowards but they will bluff you if they can. If they see you are afraid of them . . . they are liable to spring upon you; but . . . if you look them squarely in the eye, they will slink out of sight." If you're not 100 percent committed to your cause, find out why. Write down the reasons for holding yourself back, then systematically go through those reasons and reveal them for what they are: traitors to your own potential for achievement. Realize that you can deal with failure but you only have one chance for success.

As Dr. Irene Kassorla writes in *Go For It!*, "No one knows what the outer parameters of his own potential may be. There are no ceilings on talent, no boundaries on excellence and no limits on creativity. Whether your goals are small or of Olympian proportions . . . you, too, can take the risks that could change your life to a win."

Because when life comes down to do or die, it's amazing what you can do.

CHAPTER SEVEN

THE HURDLES: HOW TO WIN AT LIFE ONE LEAP AT A TIME

The first thing to realize about the 110-meter hurdles is the absurdity of the exercise. From the perspective of the starting point, you stare down a narrow lane where ten hurdles, each three and a half feet high and ten meters apart from each other, are so close together that they look like one long, insurmountable hurdle. Bang! *The gun sounds and the race, which lasts approximately fourteen seconds, begins. The hurdles start coming at you, one after another, like emergencies on a bad day. Run, drive over one hurdle, take three steps and attack the next one . . . then the next, then the next. Hurdling requires a rhythm that you can't think about; you just have to do it. "I don't really see the hurdles," said Olympic gold-medalist hurdler Edwin Moses. "I sense them, like a memory." The idea is to run as fast as possible, getting as little clearance as needed over each one. Points are awarded for speed, not height. Too much height will slow you down; too little will knock you into the wood and onto your butt. The hurdles are a mousetrap with a million ways to fail: miscalculated steps; midleap collisions, in the case of*

Jeff Bannister in '72, slipping and falling on a wet track.
The only way to win is by taking them one hurdle at a time,
until your mind gets out of your body's way and your motion
becomes as fluid as a dancer's.

O f the decathlon's ten events, the hurdles best mimic the momentum of life. You're tight-muscled, sore and tired from the previous day's competition, and what do they throw at you first thing the
next morning? A near-impossible event that requires speed, flexibil-
ity and more than a little magic. But the hurdles in the Games are
mild compared to the hurdles of everyday life.

Bang! You're out of the blocks in the morning, facing a line of
hurdles that, if you stare at them from the beginning, looks like one
insurmountable line. But you must begin, driving over each hurdle
one at a time: from alarm clock to spouse to kids to breakfast to job to
boss to relationships to health to finances to . . . *whew!* The decathlon
has but ten hurdles, but the Decathlon of Life throws a zillion at you,
all at the worst possible moments. With nine kids, a half-dozen businesses and a constant speaking schedule, I run more decathlons in a
single day than I did in my entire athletic career. Like the decathlon,
taking the hurdles of life requires action, speed and a dancer's sense
of coordination and grace, so ideally by the time you cross the finish
line, you have not crashed into any one particular hurdle nor tripped
up in the distances between.

Let's consider a few of the disciplines required to run this event:

Technique: In the hurdles, style is everything. Anything
short of perfection will send you crashing before you even
get over the first one. Slouch in your life and you send a signal that tells the world everything. Stand erect! Your pos-

ture tells the world, "Look at me! I'm a contender," just as your slouch tells the world, "Pass me by."

Speed: In a fourteen-second footrace, with ten hurdles to overcome, there isn't a second for wasted motion or emotion. So how can there be a second to waste in the even relatively shorter span of a lifetime? In the context of eternity, one person's life is not even fourteen seconds. It's not even one tick of God's stopwatch or the beat of one heavenly drum. Don't waste a second to get out of the blocks and start driving toward your dreams.

Agility: Challenges do not arrive in a leisurely, organized fashion. Challenges come crashing one right after another, each demanding immediate attention. You've got to be fast on your feet, able to juggle one thing after another and agile enough to correct your course whenever necessary. Life, as in the 100-meter hurdles, is not run in a vacuum; circumstances demand split-second reactions, corrections, readjustments. Live by the words of writer Aldous Huxley: "Experience is not what happens to you. It is what you do with what happens to you."

Focus: One split-second side glance in the hurdles is an invitation to a fall. Take your eyes off the target in life, and you're going to similarly trip up on your journey. The eyes must be as focused as a hawk's, constantly searching for any potential pratfalls ahead. Take your eye off your course in life and you're not going to reach your dreams.

The hurdles offer not only a lesson in style, but also a secret to achieving your major goals. Break any great accomplishment down to its essence and you will see the hurdles, which can only be surmounted one at a time. The only way to accomplish something major is to deal with the minor, jumping from one hurdle to the next and then the next until you arrive at your desired destination.

I believe each life can be broken down into a road map of hurdles crossed, accomplishments attained. As an example, let's study an individual from the history books. Although the source is unknown, the list was included in the book *Chicken Soup for the Soul.*

1816 Family was forced out of their home. Had to work to support them.

1818 Mother died.

1831 Failed in business.

1832 Ran for state legislature—lost.

1832 Also lost job—wanted to go to law school but couldn't get in.

1833 Borrowed some money from a friend to begin a business and by the end of the year was bankrupt.

1834 Ran for state legislature again—won.

1835 Engaged to be married, sweetheart died, was heartbroken.

1836 Had total nervous breakdown and was bedridden for six months.

1838 Sought to become speaker of the state legislature—defeated.

1840 Sought to become elector—defeated.

1843 Ran for Congress—lost.

1846 Ran for Congress again—won, went to Washington and did a good job.

1848 Ran for reelection to Congress—lost.

1849 Sought the job of land officer in his home state—rejected.

1854 Ran for Senate of the United States—lost.

1856 Sought Vice Presidential nomination at national convention—got less than 100 votes.

1858 Ran for Senate again—lost again.

1860 Elected President of the United States.

These hurdles—some of success, but most of defeat—are the road map of the life of our sixteenth president, Abraham Lincoln. After one of his Senate race losses, he had this to say: "The path was worn and slippery. My foot slipped out from under me, knocking the other out of the way, but I recovered and said to myself, 'It's a slip and not a fall.'"

Study the life of any successful individual and you will see a similar progression, a graph of up and down and up and down but always moving forward. I have discovered that it's the journey, not the destination, that makes life a marvelous adventure. The notion that some people are born to victory is a fairy tale. The real wonder, the true magic, is that each of us has an opportunity to take life in manageable leaps and follow those leaps wherever they lead.

Direct your sights toward a destination of high purpose, make your goal one of true accomplishment, and the hurdles you cross will become galvanized with power and meaning. Direct your sights toward nothing and your hurdles will guarantee you of becoming one of those, in Teddy Roosevelt's words, "cold and timid souls who know neither victory nor defeat." Once you have a sense of mission, you will find hidden reserves of energy and the feeling that you are using your whole soul—not merely a fraction—in your quest.

Let's take a brief accounting of your progress thus far. It's the start of the second day of the decathlon, five events to go. You're gotten started in the 100-meter run of your new life. You've set longtime goals in the long jump. You've learned to play to your strengths and downplay your weaknesses in the shot put. You've systematically begun raising the bar on your aspirations and abilities in the high jump and learned how to escape your fears in the 400-meter run. Now it's time to put it all together in the next event, the hurdles.

For me, the supreme example of hurdling occurred during the 1976 Olympic Games, when peak performance in ten separate events built to a victory in the whole. Let me tell you the story of how I used my "hurdling technology" to win the decathlon at the '76 Games, then show you how to use it in the games of your own life.

"Slow and steady wins the race."

—*AESOP*

"Instead of rising rapidly in the beginning and flattening out later, the earnings curves of most of those who eventually became millionaires was the reverse: their income increased slowly, if at all, for many years. And then, after two to three decades, it suddenly went through the roof."
—SRULLY BLOTNICK, AUTHOR OF THE CORPORATE STEEPLECHASE AND AMBITIOUS MEN

By the time I stepped off the bus in Montreal for the Twenty-first Olympiad in 1976, I knew my steps so well I could run the decathlon in my sleep. I was at the peak of physical perfection. I had conquered the fears that my mind had thrown before me as roadblocks. I was now ready now for the supreme hurdles—the ten events, coming after another, the near-suicidal succession of athletic tests.

The pressure, of course, was intense. The Games are the biggest pressure cooker in the world: 192 countries assembled for peace, for goodwill, for good competition. It's the largest assemblage of countries in the world, larger even than the United Nations. From the U.S. and the USSR, from the Orient and the Outback, from Europe and Asia, from Africa and South America . . . from every corner of the globe, the athletes stand as representatives of their countries—not merely themselves.

The Games bring together a community of winners, ordinary people who have accessed the extraordinary within themselves. As we noted earlier in the words of Olympian Bob Richards: "There are many people who could be Olympic champions, All-Americans who have never tried." These are the people who tried and, in doing so, accessed the power of the Champion Within. Having passed untold tests and trials, each athlete represents a magnificent journey of mind, body and spirit. In their eyes you can see an unblinking fire, the gift of arduous minute-by-minute preparation that has now culminated in the realization of a dream. Dreams are what separates mankind from the animals, and at the Games, dreams are elevated to their proper pinnacle.

I felt the pressure ten months before the Games. My family, friends and relatives all bought tickets to Montreal. A great wagon train of recreational vehicles traveled across the United States, picking up Jenners along the way, all congregating in Montreal to watch Bruce win.

But I wasn't there to party. I'd arrived in Montreal with a whole different attitude than I'd had in 1972. Then I just felt lucky to have made the team. I was a young kid, overwhelmed by the size of the Games, the pageantry and the history. This time I didn't care about

anything but *winning*. I was a representative of a country that had offered me boundless opportunities to develop my body and mind to the
fullest potential, and this was payback time. I was a team player, determined to make my contribution as one of the hundreds of athletes
representing the good old USA. But to say I was high-strung would've
been a gross understatement. My day was divided in two halves—
training and sleeping. Nothing else was allowed to intrude upon that
discipline.

But five days before the competition, the forces of dread, doubt
and self-destruction found me, thundering right through the door of
my Olympic Village room. I was watching closed-circuit TV as the
greatest pole-vaulter in the world, the unanimous choice of every
track writer, the world-record holder, my roommate in the Olympic
Village, Dave Roberts, got the *bronze* medal—third place—not because he wasn't the best vaulter in the world but because of something else: rain. Pouring-down rain.

Dave jumped at a lower height and passed the next height to go
with what he thought would be the winning vault. But when he finally
got to the height that would have won him the Gold, the clouds
opened, a thunderstorm erupted and Dave Roberts had to take his
jump in an absolute downpour. Obviously, he didn't make it, and he
wound up with a bronze medal, third place.

In every dream I'd had about the Games, it was a beautiful sunny
day. Suddenly, I realized . . . *it could rain!* Maybe somebody else is in
control of my destiny, I thought. Maybe Mother Nature is going to direct my game. For the first time, I didn't feel in control. I could feel
the pressure coming down on me as hard as the rain. I was thinking,
I've spent the last twelve years of my life preparing for this moment,
this one moment, and now I'm going to have to run the decathlon in
the rain.

I felt the pressure from those sixty-five Jenners up in the stands with their yellow GO JENNER GO T-shirts. I didn't want to let my family down. I certainly didn't want to disappoint my team. But there was an even bigger family to think about. I had USA written in big block letters across my chest. It was late July 1976, our Bicentennial year. Every American from California to Maine had a flag in their front yard.

I wanted to win for myself, my family and the good old USA.

Angry over the rain, sick and tired of hearing the West German and Russian anthems playing over and over to celebrate the winners thus far, I switched off the TV, walked outside my Olympic Village room and stood on the third-floor balcony, where I could look through the thunderstorm at the Olympic stadium about a mile away. I was staring at that stadium, thinking, The greatest pole-vaulter in the world is in that stadium right now with a bronze medal. Just then, a good friend of mine, the 260-pound shot-putter Pete Schmock, walked by. He looked at me staring dolefully into the night, slapped me on the back with one of his big ham hands and said, "Hey, Bruce, it looks like you're going to have carry us now."

My knees literally buckled.

"You're going to have to carry us now."

It seemed as if my adrenal glands had swelled to the size of basketballs. I felt pressure, fear, anxiety, doubt. I started asking myself, "Do you remember how to throw the shot and the discus, do the pole vault? You haven't done them in three days."

I took a deep breath and got hold of my emotions.

Rely on what you know, I thought. What you know is that you've done your best in times of the greatest pressure. What you have to do now is use that pressure to propel yourself forward.

If you're systematically jumping the hurdles in life, things are eventually going to come to this: the pivotal moment, the point where

you've got to put up or shut up, when it becomes time to show what
you're made of. The big meeting, the big sale, the major speech; the
pressure is going to be intense. To get through it, you've got to reframe
your thoughts about pressure. You've got to make pressure *positive*.
You've got to use pressure as the switch that jump-starts your brain,
not the force that shuts it down. Pressure must become a signal that
you're doing something right.

I knew what I had to do: concentrate on the minor to conquer the
major, jump the hurdles of the Olympics one by one. View every
action as a separate hurdle to leap that, jumped one after another, link
up like a freight train with the power to deliver you safely onto
the doorstep of your dream. What were the hurdles of the Olympics?
Not merely the ten events but *specific scores* in each event, scores I
knew I'd have to make to win the gold medal and set a new world
record.

Weeks before the Games, I had created a "dream sheet" of
scores that could push me over the top. Here are the events with my
"ideal" times, events that I've used as metaphors in this book:

100 meters	10.9 secs.
long jump	23' 8"
shot put	47' 6"
high jump	6' 8"
400 meters	47.9 secs.
hurdles	14.4 secs.
discus	170'
pole vault	15' 9"
javelin	225'
1,500 meters	4:14 secs.

At this point, write down your own long-term goal and the expected hurdles along the way. Your list will tell you what is required for you to arrive at your goal, just as I knew what I had to do to arrive at mine.

Consider the early hurdles in the life of Helen Keller, taken from the book *Notable American Women,* edited by Barbara Sicherman and Carol Hurd Green with Ilene Kantrov and Harriette Walker.

1880—Born in Tuscumbia, Alabama.

Stricken with a variety of afflictions at the age of nineteen months, leaving her deaf, blind and mute.

Her afflictions turn her into a wild, destructive child, but one who also displays a native intelligence, inventing sixty ways to show what she wanted.

Her mother, Kate Keller, takes her daughter to be examined at the Perkins Institution in Boston, where a tutor is suggested.

The tutor, legally blind Anne Sullivan, twenty, arrives at the Keller home in 1887 as Helen's teacher and governess.

Within two weeks of her arrival, Ms. Sullivan establishes mastery over the unruly child.

Two weeks later, Helen stands with Ms. Sullivan at a water pump, learning that everything has a name and the alphabet is the key to everything she wants to know.

Several months later, Helen has learned 300 words.

Within the first year of Ms. Sullivan's arrival, is known internationally as "one of the most remarkable children in existence."

The next year, Ms. Sullivan and Helen move permanently

to the Perkins Institute, and Helen Keller begins her
life's mission: to help the disadvantaged, especially
the blind and the deaf.

Helen Keller's emergence as a living symbol of the limitless nature of human possibility did not happen overnight. Rising from
blindness into light into becoming a beacon for others was a gradual
process, a mission that began in the ordinary and progressed step by
step into the extraordinary.

Pay special attention to the word "mission." In his landmark
book, *Peak Performers,* Charles A. Garfield breaks down the concept
of "mission" to its essence:

"Putting preference before expertise. Drawing on the past.
Trusting intuition. Having no preconceived limitations. Combining
profit with contribution. Being pulled by values."

Explains Garfield in *Peak Performers:* "These six principles are evident in peak performers' ability to formulate missions with real power."

Once peak performers identify their mission, accomplishment
follows from systematically taking one hurdle at a time. "Whether
they are focusing on family, developing talents, or getting to the top of
a particular field, peak performers refine their capacity to see clearly
what they want and to state it in terms that motivate," writes Garfield.
"The mission statement provides the *why* that inspires every *how.* It
points the way. Then comes action, and in peak performance it is action based on a long view. Peak performers want more than merely to
win the next game. They see all the way to the championship."

I love that sentence: "The mission statement provides the *why*
that inspires every *how.*" Think of your mission as the finish line and
your hurdles as the "how" to get there.

Garfield lists several examples of systematic action:

The brothers Joe and Ben Weider, who, with no money and next to no formal education, hurdled obstacle after obstacle in the thirties and forties to establish their weightlifting organizations and magazines. The hurdles were even more intense because, at the time, few people had even seen a barbell, and exercise was considered a dangerous folly.

Dallas Cowboys coach Tom Landry created "yardsticks" to measure the step-by-step progress, of both individual players and the Cowboys as a team, in tangible terms: passes completed, yards run and touchdowns scored.

But the story I like best in Garfield's *Peak Performers* is the tale of Victor Kiam, who, at fifty-two in the late seventies, had turned around the once-embattled Benrus Watch Company, then set his sights on the Remington Corporation. Remington was definitely not a cash cow; the firm had lost 30 million dollars during the recession of 1979 and was being brought to its knees by Norelco, a Dutch company. Its fate seemed written in stone: another U.S. company being driven out of business by foreign competition.

According to Garfield, Kiam bought Remington back one hurdle at a time. Let's trace his steps:

- Ellen Kiam bought her husband a Remington electric razor so he could see if the product was any good. It was.

- Kiam, not having anything near the 25-million-dollar asking price for Remington, secured a loan from Chase Manhattan Bank.

- In his first week as CEO, Kiam fired 70 percent of the company's executives, trimmed 2 million dollars from the company payroll, disbanded the company's car fleet, cut first-class air travel, put a stop to frequent shaver model changes and cut back the use of chrome.

- He then personally hit the road to reassure shopkeepers that Remington was stable and its products were sound.

- He then did his own television commercials in his bathrobe, holding up a Remington shaver and saying, "I liked the shaver so much that I bought the company."

- He did the commercial in Italian, German, Spanish, Norwegian, Japanese and a dozen other languages.

- He made a profit his first year, turned Remington around in four, paid off his bank loan three months early, retired the company's entire debt eleven years ahead of schedule and doubled the company's payroll.

- He went on *Sixty Minutes* and said, "What's really important in life? Sitting on the beach? Looking at television eight hours a day? I think we have to appreciate that we're only alive for a limited period of time and we'll spend most of our lives working. . . . That being the case, I believe one of the most important priorities is to do whatever we do as well as we can."

In *Rocky* terms, Victor Kiam "went the distance." In decathlon terms, he "ran the hurdles." In any language, Kiam proved that he had greatness within him and that greatness manifested itself one step at a time.

"Take those small steps," instructs Chicago Bulls champion Michael Jordan in his book *I Can't Accept Not Trying.* "Otherwise you're opening yourself to all kinds of frustration. . . . All those steps are like pieces of a puzzle. They all come together to form a picture. If it's complete, you've reached your goal. If not, don't get down on yourself. If you've done your best, you will have had some accomplishments along the way. Step by step. I can't see any other way of accomplishing anything."

> *" 'Give me something to say!' said the thirty-eight-year-old, 250-pound George Foreman to Jesse Jackson after he lost a pivotal comeback fight, the 1991 World Championship, to Evander Holyfield.*
>
> *" 'Tell them we didn't retreat and we kept our dignity,' said Jackson.*
>
> *" 'We didn't retreat and we kept our dignity!' the soon-to-be-once-again-heavyweight-champ Foreman told the crowd. 'So everybody at home can take pride that, while we may not win all the points, we made a point. Everyone grab your Geritol and let's toast! Hip-hip-hooray!' "*
> —GEORGE FOREMAN IN HIS 1994 AUTOBIOGRAPHY, BY GEORGE

The day before the '76 decathlon, it rained all day long. Rain was predicted for the next day. I went to bed that night, woke up the next morning and stared outside at the heavens. They sky was gray and overcast, but at least it wasn't raining. I walked downstairs to the dining hall, ate a quick Wheaties breakfast—see how I sneaked that little plug in there?—all the while thinking to myself, This is the day you've been waiting for, and it is yours. Nobody is going to take it away from you.

I grabbed my two pairs of socks and five pairs of shoes—different shoes for practically every event—and headed down to the practice track to begin my warmup. Every day of practice I'd wondered, How am I going to feel on that morning of the decathlon? Am I going to have a cold, any aches or pains? When I got down on the practice track and started warming up, I felt . . . good. As good as a young leopard ready to pounce. Everything seemed right! The legs were bouncy. The arms limber. The mind clear. It was a great, empowering feeling. I got a rubdown, stretched out and then walked up to this little platform, where I could see the practice track stretching in front of me.

From that vantage point I envisioned the figures from my dreams, the greatest decathletes in the world. I saw Nicolay Avilov, the '72 champion, the godlike figure who had motivated me over the past four years. I saw Leonid Litvenyenko from the USSR, who took the silver in '72, Ryszard Katus from Poland, who won the bronze, and Fred Samara and Fred Dixon, the other two Americans on the team.

All stood on that practice track, ready to go into that stadium and do battle.

I felt it was going to be a glorious day.

We walked down the long and complicated tunnel from the practice field to the stadium. The closer I got, the more eager I was to get started. I kept thinking, I've been waiting so many years. Let's get it going. Once inside the stadium, I felt completely at home, because I had already visualized every move I had to make once I got there.

The gun sounded for the first event, the 100 meters. I leaned down in the blocks, hands on the starting line. It's always a scary event, because you haven't had a chance to test yourself for so long. So the question rages: What type of shape are you really in? I'm not the best 100-meter man; it's a weak event for me. But I figured if I could come up with a great time in the 100 meters, I'd be off to a strong start.

I ran the race, leaned at the tape and everything felt pretty good. But then I sort of had a hard time slowing down. I thought, Ooooh, that's kind of a good feeling. Maybe I was going kind of fast back there.

I had to wait a few minutes for the officials to post my time up on the scoreboard, and then I saw it: 10.94 seconds, the fastest time I'd ever clocked in the 100 meters.

Oh, yes, a glorious day!

I looked at everybody else's times, and they were just average, some even below average. Right then, after the first event, I knew: I'd just won the decathlon.

I believe we all know when we've prepared ourselves for victory. It just feels right. The seeds of success, watered regularly, bloom just like a glorious flower. When Miami Dolphins coach Don Shula took the team over in 1970, he knew the secret of growing success. When the press asked him about his three-to-five-year plan, he answered, "My play is day-to-day." He broke coach George Halas's coaching record in the 1993 season with a systematic, hour-by-hour, day-by-day progression. Here's a page from Don Shula's date book from his 1995 book with Ken Blanchard, *Everyone's a Coach:*

7:00 A.M.	Practice 1: Work on special teams and kicking game
7:45	Breakfast

9:30	Meeting to cover morning practice points
10:00	Practice 2: Work on running game, both offense and defense
11:30	Lunch
3:00 P.M.	Meeting to cover afternoon practice points
3:30	Practice 3: Work on passing game, both offense and defense
6:00	Dinner
7:30	Practice 4: Work until dark on making corrections
9:30	Meeting
10:30	Dismiss

Added Shula: "My players couldn't believe what I was asking them to do. There was a lot of moaning and groaning from the guys. 'Four practices a day!' 'This is unheard of.' 'What's he trying to do? Kill us?' . . . [But] what has produced winning football teams for us over the years has been our willingness to create practice systems and procedures that are aligned with our vision of perfection: *We want to win them all.* Everything I do is to prepare people to perform to the best of their ability. And you do that one day at a time."

That's exactly how I felt after winning the 100 meters: I not only wanted to win them all; I *knew* I was going to win. Now, you don't go around telling everybody that you've won before the game even gets started. But in my heart and in my soul, I felt like I had won the gold medal in the 100 meters. I only had nine events to go, two days of competition. I knew that if I took them systematically one at a time, one after another, looking at them as parts of a whole, nobody could beat me.

In the next event, the long jump, I made the longest jump of my life by a centimeter. The shot put posed a problem. I had a bad pinky finger that had kept me from throwing the shot at 100 percent for a long time. But I took that little finger and put it right behind the ball, thinking, What the heck—this is the last shot put of my life. I've got forty years to heal a busted finger. *Boom!* I could hear the finger snapping. But I had the best shot-put throw of my life.

The high jump, the same thing: 6.8 feet, the best of my career.

By this time, my confidence level was so high that I attacked the 400 meters—the Bear—like some hungry hillbilly with a double-barreled shotgun. *Blammo!* I had predicted 47.51 seconds. When I looked up at the scoreboard it said 47.5—my best time ever and only a fraction of a second away from my prediction.

At the end of the first day, I'd had the best five events that I could have ever imagined, better than I had ever dreamed. Because the second day was my strong day, I expected to end the first at least 200 points out of the lead. But I was only thirty-five points out of first place.

I was running at potentially world-record pace, with five more events to go, but then the first day was over and I had to head back to my room and . . . *sleep!* How could I sleep? How could they throw sleep into the middle of the decathlon's two days? It just didn't work. My adrenaline was pumping so hard and my heart was beating so violently that the sheets were bouncing off my chest.

All to the rhythm of rain.

Fear played tricks on my mind. I saw Jeff Bannister, America's favorite to win the decathlon at the 1972 Olympic Games, slip and fall in the hurdles, the first event of the second day, because the track was wet from rain the night before. I kept thinking of Dave Roberts, whose gold medal was stolen by the rain. The pole vault was ahead of me on the second day. Would it rain, turning the track into an oil slick and my performance into a disaster? As I lay there, listening to the rain coming down all night long, I tried everything to get to sleep: counting pole-vaulters, high-jumpers, hurdlers, trying valiantly to concentrate on the moment and not the hours that lay ahead.

I should've been counting vacuum cleaner salesmen, specifically the Swedish vacuum cleaner salesman Ove Sjogren, featured in the book *Secrets of the World's Top Sales Performers* by Christine Harvey.

Sjogren became the number one Electrolux salesman by practicing a supreme example of hurdling, the philosophy of "twenty seconds at a time," breaking down cold calls into three hurdles to surmount:

1. Getting past the door.

2. Getting into the demonstration.

3. Getting over the price objection.

"First impressions count the most," Harvey quotes Ove Sjogren as saying. "In fact, the first twenty seconds are the most important. Everything from the way you ring the doorbell to the way you look counts."

Sjogren lives each sale one second at a time, a technique he recounted for Christine Harvey:

> He sets a structure in his mind for each phase. "Two short rings of the doorbell sound friendlier than one long ring," he says. And so he gives it two short rings.
>
> "When they open the door, they must see more than you. **They see what's behind you, too.** They must make the right professional impression." So he washes his car every night and parks in front of the house to frame the picture with the right impression.

"They must first take you in **at a distance that won't frighten them**, but you have to move up to start direct contact," he says. So he stands well back from the door and off to the side where they'll see him upon opening the door. Then he pauses a moment and moves forward to shake their hand.

"You must look absolutely professional to gain their trust, or you won't get in." And, if you don't get in, you don't sell. So he advocates a tidy shirt-and-tie business look. Nothing should be forgotten—clean collar, clean-shaven, immaculate hygiene—body odor and dirty fingernails won't do. "Anything that detracts from your professionalism will ruin your first twenty seconds."

"They must instantly **associate you with a reputable organization**," he says. And so he holds his Electrolux black leather binder up where they can see it. The company name shows as well as his company ID card with his photo.

"You must come across **unobtrusive, but friendly** at the same time." And so, after they open the door and take him in visually, he steps forward and says, "Excuse me for calling."

"Names are important to people." So if there's a nameplate on the door, he'll say, "Are you Mrs. Andersson?" Then, he follows with, "My name is Sjogren and I'm from Electrolux."

And last but not least of the twenty-second first impression is the handshake. "You have to make direct contact with the customer," he says. "If the customer doesn't shake your hand, you won't get that necessary direct contact." He always pursues because he thinks sales fail 99 times out of 100 without that personal-contact handshake and the trust that results from it.

Then he leaps right into the **question:** "Do you mind if I come in for a moment?" If the twenty-second trust has been successful, he gets in.

As Napoleon said when asked how he won so many battles: "Because I understand the value of five minutes."

"By the mile, it's a trial.
By the yard, it's hard.
But by the inch,
It's a cinch."

—*ANONYMOUS*

Concentrating on the moment instead of the hour, I got a few hours of sleep, then awoke at six A.M., raring to go. I looked outside. It had stopped raining, but the clouds were so low they were touching the top of the stadium. I went to the first event, the hurdles, and—*bang!*—the gun went off, I stayed on my toes and made it all the way down to the finish line in record time. What a way to start! I threw the discus just as well. By the time I got to the pole vault, the eighth event in the competition, I was so far ahead of myself in points that I knew: all I have to do is make the opening height and I can win the gold medal. The javelin is always a fairly easy event for me; I knew I wouldn't die in the 1,500 meters. All I had to do was make the opening height, and I could win.

I stripped off my T-shirt, the one that said FEET DON'T FAIL ME NOW across the front, stood down at the end of the runway and looked at the bar, set at fourteen feet. I put my foot on the line, flew down the runway, planted the pole and soared, clearing that baby by three feet.

My feet hadn't failed me. I had enough points just in the opening height to win the gold. In the half-hour before the javelin, I lay down on the grass with a towel over my face as a wave of emotion washed over me. I started to cry. I knew I was going to win the Gold, knew that I'd break Avilov's 8,454 world record if my javelin throw was decent. I knew that within the hour the decathlon would be over. I wiped my tears and took the towel off of my face. I stared into the stadium and took it all in: the faces, the cheering, the pageantry.

Then I heard that voice again, coming from someplace within.

"Wait a second," it said. "You got your goal of 85 in '75, but what about 86 in '76? You didn't score your 8,600 points yet. Keep raising the bar. Let's see how hard you can push yourself!"

I threw the javelin far enough for the world record, leaving only the 1,500 meters, the final event in the decathlon. If I tied my best time ever in the 1,500, I could just sneak over 8,600 points. But I've always believed that the 1,500-meter run separates the men from the boys. Most decathletes dread the 1,500. It's that ultimate, tough challenge that sits there at the end. After putting you through sheer hell for two days—after you've given the events your all and your legs have lost their bounce and your spirit has been drained of momentum—they throw in one last hurdle, perhaps the most incredible hurdle.

They make you run the metric mile.

Most guys fold in the 1,500, just like most people fold in the most crucial tests of a lifetime. They haven't trained for the 1,500 meters. They're not in shape. They don't like to run distance. I've seen decathletes go out and literally jog the 1,500 meters. But the 1,500 meters is the time when "giving your all" is most important; it's a true test of your character. These are the moments in which to persist, not retreat. To me, the 1,500 has always represented a chance to kick the decathlon's butt instead of letting it kicking mine.

The announcer boomed, "At seven, we'll have the final event in the decathlon, the fifteen hundred meters." I stared up at the clock in the stadium: twenty minutes to seven. And then it hit me: in twenty minutes, it's going to be over. I loved what I was doing, I was the best in the world at what I was doing, and in twenty minutes I would have to walk away.

It was like I'd finally found a best friend or an incredible soulmate and, in twenty minutes, we would have to part. I'd have to walk away from the security of the one sport I'd lived, breathed and dreamed about, that had been the center of my life for ten years, consuming me so totally that I'd never had to deal with the outside world. Now, in twenty minutes, I'd have to pack my bags, walk away and go into a new world that was one big, scary, unfamiliar void.

I got into the starting position, put my foot on the line and, when the gun sounded, took off. I ran the first lap right on pace. Then I said to myself, "Let's start picking the pace up a little bit; let's see how you feel." *The faster I ran, the better I felt!* I came around the next lap, looked at the clock on the inside of the track and saw that I was running one second slower than my fastest pace ever, with 300 meters to go.

Something screamed from deep within me, a voice that began booming in my brain: *"You've got fifty or sixty years to recuperate from this thing! Open it up and let it go!"*

Down the backstretch, I exploded, sprinting as hard as I possibly could. I heard a tremendous roar from the stadium, and then the ground trembled beneath me like a six-point earthquake, and I knew: I had reached the part of the race that I'd always dreamed about. Not the finish line but the final turn. All I had to do was follow the dream and it would bring me across the finish line. I had that little lean going, just as I'd had in my dream, and I was headed for the tape, listening to that gold medal jingling in my back pocket.

"Hold on to the moment!" screamed the voice in my head.

I followed the order, taking little mental snapshots of everything going on around me. I noticed the stadium and the faces in the stands. I noticed the other athletes. I breathed in every ounce of the experience, six years of hard labor crystalizing into one single action. Because I knew that once the race ended, the decathlon would be over for me forever. I always wanted to remember what it would look like coming off that final turn with 100 meters to go. When I rounded the corner, it was like I left my body and was watching myself as an observer. I saw the arms churning, the legs pumping, the eyes focused on the single goal.

My butt was literally on fire with lactic acid buildup. My thighs were so tired that I had a hard time lifting them up to sprint that last 100 meters. But because of all of the training and a tremendous will to get to that finish line, the knees kept coming up and the arms kept pumping.

The next thing I knew I was crossing the finish line and, in an absolutely unconscious reflex, my arms shot into the air and I screamed. I screamed a cry of release, a cry of pain and accomplishment, a cry of completion. Right then, it was like taking a key and sticking it in my brain and locking it shut. The accomplishment would be mine forever. Nobody could ever take it away from me. I'd seized the moment; I was living my dream.

A spectator named George Elliott jumped down from the stands and, amid the incredibly tight security, managed to hand me a small American flag before being dragged away by the Mounties. I held it aloft as I jogged a complete lap of the track, trying to wind down from the race. As I ran, the roar of the crowd of 70,000 grew louder and louder in what would later be called the longest, loudest ovation of the Twenty-first

Olympic Games. At that moment, I knew the glory of the ages, of that spirit that Homer described so perfectly centuries ago in *The Odyssey:*

> *So long as a man lives*
> *He has no greater glory*
> *Than what he wins*
> *With the strength of his hands*
> *And the speed of his feet*
> *In the athletic games.*

I'd won.

My scores were so close to my personal-best predictions before the decathlon, it seemed psychic. I'll list my predictions, then the actual score in parenthesis: 10.9 seconds in the 100 meters (10.94); long jump 23' 8" (23' 8¼'); shot put 47' 6" (50' 4¼"); high jump 6' 8" (6' 8"); 400 meters 47.9 seconds (47.51); hurdles 14.4 seconds (14.84); discus 170' (164.2'); pole vault 15' 9" (15' 9"); javelin 225' (224' 9½"); 1,500 meters 4:14 seconds (4:12.61).

I'd predicted five of the ten events to the second, inch or foot, set personal records in the long jump, shot, high jump, 400 meters and 1,500 meters, equaled my career bests in the 100 meters and the pole vault and exceeded my goal of 8,600 points by 34. "Jenner has an almost mystical ability to divine his own limits, and those who have been with him at meets say that by studying his opponents as the events go by, he can perceive their exact capabilities that day," wrote Frank Deford in *Sports Illustrated* shortly after the '76 Games. "Montreal, he felt, was his destiny."

There was nothing mystical about my victory, however. It was purely scientific. I'd taken an incredible mission one hurdle at a time, and the successive hurdles had delivered me onto the doorstep of victory.

Hurdles from the life of Joel Staadecker, the "reinvented CEO," as described in the July 1996 issue of *Life* Magazine:

> His father, an insurance broker, died a month after he turned sixteen.
>
> The insurance broker left no insurance.
>
> His mother took over his father's business, and Joel spent his high school years working odd jobs to bring home extra money.
>
> He brought home Ds on his report card.
>
> He still hadn't "completely processed" his father's death when he graduated from high school; he knew nothing of the direction of his future.
>
> He got his pilot's license and joined the Air Force reserves at seventeen.
>
> He was hired as an airline pilot, then laid off before his first official flight.
>
> He told his wife, "Each person is given enough energy in a lifetime to mount one career. I've spent mine." He was twenty-three years old.
>
> He returned to school as a radical: his life was one long rebellious, angry march.
>
> On New Year's Day, he saw a plane fly overhead. "In that instant, I decided to rejoin the culture."
>
> He drove seventeen hours straight to Seattle, got a haircut and talked one of his old employers into starting a branch of his pilot-training operations in Southern California. He launched his first entrepreneurial venture.

He was hired to start a private airplane charter company in
the North Sea.

Less than forty-eight hours after he arrived in Scotland, he
was in a head-on collision. His nose was ripped off his
face and had to be stitched back down; his legs were
in a cast. Worse, a coal strike crippled industry and
Joel's newly founded enterprise.

He was offered a job with a Houston oil company; for three
years, he was part of a corporate rise, from 13 million
dollars in sales to 180 million.

This was followed by eight years building a real estate firm.

Then the price of oil dropped, taking his fortunes with it.

He became a father and vowed to build a new life for his
wife and child.

He moved back to Seattle, running a company making corporate education training programs, then decided to
go back into business for himself.

He found personal and professional fulfillment as CEO of a
software company that has grown from four people in
1994 to twenty-eight by 1996.

Joel Staadecker believes that the magic is how you react to each
moment: "It's possible to make these jumps. What's difficult is the belief that it's possible. . . . You have to go through the cycle and come
out on the other end. There's birth and renewal. Forget the past. Look
at the future as a new day. Embrace all it has to offer. If you can face
life that way, you can succeed at anything."

Every life is a trajectory of experiences, a book of chapters that
tell the story of the whole. Mine led me to the top of a platform that

represented the top of the entire world. It had stood as a beacon in my memory, the final destination of a million actions, and when I first saw it that evening of July 30, 1976, a tiny, pristine, three-level white carpeted platform in the middle of the Olympic Stadium, the sight didn't let me down.

This would be my last hurdle, and it would be the toughest.

Staring at those steps, I thought, Those are the last two steps of my career. Once I get on top, it's over, it's done with. I've got to retire from sports and go on with life.

The officials announced that the awards ceremony was about to begin. I stood beneath the stadium, where they had led us, in sort of a daze. I was thinking about how the years of practice and thousands of miles run had delivered me to this incredible moment. I thought about how every time I had come to a Y in the road and could've gone one way or another, for some reason I had always picked the right way. Now, as I left my vaulting poles on the field in Montreal, knowing I'd never need them again, that road stretched behind me, leading to the top of that platform where this part of my life would finally come to an end.

The Olympic theme song blared over the loud speakers, and the names of the top three finishers were called to stand on the platform: first, winning the third-place bronze medal, Nicolay Avilov; then, winning the second-place silver, Guido Kratschmer; and then me. When they called my name, I took the two steps slowly, tentatively, and stood at the top, looking out over the surreal landscape of a dream realized.

Let me tell you what I learned at that moment: when you win, life treats you differently. Life opens its arms wide. Life will give you holy hell on the way up, but it doesn't let you down when you fulfill your dreams. It rewards you with everything you've ever imagined— and much, much more.

God, I felt good. I felt satisfied. I had scored 8,634 points. I had achieved my 86 in '76, my gold medal and the new world record. When the gold medal was hung around my neck, the ending I'd heard in my dream came true: the National Anthem thundered from the stadium speakers.

This is the reward you're going to receive once you've reached your dreams. Whether it's 70,000 people or seven, the National Anthem or your favorite song, when you reach your dream it's going to be nothing but anthems and applause. You are going to revel in it, bathe in it, take it in with all of your five senses and never want it to end.

"Mr. Jenner?"

The voice was loud, insistent, but I was too busy reveling in the moment to give it much notice. I guess that National Anthem that had sounded so good had ended some time ago. The crowd was beginning to leave, and I looked around me on the platform and saw that I was all alone up there.

"You're going to have to get down now," said the voice, which belonged to a very serious-looking and -sounding official.

"No," I said, then added quickly. "Sir, I've got nowhere to go! No dinner reservations, no nothing. I'm kind of happy right here. Is it okay if I stay here awhile?"

He looked at me a little strangely, and I thought I'd better climb down. Didn't want to make an international incident out of this thing. I could imagine the headlines: WHY DIDN'T JENNER GET DOWN OFF THE PLATFORM?

I jumped down, walked across the track and, just before I went inside the building, I stopped for a second. I looked back over my left shoulder. I looked back at the track that had given me so much, imagining each and every one of the hurdles that had brought me here, and I said, "Hey, thanks for the memories. I had a wonderful time, but I leave it to the next guy."

From that experience, I learned the power of the human spirit. Not just the potential that lies deep inside me but the potential that lies deep inside *every* human being. I didn't start off an Olympic champion. I was a dyslexic kid. I flunked second grade. I had an image of myself that was about an inch big. That simple thing called reading was extremely tough for me; my biggest fear in my life was showing up for school, because I was terrified that the teacher was going to make me read in front of the class. I thought everybody was smarter, better and faster. Athletics showed me that we are all given strengths and that mine lay precisely in the one place I thought I was the weakest: my mind.

In the movie *Phenomenon,* John Travolta plays George O'Malley, an absolutely ordinary auto mechanic who is suddenly struck with extraordinary powers of perception, learning and love—gifts that he learns are inherent in all of us and will emerge if we have the faith to tap into them. "Everything is on its way to someplace," he says in one pivotal scene, voicing the essence of how the parts make up the whole of everything in life.

Sail your own voyage of discovery one knot at a time, and pay no attention to those who try to tell you the world is flat! Break down your major goals and follow the steps toward your dreams. You have the ability to build on your experiences, to make your life a grand adventure.

Taking the hurdles of your life will give you a start. But when you get to that part of the race where the hurdles end and the finish line looms, you've got to accelerate.

You've got to lean into the finish line.

You've got to know when to make your move.

CHAPTER EIGHT

THE DISCUS: HOW TO MAKE YOUR MOVE

It's a four-pound, six-ounce piece of history, a relic from the days of Achilles and Apollo, the inspiration for art, poetry and sculpture. In Greek, the word literally means "a thing for throwing," and the discus is perhaps the most perfect throwing implement known to man. A descendent of the throwing stone, which David slung against Goliath, the essence of the discus is guided force. You begin in the back of the circle, knees bent, back straight, throwing arm fully extended, with the discus in your fingertips. You begin swaying back and forth, building up momentum, preparing to mimic the motion of a spinning top. Finally, you take a big gasp of oxygen and rotate over your right foot; then, once your feet are firmly planted, you unwind, so when you release the discus it explodes like David's rock from his slingshot. If the spin is right and the wind is with you, that little piece of flattened wood and metal can soar into the stratosphere, knocking out giants in its path.

"Hey, Bruce, baby, right this way. Step into the world's parlor and let us take a long look at you. Have some champagne and caviar! You deserve it, babe. And oh, yes, a contract. You'd like a contract, wouldn't you, kid? Television or film, commentary or drama . . . all ya gotta do is sign on the dotted line. You don't have any acting experience? No problem! We're gonna make you a star! Prince Valiant with muscles—that's what you are. Is that hair real? Are those eyes brown? Can you smile bigger? Stand taller? Look older? Speak clearer? Gimme five, bay-bee! We feel like we know you! Just stare into the camera and speak into the microphone. NBC, CBS, ABC . . . deadlines, Brucey baby, deadlines. Say hello to Hollywood! Bid good day to the Big Apple! Say good-bye to San Jose and hello to dinner at the White House! That's your chair, right next to the First Lady. Ralph Lauren will be here soon to fit you for your new wardrobe. You're gonna look slick, babe . . . and everything's on the house! Francesco Scavullo wants you in his photography studio at three P.M. The great producer Ilya Salkind is expecting you in Rome for your screen test. How would do you feel about playing Superman? The telephone's ringing off the hook! Can you/will you/won't you . . . attend/pose/ endorse? *What are you gonna do with your life? What are you gonna do with your life? What are you gonna do?* And oh, by the way, we're watching you . . . so don't you dare let us down."

Like a discus spins dizzily, such were the days of my post-Olympic life. You just cannot imagine the chemistry that occurs when millions upon millions upon millions of people watch you win a gold medal on television. It's like a nuclear reaction which leaves you transformed. Overnight, *bango!* You're known in every household with a TV set or a newspaper subscription. Everybody knows you. Everybody *wants* you. I was a product, a freshly minted Olympic champion, and the world was ready to hoist me up onto Celebrity Mountain.

I was so proud of what I'd just accomplished that I swore never to do anything that would tarnish the medal that represented so much achievement and pride. But at the same time, I had to be smart. This was a once-in-a-lifetime opportunity, and the time to strike was *now*. So I had to pull myself out of the spin and employ the lesson of the discus. In the decathlon, this was the one event where I felt totally secure of my abilities, the event I could always win. When it came time to throw the discus, I knew it was time to make my move, to *act*.

In ancient Olympics, the victors were taken care of for life, literally given the keys to Greek cities. Many became the equivalent of millionaires; most never had to work again, giving rise to the term "resting on your laurels." These days, even Olympians have to act or they rust. When I stood buck naked before the mirror with that gold medal slung around my neck on the morning after the Games, flat broke but facing boundless opportunity, I was staring at my only commodity. Now I had to act to turn that commodity, that victory, into currency, into both financial and personal fulfillment. Now I had to throw the discus. I had to go for it, to make my move, to prove myself in the field of life.

It was my big moment.

Let me help you learn what to do with yours.

"The basic difference between an ordinary man and a warrior is that a warrior takes everything as a challenge, while an ordinary man takes everything as a blessing or a curse."
—*DON JUAN*

There comes a point in every person's life where dreams, preparation and strategy must galvanize into action, when apprehension and doubt must step aside to let the essence of the life force step up to bat. Preparation and ability are only talk; it's the doing that makes the preparation pay. The ability to act is what separates the winners from the losers in life. It's the force that sends a man to the moon or an athlete to the stadium. Action is power in its rawest, most elemental form.

It's Michael Jordan scoring forty points in the fourth quarter.

It's Mike Tyson turning ferocious in the tenth round.

It's Michael Johnson becoming the first man in history to win world championships in both the 200- and 400-meter runs in the same year, saying, "When I heard that no man had ever done that, I made it my goal."

Champions listen to an inner voice, a voice perpetually repeating "Do it!" "Go for it!" "Make it real!" Action is the force that can literally move mountains.

"We are born to action and whatever is capable of suggesting and guiding action has power over us from the first," wrote U.S. sociologist Charles Horton Cooley.

"The soul is made for action and cannot rest till it be employed," wrote English poet and mystic Thomas Traherne in the 1600s. "Idleness is a rust."

How will you know when it's your time to make your move?

Look for a flash of light, a moment of clarity, a glow of feeling.

"A man should learn to detect and watch that gleam of light which flashes across his mind from within," wrote Ralph Waldo Emerson in his landmark essay "Self-Reliance." Reject that gleam, either out of insecurity or a feeling of inferiority, and you're sentencing yourself to failure and eventual shame. As Emerson wrote: "Tomorrow a stranger will say with masterly good sense precisely what we have thought and felt all the time, and we shall be forced to take with shame our own opinion from another."

Author Erskine Caldwell saw the gleam of light at twenty-six so strongly that he quit his stable newspaper job to move to Maine and spend the next five years of his life learning to write fiction.

Passing Nashville on his way to West Point, then U.S. Army officer Kris Kristofferson saw his gleam of light to become a songwriter so vividly that he resigned his Army commission and moved to Nashville. His wife left him. His family disowned him. Kristofferson endured jobs as a ditch digger, oil rig laborer, bartender and janitor to work at his dream until it came true.

For Federal Express founder Fred Smith, the flash of light came in a sign that said LAS VEGAS. According to the book *Absolutely Positively Overnight* by Robert A. Sigatoos with Roger R. Easson, he was standing in the Chicago airport after being turned down "for the umpteenth time" by a corporate giant that was supposedly going to acquire a portion of his then-faltering company, and he needed money to send home to help make payroll back in Memphis. The flash of light was the airport sign announcing a flight to Las Vegas, but it was the *action*—switching his ticket from Memphis to Vegas, then sitting at the tables and running up a couple of hundred dollars into 27,000 dollars—that made the difference in the destinies of Fred Smith and Federal Express.

How do you take action on your own flashes of light? By following three basic principles:

ACT UPON EVERY SECOND.

People are either driven to action or complacency, mission or rust. You're either participating in the Game of Life or you're watching it from the grandstands. Herein lies a crucial difference. A champion *plays* the game; a spectator observes, criticizes and never really gets to live. A champion knows what he or she wants and goes after it with carefully calculated goals and no-holds-barred action. A spectator feels that his or her life is not their own. They let others dictate their destiny. They become victims of life instead of masters of it.

Champions know that whatever their arena, every second represents a chance to act, an opportunity to use that second as a stepping-stone toward an eventual goal. They realize that few of us step immediately into our dreams but that all of us are blessed with the power to see what we want in life, and, if we have the discipline to keep that vision burning brightly in our minds, the ability to make it a reality.

A story that illustrates this perfectly comes from Charles Garfield's book *Peak Performers*. Driving from his home in the Bay Area of California, Garfield had driven through every one in the row of seventeen tollbooths on the San Francisco–Oakland Bay Bridge for years without incident, until one day he stumbled upon something wonderful. He pulled up to a tollbooth and heard music blaring as loud as a Michael Jackson concert. He looked around. No other drivers had their windows open. There wasn't a boom box on the sidewalk. The sound was coming from the tollbooth, where the attendant was . . . *dancing*.

"What are you doing?" Garfield asked.

"I'm having a party!" the attendant shouted gleefully.

Garfield motioned to the other sixteen attendants, all stern and dour in their booths.

The attendant smiled. "Vertical coffins," he said. "At eight-thirty every morning, live people get in. Then they die for eight hours. At four-thirty, like Lazarus from the dead, they reemerge and go home. For eight hours, the brain is on hold, dead on the job. Going through the motions."

He pointed to the administration building.

"I'm going to be a dancer someday," he said. "My bosses are in there, and they're paying for my training."

Garfield was astounded. "Sixteen people dead on the job and the seventeenth, in precisely the same situation, figures out a way to live," he writes in *Peak Performers*.

In life, the ratio is, sadly, roughly the same: out of every seventeen attendants, sixteen are spectators—only one's a player. Become the one in seventeen in your own arena of endeavor. Fill your heart with mission. Look at your current situation and find the gifts that can help you toward your goal. Take every moment as a chance to learn, to grow, to do.

Realize that you have control of your life and that action is the ammunition that guides you toward your target. Expect the best, not the worst, and you'll find the world will clear a path for you.

OBEY THAT IMPULSE.

"Have you noticed that from time to time, for no particularly good reason, you will get a sudden impulse—feel a sudden urge?" asks the late motivational authority Earl Nightingale in his book *This Is Earl Nightingale.* "Everything about the idea seems good at the moment; you can't find a thing wrong with it. But instead of acting on the impulse right then, you wait, you sit back and begin thinking of it critically. Pretty soon you can find a lot of reasons for not doing it, or it just passes, and an opportunity is gone forever. These sudden impulses often come straight out of our subconscious minds, giving us valuable direction—direction we should be taking. By vetoing them, we miss all kinds of opportunities."

The book *This Is Earl Nightingale* quotes the psychologist Dr. William Moulton Marston, who once said that most people stifle enough good impulses during the course of a single day to change the current of their lives forever! Writes Nightingale, "On this very subject William James has said, 'Every time a resolve or fine glow of feeling evaporates without bearing fruit, it is worse than a chance lost; it works to hinder future emotions from taking the normal path of discharge.'"

Think about every "glow of feeling" as a supreme gift from life, a call to action, a direction in which to go and grow—and you'll be able to act upon it. Realize that life is constantly giving clues and directions, if you'll only take time to see them. Find meaning in the seemingly mundane, for this is where the signposts of life are to be found.

TAKE THE LEAP.

As he explains in his book *Over the Top*, motivational speaker Zig Ziglar was still in the cookware sales business when he hired an assistant named Gerry Arrowood, whose entire professional work experience consisted of baking cakes and taking in sewing to earn extra money for her family. "She assured me that she did not mind washing dishes or cleaning the kitchen; however, she was shy and did not relate to people," writes Ziglar of the experience. "Therefore, I must never call on her to participate in the [cookware] demonstration."

Everything went fine until one day Zig overscheduled his cooking demonstrations and had to call upon Gerry to help him. All she had to do was deliver cookware to six couples Zig had already sold and show them how to use it. "Terror appeared in Gerry's eyes. Her hands shook as she said, 'I can't do it! I can't do it!'"

But Ziglar has a way of motivating people and, after thinking about it for a while, Gerry consented, even though she said she wouldn't sleep a wink or breathe an easy breath until the demonstration was over.

"The next night I got one of the most exciting telephone calls I've ever received," Ziglar writes. "Gerry was wound up tighter than a nine-day clock. With enormous enthusiasm, she said, 'Zig, you cannot believe how much fun I've had today! The first family I delivered cookware to had the coffeepot on and a piece of cake waiting for me. They really bragged on me and told me how professional I was, what a nice personality I had and how much they enjoyed having me in their home. . . . I don't ever remember having this much fun or feeling so good about myself. I'll be glad to do this for you anytime you want me to!'"

From demonstration to demonstration, Gerry's confidence grew, until, by the end of one evening, she had made the leap from office assistant to full-fledged salesperson in her mind. Today, Gerry Arrowood owns her own company—all because she was forced to act! By overcoming her fears and taking action, she discovered that life had laid out a picnic for her.

She had found her Champion Within, an inner strength that she didn't even know was there.

DIRECT YOUR ACTIONS
OR THEY'LL LEAD YOU NOWHERE.

Look into the history of any successful person and you'll find not merely action but action directed toward a greater goal. The secret that successful people share is the selection of an arena in which they have room to grow, not where their actions will eventually hit a dead end. No great tree can grow tall in a glass jar. A redwood requires room to spread its roots.

So do you.

As noted in previous chapters, we all know people who are perpetually busy, slaving away their days routinely checking off innumerable items on endless to-do lists. They spin their wheels furiously but end up getting nowhere. Successful people decide in advance where they are going to throw the discus; their target is never out of their minds.

To accomplish your goal, you can't just "want." You must be perpetually becoming. You must truly *become* your cause, your goal. You have to become like a logo for your endeavor, just as a magazine's logo tells the reader what to expect inside. Pick up *Rolling Stone* and you immediately know its mission is rock 'n' roll. Pick up *Cosmo* and you know immediately that it's a young woman's guide to life. Pick up *Outside* and you're in the great outdoors of sports and adventure. No magazine is called *Maybe*, *Whatever* or *I Don't Know*. But they could be fitting titles of a great many lives. Create a logo for the magazine of your life and live every day with that logo emblazoned in your mind.

The key is this: You must see the outcome, and that outcome must be simultaneously attractive and empowering. You must be able to reach out and touch it, just as I felt I was able to reach out and grab the gold medal long before I'd run even one event. You must act as author Michael Crichton does when he dresses in the same clothing and eats the same lunch for thirty-five days, acting *as if* he's writing the first draft of one of his novels in one long single day. You must act *as if* you've already done the thing, achieved the goal, written the book, won the reward, accessed the Champion Within. When you act *as if* you have the qualities to complete the action, you will amaze yourself at what you can accomplish.

I know this strategy works because it worked for me, when I stood before a national TV camera and began to act *as if* I could read well.

> *"Opportunities have an evanescent quality about them. The stock market builds and builds, finally reaching a crest and then hesitating for a moment, plunging downwards. . . . A coveted painting appears at auction. The bidding takes place, the gavel falls and it disappears from sight perhaps for generations. Opportunities are usually for the moment, and as they pass by there is often only a brief moment to grab them."*
>
> —*EUGENE GRIESSMAN*, THE ACHIEVEMENT FACTORS

"Become a spokesperson."

The words were deep and resonant, more pronouncement than suggestion, and they were coming from a dozen different voices. Every person who had parlayed sports success into winning seasons off the field seemed to have one word of advice for me, a young lion eager to go from one field into another.

"Remember this one word," they would say. "*Spokesperson.*"

I was totally confused. "What?" I'd ask.

"You don't want to just do commercials," they'd reply. "Anybody can do commercials! You want to get involved in the company. You want to become a spokesperson."

I carefully considered this advice amid the flood of offers being presented to me in the days and weeks after the Games. *Become a spokesperson.* It has validity in any field of endeavor. Make your every action have meaning, resonance, the ability to connect to an even higher action. Don't just go for the short buck but focus on the long haul. Let your every movement become a spokesperson or, as we said earlier, a logo, for your larger mission.

I had four years to learn a new business, to become a spokesperson for something more than my athletic ability. Setting a four-year time period for accomplishing your goals is much more effective than allowing yourself twenty years. Twenty years seems an eternity, so what's the rush? But four years hence seems right around the corner. It propels you to *act!* In my case, once that four-year period was over, there would be a new Olympic champion in the spotlight, a new name to celebrate and, without further action, my own name would be destined to fade. My name recognition could get me into any door in the world, but now I had to discover which of the millions of possible doors I wanted to enter.

I couldn't take forever. A hundred voices were telling me, "Strike while the iron is hot, kid, because Olympic champions come and go." I had to become a spokesperson, a player, not a spectator, in the larger Game of Life. I had to follow Charles Garfield's advice in his 1986 book, *Peak Performers:* "Don't juggle; choose. You turn away from things you might like to do in order to focus on those you must do."

I had vowed not to tarnish my gold medal by going for the fast buck or the short-term deal. So I began the process of rejection, turning down the things that weren't directed toward my goal of becoming a spokesperson for the Champion Within.

Aside from sports, I had one natural talent, a talent I'd discovered and polished as a student at Graceland College. To help defray my tuition, Graceland's development department had agreed to trade education for speeches. I'd go around the country, speaking to schools, churches and civics groups, and they'd pick up my tuition tab. It was a good tradeoff and an even better education. I discovered something I loved doing: being out in front of the public and passing on the incredible lessons of accessing the Champion Within.

I decided to build upon that talent.

In doing so, I turned down everything that didn't fit in with the larger cause of becoming a spokesperson for human potential.

One-shot commercials for cologne, toothpaste, hair gel—rejected.

Throwing fluorescent lightbulbs for a major lightbulb company—rejected.

A four-year professional track meet contract, which would've netted me 200,000 dollars—rejected. Here I was, flat broke, and turning down 200,000-dollar deals! But very quickly I learned to think like a champion and not a spectator: every action must lead to a higher action, just as every rotation of the discus leads to a longer throw. I knew I couldn't do everything, so I chose the things that would further my long-term goal. You must do the same.

I accepted activities of which I could be immensely proud. I appeared, of course, on the Wheaties cereal box for five years. I did

Wheaties TV commercials. (My line: "I logged a lot of miles and downed a lot of Wheaties.") I was head of the Wheaties Sports Foundation, which involves giving speeches to young people throughout the year. Twenty years later, I'm still on the Wheaties team, both by eating the cereal every morning and working for General Mills in various capacities.

> *"Bruce Jenner is a real-life version of the American dream, fairly bursting with honest vitality, infectious health, and cheerful good humor. . . . He's direct, self-assured, sincere."*
> —KENNETH TURAN, THE WASHINGTON POST

The second step to productive action—Obey That Impulse—came easy for me. I didn't have to search very hard for a "flash of light" or a "glow of feeling" to point my way. The lights were literally exploding all around me. All I had to do was see my way through them toward the brightest one. To do this, I had to gingerly sidestep the minefield of media, which, I knew, would depict "The Bruce Jenner Story" one of two ways: positive or negative.

At twenty-six, I would be either be labeled a has-been or a going-to-become.

Because in the middle, who cares?

My life became an open book for the world's consumption. The press watched my every move. They sat their with their cameras and notebooks ready, eager to celebrate my success or jeer at my failure.

What did I learn? First of all, don't rise too fast in the media spotlight; secondly, don't give them any ammunition to shoot you down. Learning a new business is hard enough; learning a new business with millions of people watching, many of them wanting you to fail, is a heart attack waiting to happen.

Once I'd learned to separate media lights for the flashes of genuine opportunity, I could begin to Obey That Impulse. The brightest light was coming from ABC, the network of the '76 Games. I knew the people—everyone from Howard Cosell to Jim McKay to sports division chief Roone Arledge to deal-maker Irwin Weiner—and felt comfortable with most of them. NBC and CBS were calling too, of course, but I didn't know anybody at either of those companies. So ABC, which really dominated sports coverage at the time, was the natural place to go.

I obeyed the impulse.

I moved from San Jose to Los Angeles in the fall of 1976 and prepared to take my talents from track to television. My first assignment? "Battle of the Network Stars," a television offshoot of the popular "Superstars" competition, in which ABC stars would take on NBC and CBS stars in athletic contests. It might have been corny, but the ratings constantly went through the roof.

I arrived on the outdoor set an absolutely green novice. Aside from being interviewed, I had never done a formal television show in my life. I had never even held a microphone. I stood there, amid snaking wires and technicians talking languages I'd never heard, mentally preparing myself to cohost a national show for a major network with Howard Cosell, the star of television sports in 1976.

I'd met Howard before, of course, but I can't say that he took an immediate shine to me. I was the big name at the Olympic Games, the one voted or at least assumed to be Most Likely to Succeed. After I'd won the Gold, I was watching the boxing finals, which, in '76, featured some of the toughest boxers America has ever produced, including Sugar Ray Leonard.

"These kids have no Hollywood contracts awaiting them," Howard said, very aggressively, on ABC.

I didn't have to think too hard to interpret his meaning: he was talking about me.

Later, I'd approached him at an ABC event. His attitude toward me could have flash-frozen kerosene.

Now I was entering his arena, an arena where I wasn't known as a champion. Now I had to become, in an instant, a sports commentator. I had to hold a microphone, interview people, interact with a TelePrompTer.

A thousand horrors invaded my brain.

Now I had to *act*.

"My dreams are worthless, my plans are dust, my goals are impossible.

   "All are of no value unless they are followed by action.

   "I will act now.

   "Never has there been a map, however carefully executed to detail and scale, which carried its owner over even one inch of ground. Never has there been a parchment of law, however fair, which prevented one crime. Never has there been a scroll, even such as the one I hold, which earned so much as a penny or produced a single word of acclamation. Action, alone, is the tinder which ignites the map, the parchment, the scroll, my dreams, my plans, my goals, into a living force. Action is the food and drink which will nourish my success.

   "I will act now."

            —Og Mandino, The Greatest Salesman
                         in the World

When I needed strength to fuel my ability to *act*—to take the leap—I thought of the story of Roger Bannister, the track-and-field legend who went where no man had ever been before.

Until 1954, no one had ever run the less-than-four-minute mile.

Everyone, from physicians to scholars to athletes, said it was impossible, that the human body just couldn't run a mile that fast. But Bannister, a young premed student, didn't allow himself to be limited by what others told him he could not do. He went out on the fringe, where the Champion Within dwells, and, using two friends as spotters—one pulling him through the first mile, the next challenging him for the second, then the third, then the fourth—began the race against the impossible.

When the stopwatch was clicked on his time, Roger Bannister had run the mile in 3:59 minutes, breaking not only the record but proving that limits are only dictated by the mind, not the body.

After Bannister's record, thousands ran the mile in less than four minutes.

Why? Because one man broke the barrier, proving that it was a glass ceiling. Physical barriers do not exist. We are limited only by our minds! You can jump higher, run faster, do better than you could ever imagine. All you have to do is *believe*, then work and dedicate yourself totally to your mission.

I've always said that success is not measured by heights attained but by obstacles overcome. Now I was facing my own four-minute mile, an arena where my limits far exceeded my strengths, one more obstacle that would separate the Champion Within from the chump.

Once again, I had to stand before the world and read.

I could already envision the headlines: BRUCE JENNER: CAN RUN BUT CAN'T READ.

So I reached back into my decathlon strategies to a lesson I'd learned on how to start the race, to run the 100 meters, when I first fell under the guidance of my coach, L.D. Weldon, and later, when I moved to San Jose: the best way to begin anything is to find a mentor. Who was the one person I needed pulling *for* me instead of *against* me? He stood there, in his conservative sports coat and slacks, with a cigarette hanging out of his mouth and a scowl pointed directly at me.

Howard Cosell.

I didn't retreat. I advanced.

"Mr. Cosell, do you mind if I talk with you for a second?"

The Great One looked up. It was just before the start of the production, and I think Howard could tell that I had no idea of my first—or second or third—move. Howard was ready to hate me, to watch me fail, but I'd caught him off guard.

"No, Bruce, come on over here," he said, thawing only slightly.

We walked to a corner of the television set and I laid it out plain.

"Mr. Cosell, this is my first day on the job," I said. "I've never done this before. I have no idea what's going on and what I should or shouldn't do."

He smiled. His glare softened. And he broke into the faintest glimmer of a smile.

"You've been doing this a long time," I continued. "You're one of the superstars of the business and I really respect your work."

A puff of the cigarette. A nod of agreement. The smile widened considerably.

"I would love to have the opportunity to watch your interviews, to see how to do things right," I continued. "I've got a two-year deal here at ABC and I'd like to learn from the best in the business."

Howard draped his big arm around my shoulder, an arm that, figuratively, never left my shoulder for the duration of my ABC contract.

"Son, stick with me," he said. "I'll take care of you."

And he did. When the producer asked Howard to do an interview, he'd say, "No, I want Bruce to do it, so he can learn." Howard taught me how to work the microphone, to conduct an interview, to look at the camera as what he liked to call "an inanimate object," a mirror which must become your best friend.

With Howard Cosell's help, I got through that first experience without tripping over my own feet or, worse, one of the television cameras. I survived and, with the world's press watching, even the reviews were kind. But I still had a lot to learn. I began traveling the country doing entertaining, off-the-cuff coverage of everything from "Superstars" athletic competitions to volleyball to surfing and auto racing. It wasn't the evening news, but it was a start. There was no script to read; all I had to do, basically, was react: to the events, to the celebrities, to the crowd. I was learning the business.

Then ABC asked me to cohost *Wide World of Sports* with Frank Gifford in a television studio. They told me it would be much the same thing as I'd done in my sports coverage, except for one small thing: I'd have to read a script off the TelePrompTer.

Oh, no! Can you imagine how I felt? No amount of applause or gold medals could give me confidence at that point. Once again, I was that dyslexic kid in the back of the classroom, praying that the teacher would not call upon me to read. But now it wasn't a teacher calling upon me; it was my employer. Once again, I was terrified. I wanted to hide my problem, just like I'd done in school. But where could I hide? I'd be working beside a sports legend, the great Frank Gifford, on one of the highest-rated shows on television.

I got no sleep that night.

When it comes to do or die, you learn to rely on your abilities, not your limitations. You think of a way. My only ability at this point was my energy, enthusiasm and naiveté. I built upon that. I decided that I wouldn't try to become a sportscaster, which, in my case, would have meant a forced, wooden delivery. Instead, I went with a casual, fun-loving, off-the-cuff style—which accommodated not only my personality but my problems with reading.

We filmed in an ABC studio in midtown Manhattan. I didn't know Frank Gifford at the time, although he and Kathie Lee have since become Kris's and my best friends and the godparents of our daughter, Kendall. I was nervous, probably perspiring, and my voice, when it finally emerged, was not as strong as it should have been.

I stared at the TelePrompTer. My eyes worked fine. My brain was ready to receive. But in between lay that gulf, where the ship of reading sank every time. It was as if I'd made my way to the top of a mountain and enjoyed the view but now I had been thrown right back into the valley.

I had reached my Roger Bannister moment, a moment you're invariably going to reach in your own life, when you've got to break through your limits and *act*.

"Don't try to be a sportscaster," I told myself repeatedly. "Just be yourself. Have fun with it, enjoy yourself, put it in your own words, not somebody else's. Get the words in your mind and . . . *go!*"

I stared into the TelePrompTer. The red light turned on and I looked *beyond* it.

I didn't read.

I spoke.

"Hi, this is Bruce Jenner and it's great to be here with the great Frank Gifford on *Wide World of Sports!*"

Did anybody notice? I wasn't reading the script word for word. So of course they did! But the producers and crew were patient, thank goodness, and I worked hard and improved. I *acted,* and the momentum of the action helped carry me through to eventual proficiency in the one area where I was weakest.

I was becoming a spokesperson, all right, a spokesperson for the companies I was involved with. But, more important, I was becoming a spokesperson for myself. The actions I'd directed toward my goal of teaching others what I'd learned were multiplying day by day. I had discovered the secret of champions: that well-directed daily action builds upon itself and leads toward eventual victory.

"You have to erect a fence and say, 'Okay, scale this.'"
—LINDA RONSTADT

It was altogether fitting that the first movie premiere I ever attended was *Rocky*. It was 1976. I had just won the gold medal and, when the lights went down and the story of Rocky Balboa unfolded on screen, I could identify completely. Rocky had used his fists and every ounce of what God had given him for a brain to prove that he was not just another bum from the neighborhood.

I was out to prove that I was more than just another jock running around a track. I was out to prove that my direction in life wasn't circular, repeating itself ad infinitum, but straight ahead and constantly moving forward to the next mountain.

You've got to move forward, always forward. I went from *Wide World of Sports* to a special correspondent's job on *Good Morning America* to eventually hosting the show on David Hartman's days off. I was running the decathlon in television and business, growing from an inexperienced novice to a seasoned pro. America came to know me like family, probably because I seemed, if anything, eminently approachable. I was the happy-go-lucky boy next door, the face of optimistic, post-Watergate seventies America, the guy who loved to disco and never met a person he didn't like.

It was David Hartman and Sara Purcell and Rona Barrett and Bruce Jenner—four friendly faces you'd be comfortable with in your kitchen. I was on the fast track, staying at ABC from 1976 to 1978, then jumping over to NBC, which got the rights to broadcast the '80 Games. Attempting to build a quality sports staff to cover the Games, NBC recruited me at ridiculously phenomenal prices. I had a five-year deal at NBC but stayed for eight, even though the network didn't send crews to the '80 Games because of Jimmy Carter's boycott.

Soon I moved on to the big screen, one action building on another in my quest to prove myself able to handle all the myriad events of real life.

First up was the 1980 TV movie, *Grambling's White Tiger*, the true story of Jim Gregory, the first white football player to play for all-black Grambling College. The movie starred Harry Belafonte, LeVar Burton and, in the starring role, yours truly. The film was named one of the top-ten TV movies of the year, and I felt I was on my way to bigger and better acting roles.

I did eight episodes of *C.H.I.P.S.* and appeared on several other television series, including *Murder, She Wrote*.

Then, also in 1980, I appeared in my first—and only—feature film. It was called *Can't Stop the Music*, and I starred with Valerie Perrine and Steve Guttenberg in an Alan Carr production. The film got a special mention in Michael Sauter's book, *The Worst Films of All Time*. Designed to capitalize on the success of *Saturday Night Fever*, it was the last gasp of disco, starring the Village People, who were represented by a nerdy, straitlaced tax attorney—me.

My character exhibited all the symptoms of someone adrift in life. He had no carefully calculated goals. He didn't understand how every action builds upon itself. He wouldn't have known a "gleam of feeling" if it hit him in the face. He was on his way to nowhere, bouncing from being a stuffy corporate business attorney to representing a group that included a musical Indian, policeman, construction worker and cowboy.

One day, I looked up and I was lost on the same misdirected road.

What I learned from *Can't Stop the Music*—or, as Kris fondly calls it, *Can't Stand the Music*—is that you can't sell a ticket if the interest is gone. I knew we were in trouble with the movie when disco was pronounced dead and young people were blowing up disco records in stadiums before baseball games across America just before our film's opening weekend.

There were a million actors in Los Angeles, so what was I doing playing their game and neglecting my own? What was I becoming a spokesperson for in my life and where had my actions taken me? I had one unique talent—I was an Olympic athlete who had learned how to tap greatness within himself and wanted to show others how to do the same. But now I was stuck voicing the lines of a polyester-suited lawyer, who was everything that I wasn't.

Swept up in Hollywood, I had somehow been swept off the course of my dreams. And when you lose track of your mission in life, you're headed toward a shipwreck. As Ernest Hemingway once said, "You can't confuse momentum with action."

I wish I'd known that back then.

The slide began slowly at first, then began to snowball, until I looked up one day and I was tumbling out of control, taking advice from others who claimed to know what I should be doing instead of listening to the voice of the Champion Within.

I was headed toward the pole vault, where you can raise the bar only so far—the one event in the decathlon where you're guaranteed to eventually fail.

CHAPTER NINE

THE POLE VAULT: HOW TO RAISE THE BAR FROM THE PIT OF FAILURE

You take a 131-foot approach down a narrow rubberized runway with a sixteen-foot tube of fiberglass on your shoulder. At full sprint, you race toward the planting box, which, from afar, looks like a small triangular-shaped hole in the ground. Two strides from the box, you start raising the pole over your head, then, with all of your strength, you jam the pole into the box. You must do this perfectly; the takeoff is critical. A million things can go wrong. The second the pole plants, it bends backwards and fires you off the ground and into the toughest position in track and field: totally inverted with your feet pointed skyward. The velocity is so strong, sometimes it seems that the pole will catapult you straight into the clouds. When you rise to your full height your legs go over the bar and your torso naturally twists as you push off the pole and gain even more velocity. That final thrust is what fires your body over the bar. Then, if you've succeeded, you begin vaulting higher and higher, until you finally reach the height at which you fail. But failure cannot defeat

you. Failure is opportunity, a line on your limits that must
be scaled. So you regroup, rest up and try again.

If you would have looked into my living room window anytime between 1984 and 1990, you would have seen failure personified. Look at that shabby one-room rented house. Who could live there, absolutely alone, with only a television set for company? Why is the house such a mess? Look at those dirty dishes stacked high on the sink and those tired old clothes slung on a curtain rod in the hall. Who is that pale, aimless, twenty-pounds-underweight man at the piano or on the sofa or lugging the golf clubs to and from his battered van? What happened to his unflagging optimism, his boundless energy, his perfect muscle tone, his abiding belief that there is always a brighter tomorrow? Where is the Champion Within, the magic at the center of every human being? What happened to his direction, his motivation, the can-do attitude that raised its arms triumphantly before millions at the Olympic Games, when the press dubbed him Captain America? This is a soul in surrender, a dream adrift.

I am looking into that window now, that window our past keeps open forever in our minds, trying to remember, to sift out the lessons from the pain. Pain was the old shag carpet I walked on. Pain filled the frames on my walls, sat beside me on my throwaway furniture and leaked from the old songs I played on the piano.

I couldn't sense any of this back then. You never can when you're in the middle of it. I could feel neither joy nor pain, just an overall numbness that left me spiritually paralyzed for six long years. But like the last ember in a dying fire, I found something with which to begin anew, something that would allow me to use failure just as it had used me. Only by failing could I learn how to redefine my mission in life and how to begin raising the bar on my aspirations and abilities again. I discovered how to make failure the planting box in which to jam the pole and soar into the clouds, higher and faster than I ever had before.

> *John Denver: "If you're so involved with us, how can you permit all the suffering that goes on in the world? . . ."*
>
> *George Burns: "I don't permit the suffering. You do. Free will. All the choices are yours."*
>
> FROM THE MOVIE OH, GOD

Champions accept failure as part of the climb. They believe in the adage "Nothing attempted, nothing gained." They know that life is a grindstone that can either wear you down or polish you up. They realize that failure is the fire that tempers us for success, that defeat is only a temporary way station on the road to high achievement.

When you've reached the top, it's easy to look down and understand why and where you've stumbled. But when you're stumbling, working so hard to find the sun through the clouds, your vision is impaired, your optimism shrouded.

Having been there, I can guarantee you one thing about failure.

When it begins to happen, you will be the last to know.

Failure can be the most deceptive force on earth. When did it start? And when did I know? I could pinpoint neither times nor dates. All I knew was that I once I was winning and working and then, one day, I was trapped in a twilight zone where everything seemed . . . *normal.*

I didn't refer to it as losing or failing. I called it "coasting." I coasted with golf, working on my handicap but playing mostly to pass the time. I coasted in business, doing speeches only when I needed the money. I coasted emotionally by playing the piano, teaching myself with the Alfred series of piano self-tutor books, working my way up from Volume 1 to Volume 3, until I could play a flawless rendition of the Scott Joplin theme from *The Sting*. I coasted in that little rented house pouring my emotions into those old songs, never realizing what I was missing, because I'd never experienced a fulfilling adult relationship before. I knew how to score points in a game, and that's all I knew. I knew absolutely nothing about how to love myself or anyone else.

There were redeeming aspects about being alone. I was learning to think for myself, to know myself. It was a regrouping, a season to get away from everybody, a period to wipe the slate clean and make room for more. I'd felt yanked and pulled and bullied from so many directions for so long that the only way left for me to go was into retreat. But there was also delusion. I thought I was free, but I had built a prison for myself and I didn't even know I was locked inside.

You will be the last to know.

I had forgotten all about being driven, being obsessed with victory. I had worked so hard for so long, and now it seemed that everyone else in my life had gotten all the rewards. All those years of work, of being on the road twenty-eight days out of each month, night after night in hotel rooms, and all the proceeds had gone to other people. I had been stripped clean: of my money and my motivation.

I had 200 dollars in the bank and was approximately 300,000 dollars in debt.

But the biggest deficiency was in my bankrupt soul. I had given up—that's why I had failed. I had been beaten by the system: in my career, in my two failed marriages, in my associations with others. I had become a cliché: one more seventies person beaten down by the System. One more rising star suddenly faded. One mistake after another—getting married for all the wrong reasons, taking whatever came my way in business, neglecting to create a plan—had led to my solitary existence. At the bottom of it all, I felt that I somehow deserved to fail. I was taking failure personally, not realizing that champions have the ability to separate personal failure from the failure of their undertakings.

Alone, my feelings of inadequacy multiplied. When I looked in the mirror, I didn't like the face staring back. I thought I was unattractive. I didn't even think I could get a date, so I spent my nights at home. I never liked the hook at the end of my nose. I always called it the "Bob Hope skijump nose," and since nobody was there to reassure me, I had no reason to feel that my opinion wasn't true. For the first time in my life, I was on my own. I was free from training schedules, from upcoming competitions, from the controlling forces of others. For the first time in my life, I could do anything I wanted. Maybe it was sort of a rebellion. Maybe it was my way of casting off my old persona, the too-good-to-be-true champion who felt like a failure off the field. Or maybe it was self-punishment. Either way, I went into the office of a Los Angeles plastic surgeon and told him to cut the hook out of my nose.

"Whatever you say, Bruce," said the surgeon.

I never thought anything was wrong with that decision. Not when the surgeon botched the job so badly he had to do it all over again; not when the rag newspapers put me on their front pages, all asking the question "Why?" If I had been in the mood for talking I would have told them, "Because I've always felt unattractive. Because when I look into the mirror, I don't see a champion anymore. I see a thirty-five-year-old man who has no money, no relationships, no motivation."

But nobody asked me anything to my face.

You will be the last to know.

After five years of suffering in self-pity, I finally awoke. It was a gradual change, a building sense of dissatisfaction, of knowing that there had to be more. One night, I finally said to myself, "I'm not happy waking up every morning and not being excited about life."

It's amazing how life will help you once you decide to help yourself. That simple decision—"There is more to life than this"—would change everything for me. Once again, I was standing on the runway with a pole on my shoulder, the bar in sight. Let me show you how high failure allowed me to eventually vault.

> *"We haven't failed. We now know a thousand things that*
> *won't work. So we're that much closer to finding what will."*
> *—THOMAS EDISON*

If you want to take your life to a higher height, you must raise your level of commitment and understand that failure is part of the game. Eventually, we're all going to fail at something. We're all going to reach a height that we just can't clear, an obstacle that we just can't get over. There are two courses of action: you can either pack up your poles and go home—and having done that once in the decathlon, I can guarantee that it leads to nowhere—or you can regather your strengths, refocus your mission and start over again.

Taken in the proper perspective, failure can be the most motivating force on earth. When I became a student of failure, examining case studies throughout history, I discovered that I had also become a student of success. For the missteps of failure are evident in every successful journey, serving as refueling stations at which to refocus on a mission and charge the bar again. The examples of great men and women failing have become emblematic of success: Babe Ruth striking out 1,330 times to get to his near-record 714 home runs; Thomas Edison persisting through 1,200 failed experiments until he finally invented the electric lightbulb; Major General George Goethals failing repeatedly before he succeeded in building the "impossible" Panama Canal. True victory is preceded and seeded by defeat, just as victory in the pole vault is attained only by reaching the height at which you fail and then finding a way to push beyond that limit. All you have to do is stay in the game. There will always be another meet, another opportunity to jump higher, another opportunity to begin again.

During the Depression, a pudgy Vaudevillian named W.C. Fields had reached the height of failure, tells Napoleon Hill in *Think and Grow Rich*. He was financially broke. He had suffered a neck injury. His arena of expertise, vaudeville, was dead. Worst of all, he was sixty years old! Most men would have retired to the old-age village or moved in with the kids. But not W.C. Fields. Failure only made him stronger. He offered to work in the new, untested show business medium—motion pictures—for free. He got work. W.C. Fields had raised the bar on failure.

The activist Mother Jones experienced failure as catastrophe, such a deep and painful experience that it would have stopped most mortals cold. A farm wife in the 1860s, she lost her husband and four children to the plague. Can you image the strength it must have taken for her to begin again? But she did. She moved to Chicago and opened a dress shop, which was totally destroyed by fire. For the third time, she started anew, becoming a leader in the labor movement, leading strikes across America. Tempered by catastrophe, she rose into new realms of achievement.

There is a pattern here. When we persist in our missions, life prepares us for success by leading us through the flames of failure. Marathon runners call it "hitting the wall," that point in the race where it seems you can run no farther, when the fatigue and pain seem too much to take. But only by pushing through that wall can you reach the higher level, a level of almost religious intensity and ecstasy.

The history books are filled with stories of great men and women rising from the ashes of physical disabilities and disfiguring accidents. Helen Keller, born deaf and blind, became the inspiration of millions. Millionaire public speaker, politician and businessman W. Mitchell spent the early part of his life as a Marine. He was burned beyond recognition in a motorcycle accident, then four years later paralyzed from the waist down in a plane crash, requiring sixteen surgeries and untold internal resources, yet he raised the bar with a bang heard around the world. His body a multicolored map of skin grafts, Mitchell ran for Congress with the slogan "Not Just Another Pretty Face." Says Mitchell, "It's not what happens to you, it's what you do about it."

But the story I like best is the story of little David Lofchick of Winnipeg, Canada, which Zig Ziglar recounts so beautifully in his book *See You at the Top.* Born with cerebral palsy, with no motor connection to the right side of his body, David's head hung limply onto his chest and drool constantly flowed out of his mouth. He wasn't expected to ever walk or talk or count to ten. Specialist after specialist told his parents to give up, to put David in an institution. But David's parents were determined. They took him to thirty different specialists until one, after exhaustive tests, finally said, "This little boy is a spastic. He has cerebral palsy. He is never going to be able to walk or talk or count to ten . . . if you listen to the prophets of doom. But I happen to be solution conscious, not problem conscious. I believe there is something that you can do for this little boy if you are willing to do your part."

David's parents followed the doctor's advice. They pushed their son almost beyond human endurance. They worked with him until they were all exhausted. They hired a fitness therapist and built a special gymnasium in the basement of their home. Two years later, while at work, David's parents got the call from the therapist: "Come home. David is ready." Mom, Dad, two sisters and assorted friends and neighbors found David down on all fours, sweat pouring off every inch of his body, getting ready to do a single—*one!*—pushup. When his frail body rose off of the floor in one perfect pushup, there wasn't a dry eye in the house.

When David Lotchick officiated at his Bar Mitzvah on October 23, 1971, the thirteen-year-old boy had done as many as 1,100 pushups in a single day. He had run six miles nonstop. He was a seventh grader studying ninth grade math at school. He rode his bike nonstop, skated on the hockey team and consistently won at table tennis. Today, David Lotchick is a barrel-chested pillar of his community, a happily married husband, father of three and the number one condominium salesman in Winnipeg, a supreme example of raising the bar on circumstances when circumstances try to crush you.

Zig Ziglar puts the story in marvelous perspective. "I wonder how much more David Lotchick would have been had he been given the same chances in life that you and I have been given?" he asks in his speeches. "Finally, it hit me like a ton of bricks. Had he been given *more*, he undoubtedly would have ended up with *less*."

"Happiness is not success," Zig says at the conclusion of his speeches. "Happiness is victory."

I love that line. Happiness is not wealth or accumulation. Happiness is victory, which, by definition, is a successful struggle over an opponent or obstacle. Without struggle, without failure, true victory cannot exist. Or as I like to say, "Success is not measured by heights attained but by obstacles overcome."

One thing I learned in the decathlon was that there are ten separate and individual events. Just because you have a bad performance in one event does not mean you're going to have a bad decathlon score. I learned that once an event was over, no matter the results, I had to throw it out of my mind and face the next challenge with a new, fresh attitude, trying to come up with the best performance possible. The decathlon taught me how to always move forward, to accept the past and then let it go.

Now I had to apply that lesson to my life.

Failure in the pole vault was an opportunity to go back and re-group, to analyze what went wrong and learn how to make it right. Failure in your personal life is the same thing. You have to regroup. I had to drop out for a while to set my sights on a higher level. Once I got back into the game, I learned something startling: that my post-Olympic level of achievement was, in retrospect, almost superficial. Opportunities came to me; I didn't have to pursue them. Whichever bell rang the loudest was the one I'd answer. If I had never stumbled, I would probably have never grown beyond a happy-go-lucky, com-placent actor/athlete/commercial pitchman.

Challenged by failure, I had to search into my soul for more. I had to reinvent myself. I had to go back to the basics. I had been do-ing so many things that just weren't truly me—everything from B movies to way-out sports competitions to appearances at events where I didn't even know the cause. Failure made me go back to the basics: speaking, athletic discipline, health, physical fitness and my major mission of bringing out the best in myself and others.

Once I knew my direction, I could begin to raise the bar on my aspirations and abilities. In that little house, I decided to get serious about the business of life again. In this very mundane existence, I dis-covered that what motivates me is what motivates everyone: a journey. I had always been at my best when I was on a journey, when I had some great challenge out there, when I could see a finish line ahead. For five years, I had been merely existing from one day to the next, without a starting point or a finish line in sight. Now I knew I could erect a finish line in my mind merely by defining it: to be the best Bruce Jenner possible.

I knew the journey was going to be different than before. But at least I knew how to once again get into the game. It was time to be the old Bruce again, the guy who started every day with a ten-mile run, who was enthusiasm personified, who had goals, dreams and tremendous direction. So I got up off the sofa, closed the lid on the piano and stepped out into the sun.

"An evolving spirit must past through every imaginable horror before reaching enlightenment, for there is no way of arriving at light except through darkness. A soul is tempered only through suffering and pain."
—LAURA ESQUIVEL, THE LAW OF LOVE

"When the student is ready, the teacher appears."
—ZEN PROVERB

"Oh my God, I should set the two of you up!"

I had just finished a little celebrity fishing tournament in Ketchikan, Alaska, and Candace Garvey, wife of the baseball great Steve Garvey, had been talking about clothes—specifically about the old sweats I wore almost as a daily uniform—when she suddenly thought of her best friend, Kris, whom she described as someone who "really knows how to dress, really knows how to shop and really has a great sense of style."

Suddenly, something clicked in Candace's mind. She was absolutely certain that Kris and I would make a perfect match and should be immediately introduced.

I wasn't so sure. The last thing I needed, with 200 dollars to my name, was a date with a woman who had her black belt in shopping.

"I don't need a woman who knows how to shop," I said.

Candace nodded. "Well, it would probably never work out anyway because she has four kids," she said.

Four kids? Now, that was a different story. I had four kids, too. I figured anybody with four kids must really love kids, just like I love kids, and that's my kind of woman.

"Okay, I'll go out with her," I said.

I thought Candace might set up the date in a couple of weeks or maybe even a month. But Candace Garvey never acts slowly on anything. Back in L.A. the next day, she immediately called up Kris and set up the blind date.

It was supposed to be dinner after a golf tournament I was playing in at the Riviera Country Club on September 10, 1990. But Kris and Candace decided to stop by the club first for an early peek. There I was standing in my cleats in front of the clubhouse when I stared at the most beautiful sight I'd seen since crossing that finish line in Montreal in 1976: great face, great hair, great body, great clothes! The physical package was perfect. I rushed over, threw my arms around her, gave her a friendly peck on the cheek and said nine words that would come to have true meaning for me:

"At last, in the arms of a real woman!"

We were introduced after the kiss. Then I noticed that Kris seemed to know everybody at the club! This celebrity, that politician, socialites and sports heroes—everybody knew Kris. She was the epitome of friendliness, personality and charm. This would be her first blind date, I later learned, and she was so apprehensive she had planned to take her own car to the restaurant, just in case an escape route became necessary. But once it was time to leave, I said, "Do you wanna go with me?"

"Yeah, okay," she said, and tossed Candace her car keys.

Things were looking up!

At the restaurant, Kris and I started talking and, frankly, I poured out my soul, right there at the table. I didn't stop talking for the whole three-hour meal. I told her I'd been miserable for umpteen years. That I'd spent the last six years of my life in a Southern California version of solitary confinement. I confessed that I hadn't had a date in eight years. That I was almost broke financially and felt broken as a man. I told her I felt like I'd spent the first half of my life preparing to win a prize and, having won it, the second half of my life repenting for it. I admitted that I'd put my life into other people's hands, and now I felt used, abused, manipulated and practically destroyed. "I'm forty years old and I've never been in love," I said at last.

Most women would've left before the appetizer arrived. But Kris is one of those people who loves to be needed. She has tremendous compassion. She would solve the problems of the world if she were allowed. It was like God had tossed her a box and said, "Open it and figure it out."

After our first date, Kris told Candace that she fell in love with my honesty, my sincerity, my sense of humor. There was incredible chemistry between us, that perfect union that's like two bodies of water merging and becoming one. We were soul mates, each filling up the empty spaces in the other. We both knew from the moment we met that we going to be together forever.

When we returned to the Garveys' house, I told Kris that I was leaving for a speech in Miami the next morning, but I added, "I'll give you a call." I called her on the way to the airport. I called her twice from the plane. I called her when I arrived before my speech and when I was leaving afterwards. I called her three times from the hotel that night and twice on my way home the next morning.

We became inseparable. I remember taking Kris to my house for the first time. She stepped inside and saw the dishes in the sink and the old clothes on the rod and the tiny, dried-out Christmas tree lying beside the front door as my home's only source of decoration. She asked me what I'd done during the holidays.

"I just stayed home and had a cup of coffee," I said.

I didn't tell her that I'd also spent the day down in the dumps.

She looked at my "files," unlabeled stacks of folders haphazardly thrown into cardboard boxes, and asked me how my business was going.

"Not very well," I said, honestly.

She looked at my clothes: faded and stretched-out shirts and shorts, socks that never matched, a wardrobe that had not been updated since the Bicentennial. Two weeks after we started dating, I took Kris to a cocktail party for President and Mrs. Reagan. Kris was resplendent in the most perfectly elegant cocktail dress and I showed up in my best brown sports coat, which had a moth hole the size of a quarter in the shoulder, and brown flannel slacks that were left over from the seventies.

Now I realize that my style of dress and the condition of my home reflected the way I felt about myself. How about you? Is there a moth hole the size of a quarter in your jacket? Chances are, there's one of equal circumference in your soul. Are there dirty dishes and unorganized files stacked up on your counters? Chances are, similar stacks are also cluttering up your mind. If chaos rules in your surroundings, chaos will rule your life, and your potential will literally dry up inside of you.

In my case, all that was about to change.

Three weeks after we met, I invited Kris to hear me speak at the Beverly Hilton Hotel. She showed up dressed immaculately as always, and I showed up in my usual circa 1970 tuxedo. Somehow, she saw beyond the old clothes to the potential that exists in us all. Escorting her to her table on my way to the podium, I stared into her eyes and said, "I think we have to so something about shortening that last name of yours."

"Like to what?" she asked.

"Like to Jenner," I said.

Was that a proposal? Kris thought to herself.

Yes, indeed, it was.

The actual proposal came months later, on the day we leased a new house together. Afterwards, at dinner, halfway through a bottle of champagne, I popped the question. We were married at the home of Warner Brothers president Terry Semel and his wife, Jane, five months after we had met. But we became married spiritually much earlier, maybe even that night at the Beverly Hilton, when I went onstage to inspire the audience with tales of my Olympic victory, a story of my past, of tapping into the potential we all have living deep inside of us, of rising from our limits and leaping into the realm of champions. When I looked into the audience, I saw Kris crying, tears literally streaming down her face—not so much because of what she saw onstage but because of what she knew I could once again become: a champion.

> "Adversity is the diamond dust heaven polishes its jewels with."
>
> —ROBERT LEIGHTON

For the first time in my life, I had found someone who believed in me, someone I loved who loved me in return, and, let me tell you, that's a bigger reward than any Olympic gold medal. Find someone who will put their heart and soul behind you and, conversely, someone you can put your heart and soul behind—it's better than having the wind at your back in a 1,500-meter race. Having someone in your life to whom you are totally committed is the foundation on which you can build your new life. No matter what failures you have experienced in your previous relationships, remember that there is always the opportunity to love and live again. Never turn your back on your emotions, for they are quite literally the heart of your existence. Without them, no amount of success can be real.

A few weeks into our courtship, which had quickly turned into our engagement, I became so overwhelmed with emotion that I stopped the car and pulled over to the side of the road and told Kris exactly how I felt: how I was in love for the first time; how I felt my life changing, expanding, growing; how I felt a calling from deep within me; how I felt like working, building a future, committing myself to a lofty goal. It was the first time I'd felt such commitment since the decathlon.

"I want to work again and build a life," I said.

It's been said that beliefs are merely ideas that we hold to be true. Kris taught me to believe in myself again, to love myself, which is the most important love in the world. Once I learned to love myself and to believe in my innate talents, I could begin to consistently raise the bar of my life again. Positive affirmations really work. We all speak to ourselves unconsciously and, frequently, consciously. Speak to yourself in terms of victory, not defeat. Become your own best cheerleader. Realize that you must love yourself before you can experience true, abiding love with others.

In his 1969 book, *Self-Love,* Robert Schuller writes, "Self-love is discovering the greatness that lies slumbering deep within you. . . . Love yourself or you will die spiritually. If you do not love yourself, you cannot love your neighbor. If you do not love people, you will not be able to love God. If you do not love yourself and you do not love people and do not love God, you are a dead man who is walking, sexing, sleeping, working, breathing, eating, excreting. *Above all else, know this: You have the freedom to form your own estimate of yourself.*

Be sure of this—self-estimation will determine what your self-development will be. Believe it. You can be greater than you believe at this moment."

A sense of self-love ignited that greatness that had been slumbering deep within me, and I began to systematically cast off the baggage of my previous life. Once I did that, I began to literally blossom in ways I never imagined. I called Goodwill to pick up my throwaway furniture, threw out my old clothes and left my one-room house with two suitcases and a couple of boxes full of files. I never looked back.

Kris and I took my 1976 van, which had never seen a vacuum cleaner, and gave it away to somebody for a dollar. In the house we leased together, my days became consumed with building a future, firmly putting family first. I eventually replaced the old van with a new Acura NSX. I replaced the old clothes with Armani jackets, new trousers, Italian shoes, shirts, ties, pocket handkerchiefs. The "free" tuxedo that Beverly Hills clothing consultant David Rickey had given me to replace the obviously dated one he'd seen me wearing during one of my speeches was the genesis of an entire new wardrobe. I began ordering suit after suit from David Rickey, until his impeccable clothing lined my closets. Pretty soon, Kris's hairdresser and manicurist were coming to the house—to work on both of us.

One day, I looked at myself in the mirror and barely recognized myself. I had gained ten pounds. I was draped in Armani from the socks on my feet to the tie at my neck. My eyes glowed with happiness; my skin radiated good heath. I wore a smile worthy of a toothpaste commercial.

People began to talk.

"Have you seen Bruce Jenner lately?"

"What's with Bruce?"

"What's with the new clothes?"

This may sound like an exercise in vanity, but it was actually a major step in my reinvention. Your clothing, the way you present yourself, the people you surround yourself with—all of these factors speak volumes about you before you even open your mouth. If you don't think clothing matters—and I certainly didn't!—just consider a costume party. What happens when you put on the clothes of a pirate? A devil? An angel? You become your costume. What happens when you put on the costume of a bum? You become slovenly. What happens when you put on the costume of a winner? You begin to act like a winner. Masquerade as a winner until you become one. It's better than masquerading as a loser!

Master showman Florenz Ziegfeld, who ordered 250,000-dollar diamond necklaces for his showgirls to wear in his Broadway shows, was urged by his associates to use rhinestones instead of the real thing because no one would know the difference. "The girls will know the difference," said Ziegfeld, who knew that what we wear has a direct effect on what we can become.

If you dress like you're a success, then you're on your way to becoming one. Reaching your full potential is a stairway that you must take one step at a time. If the shoes on your feet are the first step, then buy new shoes! Everything on your exterior is symbolic of the way you feel inside.

Remember: you only have one chance to make a first impression.

Just like the clothes that you wear, you must take care of yourself physically. The designer who can make a slovenly body look fit has not yet been born. Beneath those new clothes must lie an equally new and healthy body. This is the vehicle of the Champion Within. It all comes down to pride in yourself, in being the best you can possibly be. Why would you live in an immaculate home and dress in incredible clothes only to neglect the most important thing in your life, the very center of your existence, your health? Take your health seriously or your health will find a way to get your attention.

In my case, that gold medal couldn't lift a single weight or do a single pushup, and my body showed the result of six years of neglect. Living with Kris, feeling part of a family and eating regularly, I had quickly gained ten pounds. But I hadn't been to a gym in almost fifteen years. However, I didn't like the idea of my wife going to Gold's Gym and working out alone with a male trainer. We were connected in every way but exercise. So I tagged along—even though I wasn't very excited about it. I had convinced myself that I didn't need to go to a gym. Why would Bruce Jenner, Olympic champion, need to seek out others to get into shape? I didn't require a trainer when I prepared for the Games, even though these days every Olympian is surrounded by literally teams of trainers. So why would I need a trainer now?

"I don't need a trainer, so why do you?" I asked Kris. "Why don't you let me train you? That's what people would pay me to do."

But Kris was insistent. So I followed her to Gold's, merely to watch her workout. One day, however, Kris was sick and asked me to take her scheduled workout.

"Okay, honey, this will be cute," I laughed in a macho tone. "I'll walk in and say, 'Okay, Perry, you've got me for an hour.' He'll get a kick out of that."

I did exactly that, and I learned something important: we never know what awaits behind a door until we walk through it. I'd never been worked out so hard in my life! When I left, my hands were shaking so badly that I could barely get my key into the car door. The next day, I'd never felt so *good!* The adrenaline, so long stagnant, flowed anew. I started working out at Gold's Gym with Perry three times a week.

Make an analysis of your own physical condition, then do something about it. You don't have to be an Olympic champion or train like one. But when you work out and take your health seriously, you're creating a tangible power that will literally radiate from within.

Kris asked to see my gold medal. I dug it out of my sock drawer and gave it to her. She asked to see the many medals I'd won in my years of preparing for the Games. I took her to the attic, where an entire inventory of my past—medals, newspaper clippings, presidential telegrams, magazine covers, memorabilia going back to my high school track days—was all packed in twelve bulging old boxes. It was so symbolic: my major accomplishments, like my life, had been packed up and hidden away in an attic. It was as if my life had been flash-frozen in a time capsule the moment the Olympics were over and then buried, along with my ambition.

It took Kris three weeks to sort through the twelve boxes. But when she was finished she mounted every medal in a frame and every piece of memorabilia in Plexiglas and surprised me with it all, neatly framed on several walls, when my father was visiting.

My dad and I broke down and cried.

Where are the medals in your life? Mounted proudly on a wall or hidden away in an attic? Take them out and allow them to shine! It's amazing what even the thought of past achievement can do for your tomorrows. Be proud of your accomplishments. Use them to build upon in the future. These are the accessories of achievement, the totems champions use to push themselves on to greater victories.

We next turned our attention to my office, even though neither of us had ever really worked in an office before. Kris had learned through osmosis; she had always associated with very powerful figures in Hollywood and her best friends included business leaders from around the world. So we hired an assistant, bought a computer, developed a first-class press kit and began sending it out to speakers' bureaus, trying to expand my prospects for public speaking.

"There should be Bruce Jenner clothes, Bruce Jenner exercise videos, Bruce Jenner this and Bruce Jenner that," Kris said. "But we'll build this house one speech at a time."

We planted seeds: mailing lists, brochures, phone calls, networking. Those seeds began to sprout big time. My speaking engagements increased dramatically. We had a million ideas on how to "take Bruce to the next level": speaking tours, videos, infomercials, books. I was more than ready. I was jazzed! I had risen from failure to build a foundation of family, filled my heart with love, made my exterior appearance reflective of the incredible new spirit that had grown inside of me and now, only now, could I once again dedicate 150 percent to my mission. Life was fun again. Life was once again an incredible journey.

Just as I'd done in the 1972 Olympic Games in Munich, when I stood in the shadows and looked four years ahead toward the victory platform that I wanted to stand atop at the '76 Games, I could see the finish line in my new life. I had my feet in the blocks and had begun the race anew. Once again, I was determined not to stop until I won.

We created our own slogan: *If somebody says no to me, I'm talking to the wrong person.* This must become the philosophy of your new life. If you knock on one door and it closes, go on to the next door. Before, if people said no, I took it personally. I'd say, "Okay. They don't like me. I'm outta here." But that's a cop-out. You have to be determined; you have to become unstoppable. If you truly believe in what you're doing, never let no be the final answer. Persistence and drive are the prerequisites for accomplishment.

Life is all about challenge. Those who challenge and push the limits of convention are the ones who are going to get more out of life. So be assertive. Ask and you'll receive. Be creative. Life does not happen under military rule. You're a freethinking individual in the freest country on earth. Yet most of us are forever trapped in indecision, doubt and fear, freezing on the blocks before the race even begins. Create your own opportunities and then take advantage of them. No one can do that for you.

Kris and I kept knocking on doors until they began opening with a resounding regularity. Our business grew apace with our abiding love and respect for each other. I was not only "back," in show business terms; I felt as if I had just been born. The astounding new heights at which I was now vaulting made my old life seem like a game of leapfrog. I learned a supreme lesson: the game is never over. What doesn't kill you really does make you stronger. No matter the lows, there's always room for growth, for expansion. You can always take your life to the next level. All you have to do is decide where you're want to be in your life. Then have the courage to go after it and not quit until you've achieved your dreams.

I had climbed out of the pit of failure and was enjoying an awesome new view. Now I was ready to throw the javelin, which, being a long spear that must be thrown perfectly through an tiny imaginary point in the air, is the essence of focus, direction and mission.

CHAPTER TEN

THE JAVELIN: HOW TO KEEP FOCUSED ON YOUR MISSION

The javelin is a thin spear, the ancient weapon of hunters and warriors, the most predominant implement depicted in Grecian art. Today's aluminum javelin is extremely light, so light that, when released, it's tremendously affected by the elements, especially the wind. If it's not released perfectly it will go left or right, too high or too low. That's what makes the event so difficult. To throw the javelin correctly, you have to be absolutely focused, imagining a point a few feet in front of you, an imaginary inch-and-a-half circle in the air, just a fraction of an inch bigger than the circumference of the javelin. This is your target, and the javelin must pass through it like it would through a bull's-eye. You take a running start, plant your feet, then bring the javelin back over your shoulder, as far back as you possibly can reach. Most people think you throw the javelin, but it's not a throw. It's a strong and steady pull. You pull it over your ear and release it with as much velocity as possible, directing all your power toward the Point. Once it's released you've lost your control over the javelin's direction. Now the elements take over and your ability to focus on the Point will have dictated whether you've succeeded or failed.

Like the decathlete hurls the javelin, you have to direct your life straight through an imaginary point in the air which represents your major mission, never allowing it to touch the sides. When the elements threaten to buffet your life like the wind buffets the javelin, you must remain steadfast, always pushing toward the direction of your dreams.

Your goals are your target, your Point. If you're off even by a quarter of an inch, you'll miss them completely, flying left or right, too high or too low, just as the slightest deviation from the Point causes the decathlete to miss his mark in the javelin event. As the poet Williams Matthews once said, "The first law of success . . . is concentration—to bend all the energies to one point, and then go directly to that point, looking neither to the left or to the right."

In life, as with the javelin, you have to achieve perfect balance, perfect symmetry, perfect focus.

To me, the definition of focus is knowing exactly where you want to be today, next week, next month, next year, then never deviating from your plan. Once you can see, touch and feel your objective, all you have to do is pull back and put all your strength behind it, and you'll hit your target every time.

Walk through life with blinders on, however, and you won't even be able to find a target, much less strike one.

To show how attention is a prerequisite for action, Mihaly Csikszentmihalyi, in his landmark 1990 book, *Flow*, uses the analogy of driving down a busy highway. Cars and people whiz by on all sides, but you don't notice them. Perhaps a particular car might catch your attention and you'll steal a second glance. But, for the most part, you are lost in your own world, while the other worlds that surround you speed by unnoticed. "It is attention that selects the relevant bits of information from the potential millions of bits available," writes Csikszentmihalyi. "It takes attention to retrieve the appropriate references from memory, to evaluate the event, and then to choose the right thing to do."

Life is much the same way. You are going through your day, routines in place, rushing to get to the five o'clock bell, never noticing the worlds of opportunity that surround you on all sides. Attention takes effort. Attention takes time. Attention takes focus. You must stop, think and listen. You must train your mind to see the opportunities that surround you.

Focus is the ability to make life real, to concentrate on a goal and make it happen. Without focus, achieving your dreams is as impossible as reading a license plate on a car speeding down the highway at 100 miles per hour.

"Some people learn to use this priceless resource effectively, while others waste it," writes Mihaly Csikszentmihaly "The mark of a person in control of consciousness is their ability to focus attention at will, to be oblivious of distractions, to concentrate for as long as it takes to achieve a goal, and not longer. . . . Attention is like energy in that without it no work can be done. . . . Hence attention is our most important tool in the task of improving the quality of experience."

In their 1960 book, *Success Through a Positive Mental Attitude*, Napoleon Hill and Clement Stone show that the power of focus is the ability to recognize gold where others see only stone. In a story about Crystal Mountain in Darby, Montana, Hill writes that those who lived around Darby had grown accustomed to seeing the mountain's ledge of sparkling crystal, a white formation that had been around so long that it had given Crystal Mountain its name. They saw only stone; it took two outsiders named A. E. Cumley and L. I. Thompson to focus not on the rock but on the treasure that was literally buried within it.

These two outsiders climbed to the top of Crystal Mountain, chipped off a piece of the ledge and brought it back to town. Right there in the Darby—*in plain sight of the entire town!*—was a wealth of the very crystal Cumley and Thompson held in their hands, a crystal known as beryllium, used in atomic energy research. They staked a claim and, almost overnight, became millionaires. From that day forward, trucks began hauling tons of the beryllium down from Crystal Mountain, where, at the bottom of the mountain, representatives of U.S. Steel and the U.S. government were "virtually waiting with dollar bills in their hands," writes Hill.

Gold surrounds us! All we have to do is take the time and develop our focus, and we can search it out.

Let me show you how to discover treasure in your own life by focusing on your mission and then, through focus, making it real.

"The giants of the race have been men of concentration, who have struck sledge-hammer blows in one place until they have accomplished their purpose. The successful men of today are men of one overmastering idea, one unwavering aim, men of single and intense purpose."
—ORISON SWETT MARDEN, AMERICAN AUTHOR

In the ancient Olympic Games, focus was everything. From boyhood, every Olympian's mission was spent in single-minded pursuit of victory. Wars were suspended. Personal time did not exist. The Olympian was, by definition, born and bred for victory and, until victory was attained, neither time nor attention was squandered on anything else.

For 1,100 years the Games thrived, generation after generation devoting their lives to their one pivotal moment, when they could prove their worth in one awesome "sledge-hammer blow" before the gods and all of Greece. But the glory of the original Olympic Games could not last. The Roman Empire conquered the Greeks and, in 66 A.D., the emperor Nero turned the games into a farce, insisting on winning all competitions himself. From that point on, Romans flooded the competitions, oblivious to the Greeks' lofty traditions. A few years later, barbarians ravaged the sacred shrine of Olympia. In 394 A.D., Emperor Theodosius of Rome abolished the Games. The statue of Zeus was hauled away; the remaining temples were later burned. A century later, an earthquake reduced the area to ruins. Once the center of Grecian honor, Olympia had become a ghostland. No one lived there, prayed there or played there. The Olympics were dead and would stay dead for fifteen centuries.

What happened? The Games lost their focus, their mission, their very narrow definition. They became something for everybody, a free-for-all, instead of the hallowed shrine of the Greek ideal. Instead of being the epitome of focus, the Games became a fracas, a brawl.

Such is the story of many a misguided life.

Focus!

This is the one-word secret of champions.

In the modern world, focus is not easy to attain. Most of us spend so much time merely trying to deal with the daily routine of life that we never get to our dreams. So we simply grab enough sustenance to get by. We take what we can get out of life. We accept our lot instead of pushing the envelope. We look at the big picture instead of focusing on the more narrow terrain of our dreams. We get what we deserve. And when our time on earth is ending, we scratch our heads and wonder what went wrong.

Those determined to fulfill their dreams focus their energies on extremely specific objectives and then, with single-minded purpose, go after them with all their hearts and minds. After one goal is achieved a new one is set, and the process continues.

Producer Ken Kragen wrote about the importance of focus in his 1994 book, *Life Is a Contact Sport*. When he started work on his Hands Across America project, which would result in 5.5 million Americans standing hand in hand from the Atlantic to the Pacific, Kragen met with Coca-Cola's head of marketing, Sergio Zyman, to discuss Coke's participation in the event. Zyman's first question: "What are the objectives for this thing?"

Zyman knew the value of focus. He keeps a copy of the Coca-Cola business plan on the back of his office door, so when people arrive to excitedly promote their own proposals to the company he can instantly determine whether or not they fit into Coke's long-term mission. "If it doesn't, we're not interested," says Zyman.

Kragen learned some important lessons from Sergio Zyman that day. First, he learned the lesson of creating a narrowly focused objective, which, Kragen's writes, could be boiled down to a single sentence: "Fill the line," meaning assemble the 5.5 million people for Hands Across America. Secondly, he learned the power of focus, employing it so strictly that when a major motion picture company offered to give a star-studded premier for Hands Across America, an event that would have diverted substantial energy from "filling the line," Kragen said thanks, but no thanks. "I saw this as a peripheral effort that would detract from our limited resources and central goal," he writes.

Think about Kragen's one-sentence mission statement: "Fill the line." That one sentence gave him immediate focus, the ability to determine whether or not the many possibilities that came his way would either propel or distract from his mission. It allowed him to run his event, to pursue his objective, instead of being buffeted by the elements that faced him, many of which could cloud his vision and derail his dreams.

What is your one-sentence mission statement? If you don't have one, create one right now. Boil your life's goal down to its essence, then write down one simple sentence that encapsulates your dream. Use that sentence to weigh each opportunity that comes your way. Choose life—don't merely accept whatever comes your way.

In my case, after the '72 Olympic Games, I could boil my mission down to one simple sentence: *I was going to win the gold medal in the decathlon in '76.* For four years, that became my focus. Anything that propelled me toward fulfilling my mission to win was accepted; anything that detracted from that mission was rejected.

In his 1987 book, *The Achievement Factors,* B. Eugene Griessman quotes three perfect examples of successful focus:

Mario Andretti once defined his mission statement with laserlike precision. "Racing is all I want to do," he said. "I don't have a plan A and a plan B. This is the only place I find fulfillment."

At bat, home-run hitter Hank Aaron found a way to block out all distractions and focus fully on the pitcher in front of him. "I would take my baseball cap, pull it down over my face, and look through a little hole in my cap, and focus on nothing but him. . . . I'm not bragging, but I think I focus on things very well."

As a child, U.S. Supreme Court Justice Sandra Day O'Connor learned how to focus on what was important in her life—her schoolwork—in the presence of a grandmother whom she loved but who loved to talk incessantly, even when her granddaughter was trying valiantly to study. "I learned to just automatically respond to what she might be saying at the appropriate intervals, but never let it deter me from concentrating on what I was doing," O'Connor remembers.

Asked to name the prerequisite for success in any field, Thomas Edison, who attended formal school for only three months, who was pronounced "stupid" by his teachers and classmates, replied that success was predicated on "the ability to apply your physical and mental energies to one problem incessantly without growing weary."

Focus is the force of champions. Focus hard and long enough on your mission and you will find yourself in the process known as "flow," a transcendent experience when what you're doing becomes so natural, so effortless, that you forget about time and space and become one with your activity. Once you achieve flow, you won't need to check your one-sentence mission statement to know if you're on the right course. You will know that you're doing *exactly* what you were intended to be doing on this earth.

I experienced flow time and time again during the decathlon, when, by focusing on one sport and one sport only for almost a decade, I accessed the Champion Within in the heat of hundreds of competitions. Having been in that state, I can tell you this is what life is all about. There's nothing magical about it. It's just that when you have a mission and a focus in life your existence takes on an enthusiasm, a vitality, that borders on magic.

A great example of focus occurred several decades ago when Tom Dempsey, born with a stub for a right arm and without half a right foot, achieved his dream of playing professional football. According to *Success Through a Positive Mental Attitude* by Napoleon Hill and Clement Stone, his parents had an artificial wooden foot in a special square-toed kicking shoe made for Tom, and the boy practiced kicking field goals, day after day. His skills steadily increasing, he progressed through high school football and then made the starting roster of the New Orleans Saints. Tom knew how to focus on a clearly defined mission: to be a great field goal kicker.

In the final two seconds of one pivotal game, when the score was tied 17–17 between the New Orleans Saints and the Detroit Lions, Tom Dempsey was called in to attempt a field goal. The distance—sixty-three yards—seemed impossible. But Tom Dempsey focused on the goalposts, not on the impossibility of the distance. He drew back his foot and kicked.

The ball sailed straight through the uprights.

The Saints won the game, 20–17.

Everybody said it was a miracle.

"Tom Dempsey didn't kick that field goal, God kicked it," said Lions linebacker Wayne Walker.

God might have helped, but it was Tom Dempsey's ability to focus over years and years of developing his skills that sent that football flying.

Starting over in my life gave me the opportunity to redefine my goals and then to redirect my mission. I had to control the flight of my life and not allow the elements to control me. I had to once again focus on the Point of my existence, then direct all of my energies toward that Point. I had to go back to study the lessons I'd learned in throwing the javelin.

First step? To focus on your mission, you have to first define it. Chances are, you've already stated it a millions times before, probably as a joke or as cocktail party conversation or merely as a passing thought. It starts with something like, "Man, if I owned the world, I'd—"

Fill in the second half of that sentence.

What would you do if you owned the world? If you can decide on what you really want in life, you have found your mission.

At least that was the case with me.

"He is a licensed pilot with his own aircraft corporation. He won a water-skiing championship. He has raced automobiles at Daytona and Sebring, raced powerboats and mountain bikes and soon will drive a Humvee all-terrain vehicle in a two-week road rally through Africa. He has been a broadcaster, producer, promoter, actor, author of several books, guest host of 'Good Morning America,' and a judge at the Miss America pageant. He has his own line of fitness

*products, has done more motivational speaking than any-
one since Norman Vincent Peale, more TV infomercials
since Kathie Lee Gifford. . . . The last American to win the
Olympic decathlon, Bruce Jenner crossed a finish line in
Montreal on June 30, 1976, and never looked back. There's
just no stopping him. A dyslexic child, Jenner, now 46,
seems to have spent his life overcompensating for a reading
disability by doing the things that others merely read
about, making up for lost time. His battle cry once was 'Go,
Bruce, Go.' Obviously, nobody told him to slow down."*
—MIKE DOWNEY, LOS ANGELES TIMES, JUNE 23, 1996

Focus is the secret of a life of accomplishing myriad things at
once, of constant motion, constant growth, constant enthusiasm, constant action. It's the tool I use to run the decathlon of my life, bouncing from diapering my daughter to delivering a motivational speech
before an audience of 35,000 to appearing on countless television
shows to running three different companies with my wife, Kris: Bruce
Jenner Aircraft, which brokers private planes to executives; Team
Jenner Nutritional Products, our nutritional products company; Jenner Communications, which handles my speaking engagements and
personal appearances.

I discovered that I could accomplish anything if I could focus on
it. First, I had to define my mission in a sentence. I knew what it was
about: to pass on what I'd learned about unleashing the Champion
Within and create a fulfilling life for myself and my family.

To help you learn how to define your mission in life, let me show
you the process I went through in defining mine. For years, I had
given the same speech, without even realizing that at its root lay my
mission statement. In the speech, I talked about the Olympic Games
and how I had somehow tapped deep into the core of myself and drew

out an awesome power that I didn't even know existed. I never gave that power a name. I just assumed that it was the result of training, preparation and pushing beyond physical pain.

To be able to pass that power on to others, I had to define it, just as you must define your own mission by giving it a name. I had to catch the lightning and put it in a bottle before I could focus on it.

"What's the name of your speech?" Kris asked me one day.

"'Olympic Memories,'" I replied.

That didn't sound like much of a name, much less one with a narrow focus. I thought about it awhile. What *had* I been talking about for so many years? What have you been talking about? Think about it long and hard enough and you'll know your mission. For me, it was all about my belief that down deep within lies a greatness, and that greatness, if recognized and given a chance to grow in a fulfilling arena, can propel us to heights unimagined. Helping others find this greatness in themselves is my way of giving something back, of contributing something vital. I've always felt that a person is defined by what they contribute and give back to life. It's one thing to accomplish great heights, but it's even more of an accomplishment when you pass the potential for success on to someone else.

When you're trying to discover what you'd most like to get in life, start by asking yourself what you'd most like to give. What would you like to contribute? What would you like to give back? If you're buffeted by the elements, merely trying to live one day to the next, you probably can't give back much.

We would all like to leave behind a mark in this world. Some people build monuments to themselves in the form of buildings, stores, landmarks. Others range from saintly individuals like Mother Teresa to wealthy philanthropists, who leave a legacy of help, often through grants and contributions to foundations. Still others are just average men and women acting as volunteers, giving nothing more than their time, which also has the ability to change lives. When you give money, it's worthwhile, but when you give time, you give a part of your life. Money, when you have it, is easy to give away. But giving time is the essence of sacrifice, because time is our most valuable currency.

Decide on what you'd ultimately like to give back. Chance are, that decision can light a pathway for you to follow.

"What do I want to give back?" I asked aloud.

Right then I knew the answer. The Games had been such an incredible experience, and my victory at that time motivated others in ways I couldn't even imagine. I wanted to make that victory live on, to make it more than just one win for one person, a victory to help others realize the potential in their own lives.

"What's the ultimate name for a winner?" Kris asked.

"A champion," I said.

By defining my mission statement—to unleash the Champion Within in myself and others—I had discovered the focus for the rest of my life. Now I could determine whether the infinite possibilities that came my way would propel or detract from my mission.

My speaking career was a natural. I could stand before an audience and tell them how I unleashed the Champion Within and how they could do it, too. I could receive the instant gratification of helping others awaken what I had so resoundingly awakened in myself.

But I quickly discovered that speaking engagements were only the beginning of accomplishing my goals. To grow, I had to move beyond one-shot jobs where you get a paycheck when the speech or project is completed and then walk away. The essence of focus is creating equity, value, reserves that multiply and flow into *your* pocket, not others'. That, to me, is the essence of being in control of your life instead of allowing other people to control you.

You have to become your own boss.

Kris and I set out to build a business that created equity in ourselves. We had to create companies that Kris and I owned and operated. The first thing that came our way was something called the Super Step, an exercise machine that a company approached Kris and me to promote in a television infomercial. We were skeptical at first. We wanted to see the product. When the developers brought it over, I was impressed, but I thought it needed some changes. They were willing to make the changes, and when they brought the finish product back, I said, "This works." Here was an inexpensive way to get good cardiovascular exercise in the home. I checked it against my one-line mission statement. It reduced the risk of heart disease and help users slim down, muscle up and live longer and better.

We signed on.

Pretty soon, our infomercial was being aired 2,000 times each month, in seventeen languages. From that foundation, more television work beckoned. Now, however, we did not accept one-shot TV series or B movies. Instead, each appearance was aimed toward unleashing the Champion Within.

I was focusing on my dream. Next, Kris and I began to focus on creating equity for ourselves in business, casting ourselves into ownership instead of merely employee positions. If you want to build financial freedom in your life, you have to take some risks. Working for others, building financial freedom for them, is the safe and easy route. But to me true success is being in control of your destiny in an ownership position. Be willing to take the gamble to start your own business, to develop your own ideas and follow them wherever they lead, to create equity for yourself. That is the only route to true financial freedom.

I found a way to focus on my mission and I was entering the transcendence of flow: effortless action. I had defined my Point and my direction: to use my strengths as a public speaker and become a spokesman for the Champion Within. It was a narrow focus but one that could encompass many things: from my business to my personal relationships.

By defining your Point you can discover a place to come from in your life. Then you'll be ready to narrow your focus on your dreams.

> *"The first rule of success, and the one that supersedes all others, is to have energy. It is important to know how to concentrate it, how to husband it, how to focus it on important things instead of frittering it away on trivia."*
>
> —MICHAEL KORDA

How do you refocus your life toward mission instead of "frittering it away on trivia"? I have discovered four major ways.

CHANGE YOUR INNER VOCABULARY.

In an audiotape called *Living Beyond Miracles,* Deepak Chopra and Wayne Dyer discuss the scientific estimation that the typical human being has 60,000 thoughts a day. But 95 percent of those thoughts are the same as the ones we thought the day before. Think about that! Every day your thoughts are a loop, and your life is run according to the tape you play repetitively in your brain, one thought after another, 60,000 times each day, assuring you that you are whatever you think you are.

Carefully consider your own 60,000 daily thoughts. What are you telling yourself? Are you giving yourself affirmations for victory or excuses that continuously open the door to failure? You've got to change that tape by refocusing your mind. Sit back. Relax. Focus. *Shhhhhhh!* It's said that God lives in the silences. Listen to them. Experience them. Then listen to the language of your heart. What is it saying? If it's a barrage of negativity, then punch the stop button on your mental tape recorder, hit rewind and make a new tape. This is literally the soundtrack that your life follows. Make it a glorious song of success, a symphony of victory.

In the Tom Landry–era Dallas Cowboys' locker room, a banner was hung that read, A MAN'S LIFE IS IN DIRECT PROPORTION TO HIS COMMITMENT TO EXCELLENCE. Not a bad tape to run in a player's mind. Or consider the mantra of basketball great Shaquille O'Neal: TWISM, reads a golden medallion Shaq wears around his neck. It stands for "The World Is Mine."

That isn't meant to sound arrogant; it's inspirational. The world *is* yours! All you have to do is claim it. What is better? Saying "The world is mine" or "The world is everybody else's" or "The world is out to get me—and pardon me while I barely exist in it"? Change your inner vocabulary and you'll change your focus.

FOCUS ON ONE THING AT A TIME.

No person alive can effectively accomplish a hundred things at once. But the hundred tasks, when taken one at a time, can be easily accomplished. One day at the Jenner household is all the proof that you will ever need. There I am, the Olympic champion, changing diapers, carpooling, making the kids' breakfasts, fielding phone calls, reading faxes, getting to the office, meeting the demands of a minute-by-minute schedule, writing letters, signing autographs, picking the kids up at school, flying off to a speech and flying back the same night in time to cook dinner, spending quality time with my wife. . . . The only way I am able to accomplish all these things in twenty-four hours is by realizing that every day is twenty-four hours long. As the writer Richard Cecil, author of *Einstein's Brain*, says, "The shortest way to do many things is to do only one thing at once." Don't try to do everything at once. Organize your life. Allot each task to a particular time, and then focus on one task at a time. You'll amaze yourself at what you can accomplish.

CLEAN THE ROOMS OF YOUR MIND.

"Your mind, which is yourself, can be likened to a house," writes American author John McDonald. "The first necessary move is to rid that house of all but the furnishings essential to success." Raise your standards. If you'll accept anything, chances are getting something of value becomes a crapshoot. But as author Somerset Maugham said, "If you expect the best, chances are you'll get it." When I was accepting whatever came my way, my life moved in a circular direction, a stagnant cycle. But once I decided to control my own ship, to become the master of my destiny, then my life assumed a straightforward path, allowing me to travel as fast and precisely as a perfectly thrown javelin. Focus on everything that comes your way; make sure that your every action propels your mission forward instead of taking you back to where you've already been.

KEEP YOUR EYE ON THE TARGET.

This is so elementary that most people take it for granted. When you drive, you must keep your eyes on the road or you'll get lost at best, end up in an accident at worst. But in life, most of us never bother to look where we're going. If you feel lost right now, then you probably are! If you don't know your mission in life, take some time to reevaluate and create a mission statement. If you know your mission but are not moving forward, stop and reevaluate. Then focus on it as clearly as you would a road map.

The story of Moses bringing his people out of Egypt is a classic example of focus, retold by author Walter Russell Bowie in William J. Bennett's 1993 book, *The Book of Virtues.*

Having crossed the sea, escaping Pharaoh's chariots, the Israelites were free. But as they trudged mile after mile for forty years through the desert, they were plunged into a wilderness of woe. With the intense sun blistering their skin, without a shade tree in sight, without food or even the promise of finding water, many of them began to complain to Moses. Maybe, they said, they would have been better off staying as slaves in Egypt. "There we had meat to cook, and plenty of bread," Bowie quoted the Israelites as crying. "And here you have brought us out of the wilderness to kill us with hunger."

Moses kept his focus. God had given him a mission. God would send them help. God sent plenty. Oases appeared. Quail fell to the ground. Manna, the bread of heaven, covered the desert bushes.

The Israelites trudged on toward the mountains, where they once again grew thirsty and increasingly demanding, asking Moses, "Is this what you brought us out of Egypt for—to kill us with thirst?"

Moses kept his focus. He led them to a rock which he struck with his staff and water began to flow from it. Then he led them to another oasis, full of green trees and bubbling streams, so beautiful that the Israelites wanted to stay there forever.

Moses kept his focus. He insisted they trudge forward over even rockier paths, which offered them even more reasons to turn back, to forget the Promised Land, to return to bondage rather than triumph in freedom. One particularly hard night, the weary Moses climbed to the top of the mountain called Sinai while the Israelites slept. He asked God what He wanted him to show his tribe. Moses was given the Ten Commandments, the laws for living, which his tribe carried high as they continued the march over increasingly tough terrain, facing repetitive trials and tribulations.

The Israelites' grumblings grew louder. Their desire to return to Egypt, where they at least knew the rules, instead of continuing a trek to a land of uncertainty, grew with each passing mile. Each time Moses heard their cries, he asked God to give him strength, and he received it.

When they were a hundred miles from Canaan, the Promised Land, Moses sent twelve scouts ahead to see if it was safe to enter. The scouts returned triumphant. The land was a paradise. The people were peaceful. There were olive trees and vineyards and flowing streams. But soon after their arrival, the scouts began to disagree over what they had seen. Some said the people were savages; others disagreed. The scouts began to turn on each other, one side calling the other cowards, the others saying the confident were trying to lead the tribe into trouble.

Moses kept his focus. He waited until the Israelites who had been slaves in Egypt had died, and then he led their descendants, men and women who had been born in the wilderness, to the borders of the Promised Land.

Four thousand feet above the Dead Sea, Moses stood, staring down upon mile after mile of the wondrous heaven that his people would now enter. But Moses, now an old man, would not go with them. He died on that mountain, his mission accomplished, his people free, his legacy a lesson in perseverance.

Every life is a journey through the wilderness toward a Promised Land. Along the way, you are going to find a million excuses to quit, to cop out, to stop for water and stay forever. We all know people who, headed toward their dreams, stop merely to rest and end up never taking up the trek again.

They've lost their direction.

They've lost their focus.

They've lost their dreams.

You must be like Moses, leading yourself from the fields of oppression into a bright tomorrow, directing your eyes forward, always forward, until you have reached the land of your dreams.

Moses' story of the majority preferring safe and dependable slavery over an uncertain trek to freedom is not an isolated instance. Today's postcommunist Russia, where some citizens voted to return the Communist Party to power, preferring the known commodity of communism over the long and arduous transition to democracy, is proof of the challenges of change.

Freedom takes courage, as does success.

But when you've stood atop the mountain of accomplishment, you will have no doubt that the rewards are more than worth the struggle.

"May you have a strong foundation
When the winds of changes shift."
—Bob Dylan, "Forever Young"

No matter how successful you are in business, you must always keep your focus on your personal life. Because business success without personal fulfillment is no success at all. Always remember that your relationships—with your partner, children, family and friends— always come first.

Lee Atwater, who managed George Bush's victorious 1988 presidential campaign, put life in perfect perspective. Dying in his forties of a brain tumor, he was asked by an interviewer what had been most important in his life. Atwater didn't answer power or politics; he said that life's most precious commodity is the "human touch." Here's a guy who helped elect a president, but, in the end, knew that success is not measured merely professional accomplishment; it's gauged by the love we've shared with others.

Kris and I wanted to build a life together, physically and spiritually, and we decided that the perfect way to begin was to create a family and build a home. We focused on it; we made it our major mission. What better way to unleash the Champion Within than giving it space to grow and flourish? We ended up buying 100 acres in Santa Ynez, near Santa Barbara. On our second wedding anniversary, we gathered our friends and family and buried our wedding cake beneath an oak tree on our new land as a symbol of our faith in our future together.

We focused on a goal of building our dream home, and we made it a reality. But once that goal was attained, we knew, there was something more. We wanted a child together. What better way could there be of sharing your love than creating a life that is part of both of you? What could be a more fulfilling focus? Not only would the child be a personification of our love for each other, but a living testament to our abiding love and our faith in our future together.

It all started on a ship off the shore of Barcelona, where we were doing some work for Coca-Cola during the '92 Olympic Games. Filled with love for my wife and absolutely joyous over our new life together, I stared at Kris and said, "When we get back home, the first thing we have to do is make a baby."

We didn't think there would be any problems. Kris had given birth to four healthy children with no complications. Within a month, she was pregnant. But over the next two years, she suffered two miscarriages, the deepest and most painful losses that anyone can ever suffer, losses that sank into our souls and stayed there until we could finally achieve our goal of bringing a new life into this world. Personally, those were the most painful experiences of my life. For so long, I had sealed off my emotions safely behind my own mental walls—first in my single-minded devotion to sports, then by living in solitude. But now, for the first time, I had put my entire heart and soul into my marriage and having a child. I had never experienced love so deep or so joyous as I did when Kris told me she was pregnant. Going to the doctor's office and watching the baby's heart beat was like watching a miracle. Then, to have all of that so abruptly and painfully taken away from us—twice—was absolutely devastating.

Our perseverance during these crises became the essence of keeping focused, because one of our attempts to have a child happened at the same time as the double murder involving our very close friend, Nicole Brown Simpson, in Brentwood, California. It dominated the worldwide press for two long, seemingly endless years. *Yeah, that's the one.* It hit our family and many of our closest friends like a ton of bricks, and we were whisked into a whirlwind of grief, chaos and disbelief.

This would put our ability to focus to the test.

From this experience, I learned that when you have built a strong foundation, you have a place to stand amid the winds of change. During this period, life became overwhelming. Kris and I literally cried ourselves to sleep at night. Inside our home, we tried to deal with both the death of our close friend, Nicole, and the feelings of loss from two miscarriages. Outside our home stood the constant circus of the media. Because we were such close friends of Nicole's, everybody wanted us to comment on the murder.

We had about 500 phone calls a day, even though we seemed to be changing our number practically weekly. Representatives of all the media were calling, from *Sports Illustrated* to *Life* to *People* to *Time* to *Geraldo*. Katie Couric and Connie Chung didn't let up. Barbara Walters knocked on the door and walked into our living room. The media attention was far more intense than what I had received when I won the Olympic gold medal—and that was intense enough.

But despite the turmoil in our lives, we kept our focus on what was most important to us: creating a child.

I remember the first time we ventured out after Nicole's murder, to attend church one Sunday, to pray to God to bless us with a child. We walked inside the church and it was as if everybody with a baby arrived at church that day. Our pain and longing were so intense. But we kept our focus, and, on November 3, 1995, our prayers were answered. We gave birth to an eight-pound, fourteen-ounce beautiful baby girl, Kendall Nicole Jenner. I stood there in the delivery room with tears streaming down my face. I have never known a greater victory than the one Kris and I experienced the moment that baby was born. It was like God had stared down, smiled and said, "Here is everything that life can be."

I tell you this story to show you the magical power of focus. When all the forces of life seem to be conspiring against and controlling you, that's the time you must keep your eyes on your mission and live one second at a time.

Stay true to yourself and your cause and, most of all, know this: when you're on the right path, the path of absolute clarity, the path known as True North, when you're doing what's absolutely right for yourself and others, then life has a way of giving you a helping hand. Focus on your mission and your life will become more fulfilling than your wildest dreams.

Now that you've learned the power of focus, you're ready to run the 1,500 meters, the final event in the decathlon, an event which holds the secret of how to run the rest of your life.

CHAPTER ELEVEN

THE 1,500-METER RUN: HOW TO RUN THE REST OF YOUR LIFE

You've been running the decathlon for two exhausting days. You've run, you've thrown, you've jumped, you've vaulted. You have put your mind, body and soul through every conceivable athletic test. You've had enough. But they save the toughest event until last. Now you have to run the 1,500 meters, just short of a mile, a race for time that's the supreme test of what you're made of. You stand at the starting line and stare down the track, gathering steam like a locomotive. Most decathletes fear the 1,500 meters, and it shows. They're exhausted. They're defeated. They're already breathing hard before the start. But it's the finish that counts. So you blast off the starting line, jockey for position on the straightaway, trying to get the inside lane, the shortest distance around the track. The idea is to run as fast and as comfortably as you possibly can, conserving your energy for the last 300 meters. This is the defining moment, the ultimate test. Your legs burn. Your lungs ache. Your spirit is almost broken. But as a true champion, you reach down beneath the physical and into the depths where greatness lies

and pull up everything you have, blasting through the finish
line, beating the odds, confounding the critics, breaking the
records and achieving your dreams.

We all have times when we're tested in life, when we have to
reach down deep inside ourselves to come up with a performance that defines who we are and where we're going.

That time is now.

I've always felt that the 1,500 meters is the true test of the decathlete, the biggest challenge of the long two days. I measure a decathlete by the way he runs the 1,500 meters. It doesn't require a tremendous amount of technique, athletic ability or God-given talent. What it requires is a lot of heart. It's four to five minutes of excruciating pain. But when you run the 1,500 meters well, you've kicked the decathlon's butt.

You've proven yourself a champion.

"No pain, no palm; no thorns, no throne; no gall, no glory;
no cross, no crown."

—WILLIAM PENN

At this point in both the decathlon and in your own personal journey, the biggest challenge lies ahead, a race that will literally define who you are and where you're going.

Only one thing stands between you and the finish line: fear. We discussed fear at length in Chapter 6. But now it arises with even greater ferocity, like ghosts guarding the doorway of your dreams. The 1,500 meters is a literal horror house of fear: dozens of varieties will arrive to haunt you. Fear of success and fear of failure. Fear of pain and ridicule and humiliation. Fear of the mental and physical challenge of running 1,500 meters in a full-bore sprint. Such a variety of fears that many potential decathletes never even attempt the decathlon because of their fear of the 1,500 meters. They're defeated before they even begin.

Fear of the ultimate challenge stops many people cold. That's why so many people never fulfill their dreams. They're too scared to even get started. But as we've discussed before, fear must become an integral part of the game, a barrier that you must break before you can become a winner at anything.

In the beginning of this book, I promised to reveal to you the secret of unleashing the Champion Within. Well, here, it is: *The race is entirely up to you.* You and you alone are in control of your destiny and in control of your emotions. You set the rules. You select the track. You choose the competition. You hold the stopwatch and referee the finish line.

What do you race against?

Your limits, your fears, your doubts.

And how do you win?

You *run.* You run every second of your life like it's the 1,500 meters in the Olympic Games. You realize that you only have one chance to get this life right, and you don't waste a second. Not on indecision. Not on negativity. Not on the myriad emotions and forces that will try to slow you down. You realize that life, like the ancient Olympics, offers no reward for second place. You win or you lose. You're either an eternal flame or a sputtering ember. It's all up to you.

You run the race of life in a flat-out, full-bore sprint.

My mission in writing this book has been to prove to you that we all have the potential for greatness deep inside us, the potential to overcome tremendous obstacles. I've certainly had proof of this in my own life. Through my own struggle, I learned to believe in myself and to connect with the powerful human being that lives within all of us. All you have to do to awaken that greatness, that Champion Within, is to believe in it, to persevere against all obstacles and allow its positive, directed energy to take over where fear, doubt and desperation once reigned.

The tools are at your fingertips. All you have to do is follow the ten events of the decathlon, ten steps that offer lessons for the decathlon of life:

You blast off the blocks in the 100 meters. You realize that the race begins with a single step. Everything depends on your ability to get started. There is power in momentum, so you do not hesitate. You become a starter, which means you're a *doer*. If you're not sure which project to start, start several, the ones that have the most potential. You never know which one will lead to fulfillment of your dreams. Tomorrow is still a dream; yesterday is already ancient history. Today is the only reality we can count on. *Carpe diem.* Seize the day! There is power in beginning. So begin right now!

You run the long jump. You create a carefully calculated set of long-term and short-term goals, then, most important, act upon them! Realize that a goal is a dream with a deadline. Set your goals and then make them real. Only when you can see, feel and practically touch your goal can it become the integral part of your life that it must become to be attainable. Decide *right now* exactly where you'd like to be, then carefully plot out every minute, every hour, every day, every week, every month, every year until you reach your destination. Goals are the stepping-stones toward your dreams. Once you lay out the steps and begin following them, not one moment will pass without progressing on to the next goal, creating a powerful journey toward your desired destiny.

You throw the shot. You realize that we all possess different strengths and different weaknesses, and that we must discover what we can do and not be limited by what we cannot. You realize that sometimes what you might consider a weakness—in my case, my mind—can actually turn out to be your greatest asset. If I had been a better reader, I wouldn't have needed to excel in athletics. I wouldn't have been hungry for excellence. I would have been content just being average. My supposed "deficiency" gave me great determination, a burning desire to become proficient in something and, thus, the ability to work extremely hard to win. My greatest weakness eventually became my greatest strength. Take a thorough inventory of your assets and liabilities. Then take what you're best at and enjoy most and run with it.

You attack the high jump. You consistently raise the bar on your aspirations and abilities. You constantly challenge yourself to jump just a little higher each time. You consistently take greater risks, always increasing the chances for greater rewards. You realize that no monumental height is scaled in one fell swoop but surmounted one inch at a time. Once you've accomplished that height, raise the bar a little higher, then a little higher, until you're jumping at levels you'd never thought surmountable.

You run the 400 meters. You face the Bear, your fears. You realize that fear comes in two main varieties: fear of failure and, even more sinister, fear of success. You realize that you are your own toughest competitor and you keep constant watch for the ways you use to sabotage your own success. You know that no human being goes into an arena without fear. This is merely part of the game. You don't let fear stop you. You use it to propel you forward, always forward.

You take the 100-meter hurdles. How? One at a time. You never stand at the end of the starting line looking down at what you have to do before you start to do it. If a decathlete stared down at the line of ten hurdles to be surmounted, one after the other, in a seemingly impossible ballet of a footrace, he would never be able to begin the race. Just the thought of it would be overwhelming. The secret is to take one hurdle at a time, just as the secret of life is taking each challenge as it comes, gracefully sailing over one before going on to the next.

You throw the discus. You know that every life has its big moments, and when yours arises you must make your move. You cannot hesitate. The time for analysis is over; action must become your only course. Preparation and strategy must galvanize into action or your dreams will never get off the ground. Action is the currency of champions; without it, nothing happens.

You pole-vault. Like the pole-vaulter who eventually reaches the height at which he can vault no higher, you realize that you are eventually going to fail at something. But you never let failure defeat you. You realize that failure is merely part of the game. What doesn't defeat you really does make you stronger. Failure teaches champions their greatest lessons. Don't seek it out; it will find you soon enough. But when it does, you ask yourself, "What can I learn from this, and what can I do to improve?" You stop, regroup, then charge the bar again.

You throw the javelin. You focus on your mission as precisely as the decathlete focuses on an imaginary point in the air through which the javelin must pass perfectly. You never allow the elements to buffet your flight but steadfastly soar in the direction of your dreams. Break your mission down into one simple sentence, then weigh every opportunity in terms of that sentence. If it will propel your mission forward, then you accept; if it detracts from your mission, you reject.

Finally, you run the 1,500 meters. This is the last event, the event that holds the greatest lesson, a lesson you can use to run every area of your life. I mentioned earlier that the original inventors of the decathlon were brilliant. The 1,500 meters is the supreme example of their ingenuity. Not only does the last event require a final confrontation of your fears, the 1,500 meters also forces the you to combine all the lessons of the previous nine events in the biggest burst of mental and physical energy in the entire two-day competition—an astounding show of strength and fortitude before you win.

You must finish the last event to truly discover the incredible power that resides within you. Only when you cross the finish line a winner will you know how to win every event in both the decathlon and life: by committing yourself to running each race as if it were the last, just as in life you must live each day as if there is no tomorrow.

You must declare yourself a winner before you can truly go out and win.

You stand at the starting line, awaiting the gun, and when it fires, you put every ounce of your physical and mental abilities on the line. You run the 1,500 meters beyond limits, beyond fears, beyond pain. You realize that pain is merely a temporary barrier, beyond which lies the greatest benefit, the greatest growth, and that you'll have the rest of your life to recover. When you blast through the finish line, arms held high, voice screaming toward the heavens, you will know the secret of the ages. That it's not the finish line that counts; it's the journey, the experience of the million steps you've taken toward your dream.

This is the true prize in life. Not the olive wreath awarded victors at the ancient Olympics; not today's Olympic gold medal, which is actually made of an inexpensive alloy called silver gilt. The value of a prize is whatever the wearer attaches to it. Having been there, I can tell you this: victory is sweet, but it's the journey that gives life meaning. The journey really is the reward. The only gold you'll find at the end of the rainbow is whatever you have amassed on your journey along the way.

Personal victory is forged from the lessons we hold in our hearts. We crown ourselves winners or exile ourselves to defeat in the arena of our minds. Declare yourself a winner! Then, and only then, will you be ready to begin the great race of your life.

There is greatness living within you, a greatness that you can awaken before the world. All you have to do is begin, and you're halfway there.

I would like to leave you with this thought, originally stated in a speech Theodore Roosevelt gave at the Sorbonne in Paris in 1910.

The credit belongs to the man who is actually in the arena, whose face is marred by dust and sweat and blood; who strives valiantly; who errs, and comes short again and again, because there is no effort without error and shortcoming; but who does actually strive to do the deeds; who knows the great enthusiasms, the great devotions; who spends himself in a worthy cause; who at the best knows in the end the triumph of high achievement, and who at the worst, if he fails, at least fails while daring greatly, so that his place shall never be with those cold and timid souls who know neither victory nor defeat.

You have the potential to accomplish great things, to make your life an incredible experience, to awaken the Champion Within. The starting gun fires now. The track stretches before you. Make each step of your life worthy of the greatness that lives deep inside.

Always believe in the Power of You!

About the Author

After winning a gold medal in the 1976 Olympic Games, Bruce Jenner, hailed as "the World's Greatest Athlete," went on to winning seasons in life. He's known to millions as a motivational speaker, TV personality, sports commentator, commercial spokesperson, entrepreneur, actor, producer and representative of companies such as Visa, MCI, Coca-Cola, and Anheuser-Busch. Still the epitome of constant motion, Jenner travels around the country speaking to corporate and community groups about finding the Champion Within, and runs several successful businesses with his wife, Kris. The Jenners live with their children in Hidden Hills, California.